Recipes for Reading

Recipes for Reading

Community Cookbooks, Stories, Histories

Edited by
Anne L. Bower

University of Massachusetts Press
Amherst

Copyright © 1997 by
The University of Massachusetts Press
All rights reserved
Printed in the United States of America
LC 97-9292
ISBN 1-55849-088-4 (cloth); 089-2 (pbk.)
Designed by Sally Nichols
Set in Centaur
Printed and bound by Braun-Brumfield, Inc.
Library of Congress Cataloging-in-Publication Data

Recipes for reading : community cookbooks, stories, histories / edited
by Anne L. Bower.
    p.   cm.
Includes bibliographical references (p.).

    1. Community cookbooks—History.   2. Women's studies.   I. Bower,
Anne.
TX652.R377   1997
394.1'0973—dc21   97-9292
                                                                          CIP

British Library Cataloguing in Publication data are available.

This book is published with the support and cooperation of the
University of Massachusetts, Boston.

In memory of my mother, Maxine Scheuer Donahue,
and my father, Frank J. Lieberman, two very different and gifted people,
both creators of wonderful recipes

Contents

Part Three
Community Cookbooks in Context 133

Illustrations

Acknowledgments

From the very beginning, this book "about" community cookbooks has felt like a community project. The essay writers themselves have been inspirational—by phone, e-mail, and snail mail, from California, Israel, Venezuela, Ontario, and elsewhere, from office, home, and vacation spots, their suggestions and reactions kept me enthusiastic. I thank them so much for their acceptance of my requests to revise essays, not only for the sake of the individual pieces but so that the whole book would have greater coherence.

Closer to home, colleagues at Ohio State University have been wonderfully helpful; my own writing and thinking about this collection of essays could not have been accomplished without the caring support and incisive questions (along with fine food and drink) supplied by Lynda Behan, Marcia Dickson, Scott DeWitt, Beverly Moss, and Amy Shuman. In addition, financial support from The Ohio State University and Radcliffe College was of invaluable assistance: the OSU Center for Women's

Studies provided a Research Grant in 1991–92; OSU's College of Humanities and Radcliffe financed a stay in Boston for work at the Schlesinger Library during the summer of 1992, along with travel costs, photocopying, etc.; and OSU's College of Humanities also provided a Seed Grant during spring quarter 1994, releasing me from teaching to work on this book.

My thanks also to Tim McNiven, another OSU-Marion colleague, who helped with many of the photographs for the book's illustrations, and Joel Fetter, an OSU-Marion student whose ability to deal with various word processing programs and their quirks allowed me to create the final manuscript of *Recipes for Reading*. Thanks as well to the fine editing of Melanie Richter-Bernburg and to Pam Wilkinson for careful supervision of the book's editing and production. Last, for my book's main title, I must give credit to Susan J. Leonardi. Her 1989 *PMLA* article, "Recipes for Reading: Pasta Salad, Lobster à la Riseholme, and Key Lime Pie," provided inspiration and insight for many of us.

Recipes for Reading

Bound Together: Recipes, Lives, Stories, and Readings

Anne Bower

Almost everyone owns or has seen community cookbooks—also known as regional, charitable, and fund-raising cookbooks. These ubiquitous works seem to vary little, although older editions are normally hardbound and have names like *Our Sisters' Recipes, From Danish Kitchens,* and *Washington Women's Cook Book;* more recent books have soft covers, spiral bindings, and "catchier" names: *Prescription for Cooking Desserts,* from the Montgomery [Alabama] Baptist Hospital Auxiliary; *Home Cookin',* compiled by the Junior League of Wichita Falls, Texas; or *Bay Leaves,* produced by the Junior Service League of Panama City, Florida. Usually put together by women to raise funds for a church, temple, school, museum, or other cause, these texts seem innocent of narrative force. After all, what do they contain? A preface explaining the group's philanthropic intent and/or a few words on how the cookbook was compiled, a few illustrations, chapters dividing food by categories, paid advertisements (sometimes), and mostly, of course, the recipes, normally accompanied by their donors' names.

It is the contention of *Recipes for Reading* that fund-raising cookbooks comprise a genre containing much more than the discrete elements listed above. The contributors to this volume find that these cookbooks tell stories—autobiographical in most cases, historical sometimes, and perhaps fictitious or idealized in other instances. The discourse of the discrete textual elements and their juxtapositions contribute to the creation of these stories, which quietly or boldly tell of women's lives and beliefs. In community cookbooks women present their values, wittingly or unwittingly (we often can't know which). Using a variety of analytic and synthetic approaches, the essays that follow demonstrate not only the different kinds of stories available in fund-raising cookbooks but the variety of ways that readers can share in the feast of these stories.

Let me tell you a story. One evening a few years ago, I was browsing cookbooks, vaguely thinking about what to fix for supper. I took down an old family cookbook—one published in 1909 to raise money for a Pittsburgh synagogue (as my great aunt had told me)—but soon found myself distracted from the content of the recipes themselves. This text, *Our Sisters' Recipes*, had some odd features.[1] Why wasn't the synagogue named? Why did the frontispiece depict an African American woman, in headcloth and apron, smilingly tasting something from a large spoon? Why weren't any "typical" Jewish dishes included? A thorough search of the pages showed no mushroom and barley soup, no blintzes, nothing featuring a matzoh, no rye bread recipe, no recipes for Jewish holidays foods. And who were "Our Sisters"? Were they sisterly, did they form a community, and did they want me or other readers in there with them? Perhaps more was going on here than I imagined; perhaps the women contributors used their recipes, in Carolyn Heilbrun's terms, to "write a woman's life."[2] Could I value this book not just as a fun source of recipes but as a literary text whose authors constructed meaningful representations of themselves and their world? Probably as a result of working on other projects concerning women's writing—analyses of letter novels, of quilting metaphors in poetry, of feminist critical styles, I began to wonder about the potential interpretability of cookbooks like *Our Sisters' Recipes*.

I remember what it felt like when I first began to really read *Our*

Our Sisters'
Recipes

—Compiled in—

Pittsburgh, Penna.

CONTRIBUTED BY MANY
KIND HEARTS
AND IN A WORTHY CAUSE

Frontispiece and title page of *Our Sisters' Recipes* (1909).

Sisters' Recipes, the moment when that book in my hands was no longer a "simple" recipe collection. It became a questioning and questing text, asking me, prodding me to inquire into its existence in this world—this world that is both the academy and my kitchen, both my intellect and my senses. I discovered that in order to fully read it, I had to enter the world of its authors, know what they had read, where they had lived, what they might have aspired to. I read histories of Jewish immigration and ethnic studies, studies of philanthropy and women's volunteerism, classic cookbooks of the period, analyses of foodways, and history texts that could ground me in the economics and sociology of turn-of-the-century urban women's experience. And I read other fund-raising cookbooks. Lots of them.

The more I researched, the more convinced I became that *Our Sisters' Recipes,* frayed and brittle, its once white pages now yellowed, had a story to tell. The story I found—part collective autobiography, part history, part fiction, involved the women's asserting of themselves as upper middle-class assimilated Americans, comfortable acknowledging the German aspect of their German-Jewish background, but worried that their Jewishness, especially given massive immigration of East European Jews at that time, could undo their secure lives.

That's the story I read, but I cannot claim that my experience of that cookbook is its only reading. Somehow the ambiguity surrounding the reading of community cookbooks doesn't bother me. Someone may accuse me of egotistic self-projection, or of overreading, or of "reading into" one of these books. But in order to do that, the individual criticizing me will have to explore fundraising cookbooks and take them seriously—and so that reader may come into contact with these writers and these texts in a new way. Based on my work to date, I think others too will then find that these books contain the writing of women who took time and energy to formulate written discourse not only to raise money for a cause but also to formulate and express their collective value system and to produce texts of their own, balancing generic cookbook characteristics with their own desires for innovation and style. Patrocinio Schweikart says that "to read a text and then to write about it is to seek to connect not only with the author[s] of the original text, but also with a community of readers."[3] How apropos for community cookbooks.

In *Recipes for Reading*, scholars in history, English studies, linguistics, performance studies, foreign languages, and culinary history provide their own kinds of recipes for working with fundraising cookbooks and related texts. My hope is that the insights collectively offered will lead to new readings and valuings of the community cookbooks, new connections between food and literature, and they will also permit greater appreciation of other "nonliterary" texts. Here, I think of the many benefits derived from research and writing about another kind of nonliterary text—patchwork quilts. Like community cookbooks, although familiar to everyone, these quilts were once deemed decorative, utile, and valuable for collectors, but otherwise silent. However, because of the work of scholars in the arts, history, literature, and women's studies, we have increasingly come to see them as *readable*, with great benefit to our knowledge of women's experiences and discourse.

The quilt's readability came to us over a period of years, as scholars began to take quilters' aesthetics seriously. The 1971 Whitney Museum exhibition, "Abstract Design in American Quilts," signaled a giant step forward in scholars' textual exploration of these objects. Elaine Showalter explains how earlier negligence of quilt-texts resulted from gender and high art/low art prejudices: the quilts were seen as "trifling" both because they came from the "female sphere" and because they were produced "outside of high culture."[4] Reviewing the recovery of these texts, and seeing in them metaphors for women's writing and for American culture, Showalter moves on to call for further "work of exploration and assembly" concerning women's writing, asking us to continue finding ways to "read American women's stories and to ask American questions about their past and future."[5] Those who have taught us to read quilts provide a groundwork for that further research.

In addition, scholars working with such fragmentary forms as women's scrapbooks and samplers, "artifacts" that were produced by women relegated to a private, domestic sphere, are learning to read the stories these texts relate.[6] As we come to see the links between what Susan Arpad classifies as "literary artifacts (diaries, letters, reminiscences, and oral histories) and material cultural artifacts (especially quilts and other needlework, photographs, and gardens),"[7] we acquire more and better techniques for reading all texts related to women's self-representation.

Focusing now on women's nonliterary *print* documents, one finds readers newly appreciating these documents' textual strategies, their values statements, and their narrative powers. Those working with women's letters, for example, can, like Sally Kitch in *This Strange Society of Women: Reading the Letters and Lives of the Woman's Commonwealth*, discover that women's "correspondence . . . incorporated both group and individual values and qualities." Kitch finds that letters are often more than a record, more than a reflection of life experiences; they can actually "shape" the values of the correspondents.[8] In like manner, women's diaries are now being read as more than transparent transmissions of lived experiences or simple, private reflections on those experiences. For instance, in *Women's Diaries of the Westward Journey*, Lillian Schlissel points out the *public* intent of the diaries she studied. Most of them were destined for either newspaper publication or distribution to relatives back east, and often became not just "an individual's story but . . . the history of a family's growth and course through time."[9]

Part of what we're coming to see about these varying texts, once considered decorative and/or private and/or trivial, is how they have served the communication needs of women. Scholars, particularly those in women's studies, or feminists in literature and history, have demonstrated that, although women were often limited in access to recognized status-bearing discourse forms such as poetry and fiction, public speaking, and journalism,[10] they expressed themselves through other print and nonprint materials. And in those materials they not only recorded and reflected the world around them, they worked to construct their world. Whether complicit with or pushing against the constraints and categories that bound them, women acted to shape the communities around them. Thus, what we may designate as fairly private activity or discourse (sewing, the writing of letters, contributing to a cookbook) may actually have been seen by women of the past as forms of public participation. This point is underscored by ideas brought out in two studies of club women and women in associations in the nineteenth and early twentieth centuries. Karen L. Blair reminds us that because a "male definition of activity" has dominated discussions of history and social change, only women engaged in public work such as suffrage have been termed active. However, as noted by Anne Firor Scott, within literary, social, and philanthropic organizations, women were able to "evade some of [society's] restraints and to redefine 'woman's place.'"[11]

As a legacy of structuralism and poststructuralism, we now easily accept that any number of texts, institutions, and events can be "interpreted"; in the academy this is such a given that our critical essays assume readers' concurrence. In a recent book, Robert Scholes could offhandedly write that "we read and write our world as well as our texts, and are read and written by them in turn."[12] Given this deep acceptance of readability, I wondered why community cookbooks had not already been fully esteemed for their textuality. I propose that three overlapping problems have blocked their wide acceptance as anything more than quaint and friendly recipe collections.

The first and most obvious problem about community cookbooks is that they have usually been produced by ordinary women and food, associated with women, has been seen as unworthy of serious study. As philosopher Deane Curtin writes in discussing the philosophy of food and why until recently such a philosophy hasn't existed: "In many, if not most cultures, food production and preparation activities are women's work and/or the work of slaves or lower classes. Certainly this is true of Euro-American cultures, and to that extent it is not difficult to determine why western philosophers have not considered food a properly philosophical topic."[13] Curtin likens this neglect (as have I) to the disregard shown for women's quilts, which were "considered crafts rather than fine arts," and for women's writing in general, which was relegated to the merely "introspective and recreational."[14] Angela Little, whose background is in nutrition, agrees that "food is viewed as a subject of *common knowledge* that removes it from academic interest"; further, "there is the problem of gender identification: that feeding and nurturing are considered the purview of the female of the species." Little adds another point in explaining academia's difficulties with the study of food culture—the "transdisciplinary" quality of food and cooking often takes its researchers into the " 'real world' of everyday experience."[15] In addition, Curtin helps us understand the tendency to trivialize food culture scholarship by explaining that the tradition of western philosophy (and scholarship, I would add), has tended to privilege questions about the rational, the unchanging and eternal, the abstract and mental, and to denigrate questions about embodied, concrete, practical experience. For example, the way in which the concept of personal identity has classically been approached by philosophers is to assume the self to be a discrete, disembodied ego, and then to ask for the logical conditions of its self-identity through time. By contrast, taking the production and preparation of food as an illuminating source, we might formulate a conception of the person that focuses on our connection with and dependence on the rest of the world.[16]

Lisa M. Heldke articulates a philosophical stand in which food-making is seen anew. Instead of the past assumption that cooking activities were merely manual, practical, and did not require particular thought, she proposes that food preparation be understood as a " 'mentally manual' activity, a 'theoretical practical' activity—a 'thoughtful practice.' "[17] It is this newer attitude that I and contributors to *Recipes for Reading* apply to the fund-raising cookbooks and the work of their group authors as well as to related food-texts / events. We consider the community cookbook as a text that enacts within it a group of women's mental, theoretical, thoughtful positions or statements. Indeed, fund-raising cookbooks are ideologically motivated, in their form as well as their content, as a number of the essays in *Recipes for Reading* will insist.

A second problem preventing full and creative readings of community cookbooks has been the very word *recipe.* It signals something formulaic—a prescription or chart that allows preparation of a particular food. Even those who never cook know that a recipe will include a list of ingredients and instructions detailing what one does with those ingredients to produce the soup or cake desired. However, those who do cook also know that a recipe can go beyond the formulaic in both content and form; those of us who enjoy cooking take pleasure in the novel possibilities proposed by new combinations of sweet and sour, of foods previously assumed incompatible, of new techniques for mixing, cooking, and presenting a dish. And beyond that content level, we also savor the style of a recipe: it can make us laugh, give us a sense of the world from which it originates, incorporate some history or an inkling of the personality of its writer.

Still, whether the recipe appears in a commercial cookbook or in a community cookbook, for the most part we read each recipe as a discrete unit of instruction in food preparation, seldom considering the overall story told by the recipes when taken together. However, commercial cookbooks, that is, texts written for personal profit by one person or a cooperating team of two or three, have been allowed a certain intentionality of discourse form. The commercial cookbook's author has been granted an ideology that infuses each recipe and connects the recipes with some kind of comprehensive, shaping, directing voice. With fund-raising cookbooks the communal authorship seems to have blocked readers from perceiving that these texts can voice the same kinds of values and identity found in commercial cookbooks.

The third problem in working with fund-raising cookbooks has to do with their ubiquity. There are so many of them; most of them aren't accessibly cataloged; and in truth, not all of them are fascinating. Some seem pallid copies of each other, either because of philanthropies' mimicking of each others' successful books (as with some church groups in the late nineteenth century) or because of reliance on commercial outfits that use set conventions to process cookbooks for organizations. One has to admit that numbers of community cookbooks do not contain particularly unique voices or truly communicate the specialness of one group of people in a certain place and time. Sometimes this discourse form, like any discourse form, doesn't live up to its full potential. But that's no reason to ignore the many wonderful times when the fund-raising cookbook surpasses its assumed limitations and beautifully relates and shapes a community's time and place and needs and longings and difficulties and delights. Again, I find parallels to the discourse of quilts. Some quilts are duplicates of a known pattern, without any hint of the invention which most of us require before we call something art.[18] But we've learned how to *read* the art and craft of quilts so that we can understand the uses of patterns and variations in the patchwork texts. We can do the same with community cookbooks.

In addition to the problems of food study's past denigration, negative connotations associated with the word recipe, and community cookbooks' lack of status because of their commonness, I see another difficulty that has prevented scholarly involvement with these texts. In gaining academic acceptance, earlier feminists often felt compelled to repress expression of interests in domestic life for fear that such expression would consign them to an essentialized "feminine" role. Fortunately, we have moved from feminism to feminisms. Nowadays, feminists (female and male!) collectively have the assurance and breadth to allow us to seek our history, traditions, and voices in the kitchen as well as the conference room. Analyzing novels with domestic plots, Ann Romines contends that "we have a women's tradition of *writing domestic ritual,* which both inscribes and interrogates women's housekeeping work and art. Such a tradition opposes the confines of essentialism. It implies, instead, that women's traditional lives are worth thinking about, worth writing about, worth reading."[19] Because of the work of feminists and other poststructuralist researchers, scholarship about domesticity and its various texts has become legitimate.[20]

Changing attitudes and methodologies provide a groundwork for those of us exploring new readings of fund-raising cookbooks and related texts. Recent work on women's autobiographies proves very helpful; explorations of personal styles of critical writing facilitates interactions with texts that *are* quite personal to many of us; increasing scholarship on lost aspects of women's lives and recovery of lost texts also aids work with the cookbooks. These factors provide an encouraging milieu in which to work. However, we also have a few studies which have been foundational for contributors to *Recipes for Reading.* These texts have served as guideposts or beckoning doors or jumping off places for our own work.

Perhaps the first researcher to celebrate community cookbooks as a worthy category was the aptly named Margaret Cook, whose 1971 bibliography, *America's Charitable Cooks: A Bibliography of Fund-raising Cookbooks Published in the United States (1861–1915),* sorts texts primarily by state.[21] A self-effacing scholar, Cook provided almost no prefatory or evaluative matter. Her bibliography still provides a starting place for scholars seeking early texts, and her work was one of the first to acknowledge community cookbooks as a special category of American (women's) writing.

Moving from bibliography to more discursive texts, one finds that in the fields of folklore, sociology, and anthropology, scholars have for a long time seen the great cultural significance of food, though they did not contribute directly to discussions of community cookbooks until recently. Mary Douglas puts it bluntly in a discussion of ethnic food: "Ethnic food is a cultural category, not a material thing." She goes on to explain that "food is a field of action. It is a medium in which other levels of categorization become manifest. It does not lead or follow, but it squarely belongs to whatever action there is. Food choices support political alignments and social opportunities."[22] This kind of insight is immensely applicable to research into the compiled or charitable cookbook.

The first scholar I have found who moves beyond that assessment is Lynne Ireland. In 1981, she published "The Compiled Cookbook as Foodways Autobiography," suggesting that in spite of its sometimes "amateurish" and often "middle-class culinary kitsch" qualities, "the compiled cookbook has something to offer those of us interested in foodways research." She introduced the idea that these books can be understood as a kind of autobiography, even if in a limited way, for they "make a statement about the food habits of the groups which produce them." She perceived, however, that these texts work rather like "puzzles" in that the books themselves only contain "clues"; and without theorizing the process of reading that allows these clues to be drawn together to provide "insights," she did suggest some of the ways one could approach the texts.[23]

Ireland includes "frequency of inclusion" and excluded foods as two major components of her approach to determining food habits; "repeated recipes" explain food fashions. The reading method she uses combines these two elements with awareness of the inclusion of holiday or celebration dishes, special ethnic foods, and typical "American" foods (like fried chicken). Wisely, Ireland questions the picture one draws from this data, asking if these texts actually say, " 'Here is what we eat' or 'Here is what we would have you believe that we eat.' "[24] Based on the texts she investigated, she concludes that for the most part, the texts *do* depict the actual food traditions of their communal authors. This conclusion is based in part on looking briefly at the life circumstances, demographics, and affiliations of the authors.

Another text that helps to open up readings of community cookbooks, although it doesn't directly deal with fund-raising texts, is Laura Shapiro's *Perfection Salad: Women and Cooking at the Turn of the Century*. Shapiro's feminist/sociological approach models a reading of women's home-centered experience as an integral part of our history. By linking the nineteenth-century Domestic Science movement to both reformism and literary sentimentalism, she opens up the textuality of cookbooks in general. Further, she makes very clear that cookbooks participated in a reformist ethic; women cookbook authors demonstrated the belief that "if they could reform American eating habits, they could reform Americans." Shapiro appreciates the shift in woman's role acted out by the Domestic Science movement with its belief in "the pragmatic value of each dish"; her appreciation helps those of us studying community cookbooks to see how these texts encode and project belief systems of the women who produce them.[25]

A broader contextualization of community cookbooks allows broader readings. Thus, when Barbara Kirshenblatt-Gimblett studied Jewish community cookbooks in a 1987 article titled "Recipes for Creating Community: The Jewish Charity Cookbook in America," she took into consideration the history of Jewish women's philanthropic organizations, history of immigration patterns, influence of other cookbooks, regional influences on foodways, and social and religious influences on woman's domestic role. This permitted her readings of these texts to go beyond food habits to a reading of "how the highly perishable and ephemeral medium of food embodies core cultural values."[26] Many of the essays in *Recipes for Reading* use a similar contextualizing approach.

Also helpful to those of us wanting to work with cookery texts was that moment in 1989 when we opened up *PMLA* and found Susan Leonardi's article about a well-known cookbook, *Joy of Cooking*. Using a combination of feminist and reader-response techniques, Leonardi presented the possibility of reading such a text for its narrativity. By connecting the cookbook to various novels, to her own work as a critic, and to her own experiences in the kitchen, Leonardi effectively broke down a number of genre and scholarly conventions.[27]

Throughout the essays that make up *Recipes for Reading* the articles and books mentioned above are frequently cited; the reader will often find other resources that we share. At times we even refer to each others' work.

Certainly the small amount of scholarship concerning fund-raising cookbooks explains this pattern; however, it also seems to me an enactment of the community ideal so common to the cookbooks themselves.

Having tasted the perceptions and methodologies provided by others, the contributors to *Recipes for Reading* have collectively proceeded to prepare something new: a full repast devoted to the community cookbook. Using reader-response, deconstructivist, feminist, and historicist theoretical approaches, we place community cookbooks in broad contexts, seeing them as documents that tell much more than just the stories of food habits. The essays in *Recipes for Reading* not only look at the cookbooks' historical significance but investigate their power to construct an ideology (national, regional, class, etc.); to demonstrate the positioning of women between private and public worlds; to establish for the cookbook makers and readers certain ideas of literacy, empowerment, and community; and to provide enduring representations of ethnic, religious, and other group affiliations.

The first part of *Recipes for Reading*, "Approaches to Texts," provides three essays that background the content, form, and theoretical potential of fund-raising cookbooks. Culinary historian Janice Bluestein Longone sets the stage (or should I say the table) in "Tried Receipts" with an historical review of community cookbooks, celebrating the origins and variety of these texts. My own piece, "Cooking Up Stories," explores narrative elements one can locate within the cookbooks. And in "Claiming a Piece of the Pie," linguist Colleen Cotter discusses how the recipe code functions in charitable cookbooks.

In the second part of *Recipes for Reading*, "Experiencing Texts," four essays demonstrate scholars' interactions with or approaches to particular texts. At times quite autobiographical, at other times more traditional in style, these essays all work with twentieth-century charity cookbooks. Ann Romines, whose scholarship usually concentrates on nineteenth-century novels, describes the surprising way cookbooks influenced her identity as a writer in "Growing Up with the Methodist Cookbooks." In a similar vein, Marion Bishop depicts her personal interactions with and reactions to a particular culture and community in "Speaking Sisters: Relief Society Cookbooks and Mormon Culture." Extending our discussion northward, as well as into the realm of orality, Elizabeth J. McDougall offers "Voices,

Stories, and Recipes in Selected Canadian Community Cookbooks." Sally Bishop Shigley's experience is different, for she explores the power of a fund-raising cookbook to draw the reader into a community not originally her own; this essay is titled "Empathy, Empowerment, and Eating: Politics and Power in *The Black Family Dinner Quilt Cookbook*."

The last part of *Recipes for Reading*, "Community Cookbooks in Context," displays the many ways that one can extend or elaborate the concept of community cookbooks. Barbara Kirshenblatt-Gimblett reads the cultural values performed in an 1888 Jewish community cookbook and the Temple Emanuel Fair that provided its context in "The Moral Sublime," while Alice Ross explores the personal politics and social constraints affecting one turn-of-the-century cookbook compiler in "Ella Smith's Unfinished Community Cookbook." Moving in quite a different direction, "A Tale of Three Cakes: On the Air and In the Books," by Nelljean M. Rice, looks at the work of one radio homemaker to see how her broadcasts and her recipes helped forge bonds among isolated farm women in Iowa. Nina M. Scott situates a well-known nineteenth-century woman writer and her cookbook in the midst of Argentinian history and culture of the time in "Juana Manuela Gorriti's *Cocina ecléctica*"; then Jeffrey M. Pilcher demonstrates how commercial and community cookbooks participated in the construction of a distinctly "Mexican" cuisine, relating that process to the concurrent creation of a national identity in "Recipes for *Patria*." *Recipes for Reading* closes with Cecelia Lawless's "Cooking, Community, Culture: A Reading of *Like Water for Chocolate*," which applies insights about community cookbooks to depictions of isolation, cooking, reading, eating, and community found in a recent, popular Mexican novel.

A number of scholars have noted the benefits and difficulties of working with "women's nontraditional literature." Suzanne Bunkers, Cherry Muhanji, and Ilene Alexander, discussing women's diaries, journals, oral traditions, autobiographies, and photographs, agree that if part of one's motive in dealing with such texts is to recover "our lives as women," then those of us working with these texts may need to allow ourselves a rather subjective stance. This subjectivity includes "having feelings about a woman, about your life, about other people's lives," asserts Cherry Muhanji. It includes connecting one's sense of personally being affected by race, class, and sex prejudices to hints and silences in texts that don't necessarily state those constraints outright. This is a kind of "self-reflexivity," they explain, that allows one to see "what the multiple 'truths' might have been, the multiple 'realities,' the multiple 'experiences.'"[28] The subjective nature of this kind of reading also leads to nontraditional scholarly forms, for the standard essay often curtails the personal. Logically, a number of the essays in *Recipes for Reading* display highly personal styles.

By presenting such a collection of essays, we hope to contribute to the ways "nonliterary" texts can be read and valued. In turn, increasing awareness of the processes at work in nonliterary texts may inform new readings of the "literary." For example, novels using "the home plot"[29] (from *Uncle Tom's Cabin* to *Country of the Pointed Firs* to *Heartburn* and *House-keeping*), novels written in letter or diary form, poetry collections or anthologies pieced together like quilts, and both biographies and autobiographies, might all look different once we're more aware of traditions and inventions in the prolific "nonliterary" writings that are part of the context and background for women's texts.

While a strong motivation for this essay collection has been my own desire to relate community cookbooks to the full world of textual production, I also have great affection for these books. I want others to value them and the women (and, more recently, the men) who made them. I want to believe that after reading the essays in this volume, you'll walk into your kitchen or library and take from the shelf that old fund-raising cookbook you'd forgotten about. Perhaps a stained page or bookmark reminds you that you have "used" this book, found in it a recipe for cookies or a casserole that pleased you and others at your table. But now I see you sitting down with no idea of preparing a meal. You're reading the book in a new way. The recipes are still there and may still be helpful. But now, you're reading the book for information about the lives and values of the people who put it together, reading the story they've bound together with the recipes.

Part One

Approaches to the Texts

The three essays that open *Recipes for Reading* provide some historical and theoretical background to help readers expand their appreciation of the community or fund-raising cookbook form. In " 'Tried Receipts': An Overview of America's Charitable Cookbooks," Janice Bluestein Longone, a culinary historian and owner of the Wine and Food Library in Ann Arbor, Michigan, provides an overview of the books' patterns and variety. Her immense knowledge of these books, delight in their ingenuity, and keen sense of their historical value make for lively reading. Jan, who often provides appraisal and development services to institutional and private libraries and collectors, also writes culinary pieces for such publications as the *American Magazine and Historical Chronicle* and the *Journal of Gastronomy*. She teaches and lectures on culinary history throughout the United States and serves as a judge for cookbook awards for the Julia Child–International

Association of Cooking Professionals Awards and for the Tabasco Community Cookbook Awards.

My own piece, "Cooking Up Stories: Narrative Elements in Community Cookbooks," links narrative structures familiar from our literary reading to the fund-raising cookbooks, asking readers to think about the many kinds of stories and narrative elements to be found between community cookbook covers. Examples from diverse cookbooks illustrate the theoretical material. As a scholar of American literature with interests in many "nonliterary" and informal kinds of communication—from quilts to letters to diaries, and with a particular interest in women's literature, I also attempt to enfold the cookbooks within a context of sociohistorical and literary forces. Perhaps because I came to academic life late, after years of work in public administration and other jobs (cooking, sales, secretarial), I enjoy connecting the literary and the nonliterary. My Ph.D. is from West Virginia University; I'm now an associate professor of English at The Ohio State University–Marion.

Colleen Cotter gives us a linguist's look at the recipe form in "Claiming a Piece of the Pie: How the Language of Recipes Defines Community," using the technical tools of the linguist's trade to illustrate her points. Her comparative analysis of various recipes provides necessary groundwork for thinking about the structural, patterned aspects of cookbook language along with possibilities for creative variations. Colleen's research concerns media language, sociolinguistics, and the Irish language. Before pursuing linguistics, she worked for many years as a daily newspaper journalist. Her Ph.D. is from the University of California, Berkeley; currently she teaches jointly in the linguistics department and the communication, culture and technology program at Georgetown University.

"Tried Receipts": An Overview of America's Charitable Cookbooks

Janice Bluestein Longone

This volume is dedicated to the American principles of democracy and progress; to the ex-service men who fought for these principles in the World War; to those of their number who gave their lives; and to those also of their number, wounded, disabled and needy, now in our midst.[1]

It is now four years since, by permission of the School Board, and the concurrence of the Superintendent and Teachers, sewing was introduced in the Colored Public School, as a weekly lesson. The following year the hall of the school house was converted into a kitchen and lessons in cooking were given twice a week. This book has been compiled by ladies engaged in this work, the proceeds from the sale of the books are to be used for carrying on this work. The ladies are greatly obliged to the business men of Winchester, who have kindly advertised in the book and thus enabled us to publish it, and also to the housekeepers, who have given us their tried receipts.[2]

If you buy this book you will help the work of the Telegraph Hill Neighborhood Association. . . . You will send more nurses and doctors to the beds of pain. You will help Education and Hopefulness in the endless struggle with Ignorance and Weakness. You will bring the browns and reds into cheeks now pale. You will let Happiness dance in eyes where Sorrow now sits and glooms. You will put one more flower on a dead child's grave.[3]

The Landmarks Club, under whose auspices and for whose benefit this book is published, is an organization of well known men and women, incorporated under the laws of the State, to preserve the historic landmarks of Southern Cal-

ifornia. . . . The largest effort of the club has been to preserve from further spoliation and decay the remains of the
old Franciscan Missions. The noblest and most impressive
ruins in the United States, these venerable piles were going to
pieces with fearful rapidity, an unprotected prey of vandals
and the weather.[4]

We cordially invite you to take an interest with us in this
reformatory work. Our labors are confined to no one class of
unfortunates; we strive to help all, the rich as well as the poor.
You may ask, What is our work? . . . We are working to
combat a terrible calamity, or call it as some are pleased to, a
disease. Whatever name it takes, whatever disguise it assumes,
it is a terrible power in our land, this demon, Intemperance.[5]

These and a thousand other causes have benefited from the diligent
work of American women during the last 130 years. Although there has
been much documentation of women's charitable work in America,[6] surprisingly little research has been done on one of the earliest and, perhaps,
most financially profitable avenues of contribution: fund-raising cookbooks, hereafter referred to as "charities."

By 1860 cookbooks had become an integral part of the publishing
business in America. However, the upheaval of the Civil War caused a de-
cline in the publication of all books, including cookbooks. Then, shortly
after the end of the Civil War, three major cookbook explosions occurred,
the effects of which are still with us. The first was a Civil War legacy:
cookbooks compiled by women's charitable organizations to raise funds to
aid victims of the war—orphans, widows, the wounded, veterans. The
trickle of these early books published in the 1860s and 1870s quickly became a flood that continues into our own time, as thousands of charitable
cookbooks have been produced to benefit every conceivable cause in the
United States. The second major historical development was promotional
literature, in the form of large quantities of small pamphlet cookbooks,
issued by the ever-growing number of national food and kitchen equipment companies. This development overlapped somewhat with the "charities," since at various times these national companies advertised and/or
underwrote some of the fund-raising books. The third important development was the growth of the cooking school movement. It began with
the influential cooking schools started in New York by Pierre Blot (est.
1865) and Juliet Corson (est. 1876) and intensified with the great cooking

Cookbooks from Janice Bluestein Longone's collection:
Landmarks Club Cook Book (1903); *M.W.C.T.U. Cuisine* (1878); *Lord Fairfax's Kitchen: A Collection of Tried Recipes from Winchester Housekeepers* (1892); *High Living* (1904); *The All-American Cook Book* (1922).

schools and their teachers—Mrs. Rorer in Philadelphia (est. 1884) and Mrs. Lincoln and Fannie Farmer in Boston (The Boston Cooking School, est. 1879, incorporated 1883). These schools dominated American cookbook publishing for the remainder of the nineteenth and into the early twentieth century. Although it does not appear that this movement influenced the "charities" directly, the cooking school movement may have increased the appetite for cookbooks. Frequently recipes from cooking school publications appeared in the fund-raisers, and it is likely that the cooking school cookbooks set an example, both in form and content, for America's charitable cooks from coast to coast.[7]

The popularity and rapid spread of the community cookbook phenomenon might be considered a prime example of female bonding and collective civic virtue. At a time when American women were without full political rights and representation, they found the community cookbook one very effective way to participate in the public life of the nation. Through voluntary organizations—charitable, educational, cultural, civic, professional, political, and religious—they created networks of mutual support, training grounds for organizing, and acceptable platforms from which to influence American life.

In *Born for Liberty*,[8] Sara Evans calls this form of participation in public life "politicized domesticity." She suggests that women deserve much of the credit for many of the major social movements in America, with perhaps the most striking example being the degree to which the New Deal and the development of the modern welfare state were the result of the agenda of women's reform movements in the preceding century. Madeline Lee, in a most perceptive review of Evans's book, suggests that "from this position of unofficial influence, women were able to move into whatever enlarged political space social and political forces allowed."[9]

The single best source for investigating the beginnings of fund-raising cookbooks remains Margaret Cook's *America's Charitable Cooks: A Bibliography of Fund-raising Cook Books Published in the United States (1861–1915)*.[10] Cook compiled her work by consulting major libraries in every state, private collectors of "charities," bibliographies, and dealers' catalogs. Her efforts resulted in a listing of more than 3000 charity cookbooks published prior to 1916. (Every edition or printing of a given book is included as a separate listing.) My own work since the 1971 publication of *America's Charitable Cooks* can probably double that number and it is my belief that a large number of additional books remain unknown and/or uncataloged in any easily accessible form. The diligent work necessary for a comprehensive study of these books, state by state, has yet to be addressed.

An analysis of Cook's work gives us a picture of American women and their charitable work between the Civil War and the First World War. Clearly, most cookbook compilers were Protestants, although of many diverse sects. The were 314 Presbyterian cookbooks from thirty-seven states; 289 Methodist and Methodist Episcopal cookbooks from forty-three states; 220 Congregational cookbooks from twenty-nine states; 151 Baptist cookbooks from thirty-three states; and 77 Episcopal cookbooks from twenty-eight states.

In addition, there were a multitude of other organizations, causes, and groups, including Brethren Church, Business & Professional Women, Catholic Church (five from five states), cemetery associations, children's charities, Christ Church, Christian Church, Christian Temperance Union, Confederate Relief, Congregational Church, D.A.R., Dorcas Society, Eastern Star, Epworth League, fairs and expositions, granges, home economics and domestic science organizations, Homes for the Friendless, hospitals, Jewish charities (twenty-two from twelve states), King's Daughters, libraries, Lutheran Church, Moravian Church, Quaker groups, Reformed Church, Sanitary Commission and Civil War, schools (forty-eight from twenty-two states including Washington, D.C.), sororities, Trinity Church, Unitarian Church, United Daughters of the Confederacy, Universalist Church, vegetarian groups (four from three states), Women's Exchange (nine from six states), Women's Relief Corps and G.A.R., women's suffrage proponents, and YMCA and YWCA.

According to Cook's bibliography, which, as indicated above, is by no means all-inclusive, by 1880 "charities" had been published in twenty-eight states, by the turn of the century, in nearly every state. In some cases, a charity cookbook was the first known cookbook published within that state, for example *The Kansas Home Cook-Book* (Leavenworth, 1874) and *The Texas Cook Book* (Houston, 1883).

Cook considers the first cookbook published and sold in the United States to benefit a charitable cause to be *A Poetical Cook-Book*, issued on behalf of the Sanitary Fair held in Philadelphia in 1864.

An examination of the early "charities" from that date to the end of the nineteenth century shows women participating in a wide variety of fairs, local and national, for a variety of causes. From Boston to San Francisco, fairs were held and accompanying cookbooks issued to benefit hospitals, libraries, YMCAs, firehouses, churches, and the causes of temperance and suffrage. In Massachusetts alone, such fairs appear to have been held with great regularity in the 1870s and 1880s.[11]

The participation of women in the great national and international fairs held to showcase America's coming of age as a great power has bequeathed to us several of the more interesting and intriguing "charities," each worthy of further study: *The National Cookery Book* (Women's Centennial Committees of the International Exhibition, Philadelphia, 1876); *Favorite Dishes: A Columbian Autograph Souvenir Cookery Book* (Board of Lady Managers, World's Columbian Exposition, Chicago, 1893); and *Tested Recipe Cook Book* (Board of Women Managers, Cotton States and International Exposition, Atlanta, 1895).

The early "charities" are described as being compiled mostly by ladies, although we also find members and friends, young ladies, housewives, best housekeepers, experienced housewives, women (many fewer than "ladies"), culinary experts, many generations of noted housekeepers, women experienced in the science of cooking, farmers' wives, mothers, or daughters (e.g., in St. Paul, Minnesota, 1894), women living one mile above the sea (Cheyenne, Wyoming, 1901), ladies of unquestioned ability in ministering to the "creature comforts of inner man" (Fort Wayne, Indiana, 1873), and a limited but distinctive number of Nashville housewives (1906).

The recipes are described as tried and true, favorite, celebrated old, tested and signed, useful, practical, tried and approved, tried and tested, choice, family, best-ever, original and selected, valuable, the very best, reliable, select, tried and found good; they are often said to comprise good things to eat or a feast of good things. The ladies of the Methodist Episcopal Church of Pontiac, Illinois (1912), not only claimed that their recipes were tried and tested but admonished that the recipes "are given to use, not to fill space, and may be relied on."

In addition to charity cookbooks published by groups of women, there have always been a small number of books written and/or edited and/or compiled by one individual on behalf of a charitable cause. Among these is an American classic, Mrs. B. C. Howard's *Fifty Years in a Maryland Kitchen* (Baltimore, 1873). Mrs. Howard was chatelaine of Belvidere, a country home famous for its hospitality, and she was always actively engaged in numerous charitable causes. In 1865 she became president of the Great Southern Relief Association, which held a fair in Baltimore, raising nearly $200,000 for the benefit of those who lost all they had in the Civil War. Her cookbook was produced "solely for the purpose of aiding certain benevolent undertakings." Mrs. Howard's recipes "have been treasured and followed by Marylanders for almost a century."[12] Several other classics in this genre include *The Refugees' Cook Book* (San Francisco, 1906), compiled by the refugee Hattie P. Bowman and issued for earthquake victims; *A Book of Dorcas Dishes* (Hollis & Buxton, Maine, 1911), edited by Kate Douglas Wiggins; and *The Woman Suffrage Cook Book* (Boston, 1886), edited by Mrs. Hattie A. Burr.

There have been a small number of bilingual "charities" such as the German- and English-language *St. Paul's Bazaar Kochbuch und Geschaeftsfuehrer* (Chicago, 1892). A Swedish translation [Hemmets drottning kokbok] of *The "Home Queen" World's Fair Souvenir Cook Book* (Chicago, 1893) was published in Chicago in 1899 to satisfy the growing Swedish population of the Midwest. Ethnic cookbooks in English appeared by the early twentieth century, for example, the *Jewish Cook Book by Temple Israel* (Omaha, 1901) and the African American *The Federation Cook Book* by "the colored women of the State of California" (Pasadena, 1910). Later ethnic books frequently offered foreign language titles for recipes, although the recipes themselves were in English. Two of the more interesting examples of this genre are the *Cook Book of Popular Norse Recipes* (Blair, Wisconsin, 1924) and *Specialita Culinarie Italiane* (Boston, 1936).

As early as 1886, commercially prepared "canned" cookbooks became available. The recipes were the same, whoever sponsored the book, although the advertising was local. Examples of this are the many editions of *The Ladies Handbook and Household Assistant: A Manual of Religious and Table Etiquette*, published on behalf of various groups, such as the Ladies' Society of the Universalist Church (Hinsdale, New Hampshire) and the Methodist Episcopal Church Society (Auburn, Maine).

Although most "charities" had straightforward titles (*The Gulf City Cook Book, Housekeeping in Alabama, California Recipe Book, Favorite Recipes, How We Cook in . . .*), many had clever, cute, or intriguing names: *Helps for Young Housekeepers* (San Francisco, 1879), *The Witchery of Cookery* (San Jose, 1889), *Cooking for Working-Men's Wives* (New Almaden, California, 1890), *Crumbs from Everybody's Table* (Salinas, California, 1895), *Chop-sticks* (Troy, New York,

1884), *Cook Book and Experiences in Original Verse* (Afton, New York, 1899),
Dainties for Dainty People (Lorain, Ohio, 1908), *Edibilia* (Indianapolis 1873),
Kickshaws (Brattleboro, Vermont, 1881), *Kind That Mother Used to Make Cook
Book* (Ithaca, New York, 1913), *No Woman Ever Has Enough Cook Books* (Syr-
acuse, New York, 1915), *Nonpareil Table Talk* (Greensburg, Pennsylvania,
1889), *Old Recipes for New Housekeepers* (Grand Ledge, Michigan, 1905), *Person-
ally Conducted Tours through our Kitchens* (Troy, New York, 1897), *Substantials and
Dainties* (Wheeling, West Virginia, 1905), *Up-to-date Cook Book* (New Or-
leans 1910), *What All Saints Eat* (Omaha, 1901), *What I Know about Housekeeping*
(Adrian, Michigan, 1898), *What We Need and How We Knead It* (Albany, New
York, 1879), and *Y's Cookbook for Wise Cooks* (Salem, New Jersey, 1891).

A passion for alliteration is obvious: *Culinary Crinkles* (Birmingham,
Alabama, 1909), *Clever Cooking by Charleston Cooks* (Charleston, Illinois, 1901),
Confections Culled (Brattleboro, Vermont, 1900), *Cooks in Clover* (Passaic,
New Jersey, 1889), *Crinkles from Competent Cooks* (Woodbury, New Jersey,
1899), *Crumbs of Comfort* (Charlestown, Massachusetts, 1888), *Culinary Clip-
pings by Competent Cooks* (White Bear Lake, Minnesota, 1908), *Culinary Con-
ceits* (Toledo, Ohio, 1894), *Culinary Cullings* (Fort Scott, Kansas, 1906),
Dainty and Delicious Dishes (Yonkers, 1905), *Favorite Food of Famous Folk* (Louis-
ville, 1900), *Fish, Flesh and Fowl* (Portland, Maine, 1877), *Food Fancies* (Worcester, Massachusetts, 1906), *Goodies for the Good* (Okmulgee, Oklahoma, 1904),
Kansas Kookbook for Kansas Kooks (Topeka, 1900), *K.K.K. The "Kute Kooking
Klub"* (Honey Grove, Texas, 1894), *Kollege Kookery Kinks* (Seattle, 1915), *Pots,
Pans and Pie-plates* (Baltimore, 1905), *Rare Recipes for Ridgewood Residents* (Ridge-
wood, New Jersey, 1910), *Rules for the Ravenous* (Brooklyn, 1914), and *Women's
Wisdom* (Owensboro, Kentucky, 1890).

Some names clearly indicated what were considered to be the duties
and role of women: *How to Keep a Husband, Or Culinary Tactics* (San Fran-
cisco, 1872), *How to Win a Heart* (St. Helena, California, 1883), *Way to a Man's
Heart* (Milwaukee, 1901), *What the Baptist Brethren Eat and How the Sisters Serve It*
(Port Huron, Michigan, 1889) and *300 Ways to Please a Husband* (Lockhart,
Texas, 1915). If the title of the "charity" did not clearly indicate womanly
duties, the subtitle might do so. This is well illustrated in the *Home Mission
Cook Book* (Council Bluffs, Iowa, 1908), which is subtitled "*The True Mission of
All Cooking Is to Minister to the Welfare and Comfort of the Home—Hence the Name.*")

More commonly, the earlier "charities" had poetry, prose, or quotations from the Bible on women's duties. The biblical quotes reflected "The
Praise and Properties of a Good Wife" and included proverbs such as "She

looketh well to the ways of her household, and eateth not the bread of idleness."[13] Almost ubiquitous was the "How to Preserve [or Cook] a Husband." The specifics of this choice bit of advice varied somewhat from book to book, but the following quotation offers a good insight into the role expectation:

How to Cook Husbands

A Few Simple Rules, Which, If Followed by the Housewife, Will Insure Domestic Happiness

Many husbands are spoiled by mismanagement in cooking, and so are not tender and good. Some good wives keep their husbands constantly in hot water; others their lives; others think they need to be blown up occasionally, and others let them freeze by their carelessness and indifference.

It cannot be supposed that any husband will be tender and good, managed in this way. But they can be made really fine and delicious when properly cooked. In selecting a husband a woman should not be guided by the silvery appearance, as in buying fish, nor by the golden tint, as if she wished salmon. Be sure to select him yourself, as tastes differ. Do not go to the market for him, as the best are always brought to the door. It is far better to have none, unless you will learn patiently how to cook him. See that the linen in which you wrap him is nicely washed and mended, with the required number of strings and buttons sewed on. A preserving kettle of the finest porcelain is best; but if you have only an earthenware pipkin, it will do, with care. Tie him in the kettle with the silken cord called love, as the one called duty is always weak. They are apt to fly out or get burned and crusty on the edges, since, like crabs and lobsters, you have to cook them while alive. Make a bright steady fire out of comfort, cheerfulness and neatness; set him as near this as seems to agree with him. If he sputters and fizzes do not be anxious, as some husbands do this until they are done. Add a little sugar in the form of what confectioners call kisses. But use no vinegar or pepper on any account. A little spice improves, but it must be used with judgment.

Do not stick any sharp instrument into him to see if he is becoming tender. You cannot fail to know when he is done.

If thus cooked you will find him very digestible, agreeing nicely with you, and he will keep perfectly, unless you become careless and set him in too cool a place.[14]

There were, of course, fund-raising cookbooks that presented a totally opposite picture of what a woman's role and duty should be. The dedication found in a Washington Equal Suffrage Association cookbook expresses this:

Dedication

To the first woman who realized that half the human race were not getting a square deal, and who had the courage to voice a protest; and also to the long line of women from that day unto this, who saw clearly, thought strongly, and braved misrepresentation, ridicule, calumny and social ostracism, to bring about that millennial day when humanity shall know the blessedness of dwelling together as equals.

To all those valiant and undaunted soldiers of progress we dedicate our labors in compiling this volume.[15]

Verification of the oft-quoted maxim that Americans are joiners is amply documented by an examination of the variety of groups sponsoring charitable cookbooks. Although, as indicated above, many are simply by *the ladies of, or the women's auxiliary of,* just about every nationally recognized charitable group is accounted for: Dorcas, King's Daughters, Women's Exchange, women's guilds, missionary societies, building associations, P.E.O., Village Improvement Associations, Ladies Aid Societies, W.C.T.U., Eastern Star, Homes for the Friendless, D.A.R., United Daughters of the Confederacy and, more recently, the Junior League.

In addition, however, we find literally hundreds of smaller groups— women meeting to further a religious, educational, civic, welfare, social, or intellectual cause. We might assume what the needleworkers guilds, the ladies sewing circles, the Belgian Relief Fund, the Literary Clubs, or the reading-room associations did, but what, I wonder, was the mission of the You and I Club, The Theo-broma Club, The Sunshine Society, the Whatsoever Circle, or the Buds of Promise Class?[16]

Earlier I alluded to the paucity of resource material on fund-raising cookbooks and their role in enhancing the common good and general welfare of Americans. This is now being remedied by the publication of books such as this one, by numerous articles in both the popular and scholarly press, by the more general availability of bibliographic material and by modern library technology. Today many of the early books can be examined in libraries throughout the country. The Schlesinger Library at

Radcliffe has an especially good collection of New England "charities," including both early and more recent ones. The library at Johnson and Wales College in Providence, Rhode Island, has an enormous number of more modern "charities" from all fifty states. The Huntington Library in San Marino, California, has an excellent collection of California "charities," as does the Los Angeles Public Library. Texas Women's University in Denton, Texas, contains the greater portion of the cookery library of Margaret Cook and her mother, Mrs. Thomas Scruggs, upon whose collection Cook based her bibliography (discussed above).

A further resource can be found at the library of the Tabasco Company, Avery Island, Louisiana. In 1990, the Tabasco Company, "to recognize a uniquely American book form—the community cookbook—and the committed volunteers who use it so effectively to benefit charitable causes," initiated two national awards: the Tabasco Community Cookbook Awards for outstanding cookbooks published the previous year by nonprofit organizations, and the Walter S. McIlhenny Hall of Fame Awards for those "charities" that have sold 100,000 copies or more. Copies of all books entered into these competitions are available for research. In addition, the McIlhenny family, owners of Tabasco, have begun collecting earlier "charities," from all regions of America, with a special emphasis on southern works.[17]

There is, alas, no way to accurately determine the amount of money raised for charitable purposes by community cookbooks since their beginnings following the Civil War. However, the hundreds of books submitted to the Tabasco Community Cookbooks Awards since their inception documents the raising of millions of dollars, and the books awarded Hall of Fame status have collectively raised more than 29 million dollars.

Today, some of the fund-raising cookbooks are expensively and professionally produced with the stated purpose of reaching a wide national sales audience, but the majority still consist of more simply gathered collections of local recipes. Some are produced by the local organization, often with in-kind support and/or underwriting from local businesses or people (artwork, desktop publishing, photography, etc.). This is in contrast to the support through advertisements from local businesses, which was ubiquitous in the earlier books, and whose appearance adds immeasurably to their use as scholarly and historic documents. There are today a number of commercial companies that print fund-raising cookbooks, sometimes very well. More often, these mass-produced books are poorly produced, with much "canned" material and little or no uniqueness or regional flavor. Fortunately, however, many of today's "charities" still do offer historical and regional information, much of which cannot easily be found elsewhere.

Almost all the causes for which fund-raising cookbooks were published in the nineteenth century are still with us. And now, there are new ones. Among recent entries in the 1994 Tabasco Community Cookbook Awards, funds were raised for Meals on Wheels, the purchase of a camcorder for an adult day center, for symphony orchestras and museums, substance abuse centers, the Nature Conservancy, the Women's Appointment Collaboration (to increase the participation of women on civic boards and commissions), Hospice, battered women's shelters, Braille translations of books, playground equipment for a Montessori School, the serving of 30,000 hot lunches to seniors each year, and eight $2000 university scholarships "from a $400,000 endowment fund begun in 1975 with the profits of our first and then succeeding cookbooks."

The volunteers who wrote and write these books often mention feeling privileged to be able to participate, to contribute, to "raise hope through generosity." Fund-raising cookbooks improve the quality of community life with the funds they generate and they provide as well a record of regional culinary cultures.[18] They also record historical, philosophical, and religious aspects of their compilers and thus of their country. They always have, and they continue to do so.

Cooking Up Stories: Narrative Elements in Community Cookbooks

Anne Bower

Reading hundreds of community cookbooks (also known as charitable or regional or fund-raising cookbooks) and studying the scholarship of others has convinced me that these books form a genre governed by distinct codes and conventions and that once familiar with those standards, one can appreciate particular cookbooks' stylistic variations and inventions.[1] Perceiving how each group of authors employs the form's conventions and then creates improvisations (or does not), I have moved toward a realization that in these cookbooks, communities of authors, deliberately or inadvertently, construct their own stories. I purposefully choose the word stories, preferring it to the term narratives, because the latter term implies a distinct narrator. And while the women who compose fund-raising cookbooks are active creators of text who do employ narrative elements, they do not usually intentionally engage in narration.

If community cookbooks are seldom shaped to tell a particular story, where does the story originate? Perhaps in our need for stories—for order, form, beginnings-middles-ends. Perhaps in our historical situation, at a time when postmodernism has allowed "an erosion of the boundaries between literature and other forms of discourse," as Jay Clayton puts it.[2] Our ideas about narrative/story have expanded. Wallace Martin sees that, while we often follow literary traditions that "treat narrative as a sequence of events" or define it as "a discourse produced by a narrator," more recently we have also theorized narrative as "a verbal artifact that is organized and endowed with meaning by its readers."[3] That last definition has been applied to a variety of texts by scholars in history, women's studies, cultural studies, folklore, and other disciplines, who have modeled interactive ways of reading material objects and nonliterary texts. Feminist scholars have used the "verbal artifact" approach to show that needlework, gardens, diaries, letters, etc., "have provided women with an important outlet for their creativity and a form for expressing their view of the world."[4]

Still, because this kind of reading is subjective, I find myself asking if the stories I discover and then recount are faithful to the storytellers' experiences? Separated from the community cookbook authors by time and space, sometimes by race and other background aspects, can I read their stories accurately? There is no easy answer. However, a broad knowledge of the cookbooks and of the social, political, and historic contexts that surrounded their production can assist a reader to feel some confidence in her ability to perceive the experiences of community cookbook authors and then transmit the stories found in these texts. In spite of the hazards of misinterpretation and misreading, working with these texts involves a fascinating, stimulating experience. More than any reading before, with these cookbooks I find operative what Wolfgang Iser finds the central process of all reading, "the convergence of text and reader bring[s] the literary work into existence."[5]

The stories in community cookbooks might best be described as communal partial autobiographies. Writing about the fragmentation often found in women's autobiographies and of conditions that led women to see their lives without the linearity or "grand" scheme often central to men's autobiographies, Domna C. Stanton finds it necessary to alter the word autobiography when referring to women's life writings. She explains her "excision of *bio* from *autobiography*" as deriving from a distrust of *bio*'s "presumption of referentiality."[6] In this sense, Stanton would see *all* women's writing of their lives as "partial," and I expect she would praise the results for their realism.

Like single-authored autobiographies, community cookbooks project their authors' sense of achieved status; authors of fund-raising recipe collections are mostly middle or upper middle class and proud of their social standing. However, autobiographies usually contain personal histories: "an autobiography is typically a story of how a life came to be what it was, or a self became what it is."[7] In this respect, community cookbooks seem lacking. They seldom detail how the recipe donors achieved their status or what that status means to them individually. Theirs is a communal but fragmented portrait. They certainly don't tell us about the full range of their experience; no matter how elaborate the cookbook, we are only granted small portions of the recipe donors' lives.

However, ideals concerning home and heritage occur in the cookbooks, either as statements or implications, just as they do in women's autobiographies, although the world of work outside the home is seldom fully incorporated. As Estelle Jelinek and others have pointed out, for the most part in women's autobiography, "the emphasis remains on personal matters—not the professional, philosophical, or historical events that are more often the subject of men's autobiographies."[8] Jelinek explains further that historically women have lacked the privilege of affirming a "private self" and so have often "masked" their writings about themselves; at the same time, their life writings often express discomfort with the "male world" and greater comfort within "a *female* culture, a *women's* world."[9] Relationships almost always occupy a central place in women's autobiographies; and in the cookbooks too, one finds explicitly stated or subtly implied links to family, friends, and community. And as with autobiography, in the cookbooks we also sense that the "self" or "family" or "community" projected may be idealized. Whether the group authors of a particular fund-raising cookbook actually cooked from the recipes in their book, pursuing the depicted heritage, lifestyle, and values, we cannot actually say.[10] All we can say is that they participated in constructing these texts, usually appending their names to their recipes, so that the recipes and names remain to us as a form of self-representation.

The *form* of the cookbook bears relevance to women's autobiographical traditions also. Jelinek summarizes women's life writings as "episodic and anecdotal, nonchronological and disjunctive" compared to the more "linear and progressive" narrative style of male autobiographies. And she wonders if "there is a direct connection between the disjunctive style of women's autobiographies and the fragmentation of their lives."[11] The sources of that "fragmentation" could be the pattern of tasks in the home, social pressures alienating a woman from the larger political and historical workings of the world, customs that sometimes separate her from education and self-concepts beyond the domestic or private sphere, or the pressures of balancing a job outside the home with the daily chores of the household.

While communal partial autobiography is the dominant kind of story in fund-raising cookbooks, these texts could also be read as fictions (idealizations or romances of home, of middle-class life, of plenty, of the domestic role, of one's subculture or local community). One could also perceive them as historical chronicles, accepting Hayden White's argument that the chronicle form verges on storytelling but lacks the "narrative closure" of a true historical narrative.[12]

I would propose that within each community cookbook, whether it is designated an autobiography or a book of instruction, history, fiction, or a combination of various elements, there are many elements of a story. As I discuss these elements, I will provide examples from a range of community cookbooks, many of them in the Schlesinger Library's fine collection.[13]

We should begin with "setting." Explicitly or implicitly, it is the kitchen, dining room, or the "table" as the center of home and domestic life. However, the serving of food is occasionally allied not solely with the kitchen but with professional or philanthropic work. Thus, in the 1955 Women's Press Club cookbook, *Who Says We Can't Cook!*, setting, while still primarily the home, includes the newsroom, the war front, ships, trains, and restaurants.[14] In *The Black Family Dinner Quilt Cookbook*, convention halls, conference rooms, hospital rooms, the YWCA, hotel rooms, and other locations are some of the additional venues for meal sharing.[15] While the recipes provided in the book conventionally provide the usual number of servings for home consumption, throughout the text, sidebar anecdotes widen the circle of the food community. These supplementary passages present the sharing of food as an integral part of community-building in the work of men and women philanthropists and social reformers.

Surrounding the kitchen and home, we have the setting of region; particularly in twentieth-century cookbooks, the regional aspect is a strong element of the texts—so much so that they're often referred to as "regional cookbooks." In my "Louisiana" file I have photocopied pages from a half dozen cookbooks that feature this particular piece of topography—its scenery, traditions, and food resources. For example, *Recipes and Reminiscences of New Orleans* boldly establishes its setting through artistically rendered illustrations on the cover and at frequent intervals throughout the book. The Thibodaux Service League's *Louisiana Legacy* celebrates "bayou country" in varied ways: illustrations, such as children fishing and a graduation scene from a school now closed; explanations of regional dishes, such as po'boys and gumbo; inclusion of local ingredients, such as dove and crawfish; and references to people, events, and places well known in the region, for instance, the L. P. Babin family, the Thibodaux Firemen's Fair, Grand Isle.[16] Similarly, The Junior League of Lake Charles's *Pirate's Pantry: Treasured Recipes of Southwest Louisiana* quite elaborately sets its recipes within a framework of regionalism. Separate illustrated passages explain "Cajun Cuisine," the legend of Jean Lafitte, and particulars of local food elements, such as filé, roux, and gumbo; additional illustrations feature swamps, bayous, pirate ships; and ingredients favor the local, including squirrel, dove, shrimp, oyster, trout, red snapper, and ling.[17]

Setting also includes historical time and social milieu, both of which are incorporated into the texts of most community cookbooks. That is clearly the case in the Louisiana cookbooks discussed briefly above, where time past is used to enrich time present, exoticizing and romanticizing, but also individualizing the recipe donors and their food. At other times cookbooks may focus on their own time exclusively. Cookbooks produced during wartime often incorporate their historical moment through economies offered; this is the case, for example, with *What's Cooking at Columbia: A Recipe Book*, which was published in 1942 by Columbia University's Committee for United War Relief. Knowing the date and motives for publication assists us in reading the book's attention to budget (for example, its "tips to tease the palate and please the purse") in terms of wartime constraints, not just as awareness of younger academics' and students' thin purses.[18] In *Nos Meilleures Recettes* (Our best recipes), issued in 1947 to raise money for French Relief, many contributors provide inexpensive dishes prepared during the war. Soft Swiss (War) Omelet, noted as being "deli-

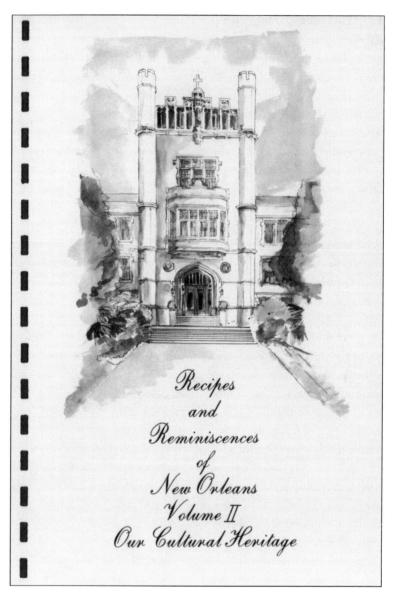

Recipes
and
Reminiscences
of
New Orleans
Volume II
Our Cultural Heritage

Cover illustration by Emery Clark from *Recipes and Reminiscences of New Orleans,* 2nd ed. (1981), courtesy the Parents' Club of the Ursuline Academy.

cious and easy to make"; gnocchi, with its attached recommendation that "children love this for supper"; and a vegetable loaf or "recipe for hard times" recall the limited choices of wartime.[19]

While setting is a strong aspect of most community cookbooks, individualized "characters"—traditionally a mainstay of both real-life and fictional stories—play a minor role in charitable cookbooks, where the community takes precedence over the individual. While certain distinctive voices do emerge, character in these stories is more collectively achieved.

The 1885 *A New Daily Food* shields the Ladies of St. Paul's Church, in Morrisania, New York, from public scrutiny by giving the spotlight to one individual—Lydia Shillaber.[20] Credited on the title page for editing and compiling the text, she appears as only "L.S." at the end of a half page preface. However, she makes clear that she speaks for "The Ladies' Society" as she states their collective belief that homemakers' work of caring for the physical health of parishioners importantly complements the rector's care for congregants' spiritual health. In a two-page "introductory" she establishes the text's legitimacy by stating that the book results from the "united wisdom of many experienced housekeepers."[21] Thus Shillaber, as a strong, capable leader, gives voice and personality to the collective character of her community. Some contributors to this book give their full names, but many of the recipes do not even carry the name of a donor, and the recipes throughout show a limited range of tone and format.

The 1897 *Florence Cook Book*, compiled by the Ladies of the Mission Circle in Florence (Northampton), Massachusetts, is a text richer in characters.[22] Here the reader gains a stronger sense of a community of women with different voices. The book's brief introduction makes few claims for the work's originality, only for its integrity; for " 'the proof of the pudding is in the eating,' so the saying goes." However, almost all recipes bear the names of donors—Mrs. Elizabeth Potter, Mrs. F. E. Campbell, and so on. Each chapter, devoted to a particular category of food, starts off with a quotation; and most of these quotations seem to have been selected by the group authors to project agreement with the dominant middle-class image of a strongly moral but highly domestic "angel in the house." For example, the vegetable chapter begins: "A Man is, in general, better pleased when he has a good dinner, than when his wife speaks Greek." Then, within the recipes, judgments and advice remind the reader that individual women have used, adjusted, and served these dishes before writing them down for *public* consumption. Thus, to learn that A. B. Moquette thinks her green mayonnaise "may be used for broiled shad, mackerel, chops or steak" gives her some individual force.

More forceful still is the 1907 *Needlework Guild Cook Book* from Jamestown, New York.[23] Here the names of the members of the Publication Committee are boldly provided, and the four members of the Advertising Committee are listed too. Each chapter states the name of its compiler (who sometimes offers general words of advice), and almost all recipes include the names of donors. Individual style survives somewhat within the recipes. Thus Eva Grier Hunter lists all ingredients for her gluten rolls first, followed by brief directions, while Anna A. Farnham names the ingredients for her bread muffins as she gives instructions on how to prepare them.[24]

By the middle of the twentieth century, the characters of contributors come through much more clearly. In *Who Says We Can't Cook!* anecdotes and background material that accompany recipes help delineate distinctive persons. We meet Henrietta Poynter, then editor of the *Congressional Quarterly,* and understand that her ability to whip together a dish called "Heavenly Hamburger" or a quick cheese wafer appetizer results not only from current necessity, balancing deadlines against social obligations, but also from her history of having to take over cooking and budgeting when her mother was away from home on a "three-month speaking tour for suffrage and left [her] to keep house."[25] Similarly, in *The Greek Palette,* published in 1987 by the Greek Ladies Philoptochos Society of Saints Constantine and Helen Greek Orthodox Church in Lawrence, Massachusetts, readers have a distinct sense of the individuals involved.[26] A staff of sixteen different women formed the cookbook committee; all recipes are signed; and contributors were given the freedom to include personal recollections within their recipes. In some cases, as in Lee Karahalus's "Island Fish Soup," with its personal recollections of night fishing off the island of Paros and of the fisherman's rituals in preparing their traditional fish soup, the recipe is no more important than the enveloping sense of the writer's personality and experience.[27]

While setting and characters are certainly conventional story elements that we expect and enjoy, it does seem that what finally makes a story a story is a plot. Searching the pages of *Cook Along with Us* or *The Best Little Cookbook in Texas*[28] for ways to prepare beef, a reader seldom thinks of plot.

The only sequence of events such a reader desires is the linear process of the recipe: for a beginning—take these ingredients; for a middle—go through these processes; and of course, for an ending, voilà!—a dish to please the tummy and the tongue. But reading for *more* than a recipe, reading the full cookbook as a text, can yield inklings of different beginnings-middles-ends and a new sense of plot.

The plots of community cookbooks unfold subtly, highly dependent upon reader interaction with the text. As Peter Brooks puts it, plot can be understood as "an activity, a structuring operation elicited in the reader trying to make sense of those meanings that develop only through textual and temporal succession."[29] One might categorize community cookbook plots under what Brooks distinguishes as a female plot of ambition. This, he asserts, formulates "an inner drive towards the assertion of selfhood in resistance to the overt and violating male plots of ambition, a counter dynamic which . . . is only superficially passive, and in fact a reinterpretation of the vectors of plot."[30]

By convention, the cookbooks, created by communal authorship and restricted by the structure of the recipe collection (an introduction, chapters devoted to different food categories, recipes contributed by various individuals, perhaps advertisements), are not *supposed* to tell stories. Thus, while some more recent twentieth-century books very deliberately propose themselves as narratives, such as *Out of Our Kitchen Closets*, which foregrounds the development through time of a gay and lesbian Jewish congregation, plot is a subtext in most nineteenth- and early twentieth-century texts.[31]

While the dominant plot in all these books can be understood in terms of Brooks's "female plot of ambition," one needs to see it also in terms of the "home plot": Ann Romines explains that "the 'home plot' of domestic ritual has generated forms and continuities very different from those of the patriarchal American canon and pushes readers to attend to texts that are not inscribed in conventionally literary language. Domestic language often seems invisible to those who have not learned to read it."[32] Harriet Beecher Stowe's *Uncle Tom's Cabin*, Sarah Orne Jewett's *The Country of the Pointed Firs*, and Mary Wilkins Freeman's short stories (such as "A New England Nun") are nineteenth-century fictions with plots in which the heroines, in different ways, come to terms with their domestic lives, defining themselves in and through their acceptance of domesticity's repeated, often ritualized tasks. Romines sees twentieth-century authors using the domestic plot as well, in particular, Willa Cather and Eudora Welty. While Romines's discussion stays with plots in fiction, her insights apply well to community cookbooks, which always, to some extent, depict their authors (who are also their characters) forcefully taking control of and constructing their own domestic lives. Within the "home plot" of fundraising cookbooks I see four major groupings:

1. *The integration plot:* This kind of plot involves a communal autobiography of social acceptance and achievement. For the most part, it proposes a story of the authors achieving assimilation and status through their acceptance of the larger society's conventions and standards.

A New Daily Food, from 1885, posits in its introduction that the homemaker who supervises servants is an "expert manager" and is inspired in her domestic endeavors equally by "love and duty."[33] The ladies of St. Paul's Church in Morrisania, New York, seem to take their own secure location in society for granted. Their recipes resonate with sense and solidity, from the initial presentation of recipes for that basic food, bread, to the establishment center of middle-class eating—meats and fish. As is customary in nineteenth-century cookbooks, vegetables and salads, while esteemed for their healthfulness, do not form a major category of recipes. Only at the end does frivolous candy appear. The selected recipes are mostly of English background, though the ladies of St. Paul's Church also include a few German and French recipes, showing their cultured status. No decorations or illustrations individualize this text, and any anecdotal or personalized writing is limited to the foreword and preface. It is a modest text.

Our Sisters' Recipes, published in 1909 to support a Pittsburgh synagogue's good works programs, assumes, like *A New Daily Food,* servants in the household (thus the African American cook depicted on its frontispiece).[34] The arrangement of food here is not from basics to trimmings, but more the order of service for a formal dinner, implying that such formal dinners are part of "Our Sisters" routine. Although put forth by a Jewish population (and the names attached to recipes attest to that background), the book includes foods no religious Jew would eat, such as dishes mixing meat and milk and those using shellfish. Thus, the "Sisters" downplay their Jewishness, recounting thereby a story of assimilation into the middle-class urban community. The advertisements at the book's end underscore that message, for non-Jewish as well as Jewish businessmen buy space.

Page of advertisements from *Our Sisters' Recipes* (1909).

The 1921 Atlanta Woman's Club *Cook Book* also tells a story of integration; the women present themselves as "professional" housewives.[35] Contributors are carefully named and those who hold office in the club are so listed. Mrs. Newton C. Wing, Chairman, Home Economics, contributes "fried sandwiches"; Mrs. T. T. Stevens, Chairman, Education, donates her "vegetable salad." The book is highly organized, and the text is often directed at practicality. For example, the foreword explains that "special menus" have been eliminated because "in our experience [they] rarely can be used exactly as printed." Rather, they have "substituted instead the order of recipes naturally followed during the day, leaving the housewife the liberty of choice."[36] Separate chapters provide information on time budgeting and kitchen equipment. While the special chapter on "Creole Dishes" indicates these women's acceptance of a particular Southern heritage, another chapter, "Recipes from Famous Homes," goes beyond the local, linking the communal authorship with society's aristocrats, presidents, authors, and other public leaders.

The plot I have labeled "integration" shows up frequently in nineteenth- and early-twentieth-century community cookbooks. Its dominant form in contemporary texts is the Junior League cookbook, which usually presents its authors as leading lights in a given town or city society or at least as consummately knowledgable purveyors of the local culinary culture. With titles such as *Simply Simpático* or *Bay Leaves,* these books quite uniformly bespeak a community of authors at home and at ease in their location.[37] Like good hostesses, these recipe donors often interject little phrases to welcome us to their corner of the world and their local foodways. *Bay Leaves* opens with a tour-guide tone explaining some background about Panama City, Florida, where "gracious hospitality and leisurely living" await the reader. With her entry for a "pineapple refresher," Mrs. Warren Middlemas, Jr., notes that it is "a dramatic beginning for a seafood dinner"; Mrs. David J. Turner tells us that although other fish can be used in her recipe for "baked scamp [sic] with creole sauce," "scamp is the fisherman's favorite."[38] The "gracious" tone of these recent Junior League books, combined with their authors' projected comprehensive knowledge of the town or city in which they live, gives the reader a sense of their firm assimilation and leadership.

2. *The differentiation plot:* In this plot, which occurs much more in the twentieth than in the nineteenth century, the communal authors define

themselves as in some way different from other women. While celebrating their difference, they never position themselves as rejected by the larger society. The difference they stress may be professional, ethnic, religious, or geographic. Actually, this plot always contains or simultaneously participates in the plot of integration. Women using this plot give equal weight to their membership within a special "different" subgroup and their assimilation into the wider society.

Mariechen's Saxon Cook Book, published in Ohio in 1955 announces its pride in a particular ethnic heritage in its foreword: the authors' goal is to pass their Transylvanian heritage along to their children.[39] Throughout, difference is marked: recipe titles usually occur in two languages, and introductions to food categories use terms many of us would not know (as with "Rindfleisch Tokana"—beef goulash).[40] Dishes are not selected to demonstrate coverage of all middle-class eating occasions but rather to mark the customs of the Saxon community, preserving the foods and their methods of preparation authentically. A chapter is thus dedicated to a national favorite, "boiled pastries." In the "Transylvania Saxon Hearth Bread" recipe, instructions specify the right way to obtain the traditional thick crust.[41]

Similarly, The Sephardic Cooks (1977) focuses on a particular group, in this case Spanish Jews of the Mediterranean basin.[42] The foreword celebrates the "pleasant tradition" of their religion and ethnicity. Again, recipe titles usually show up in two languages (English and Spanish). Not only national difference, but religious difference is represented in this text, for verbal traditions (prayers and blessings) are printed along with the recipes for dishes to prepare for special religious occasions.

Another kind of differentiation occurs in the cookbook of the Women's National Press Club, Who Says We Can't Cook! Difference here is announced on the title page, where the illustration, instead of presenting a woman with spoon or loaf of bread, shows us a woman in a hat sitting on a trunk, typing. The contents page doesn't mention the conventional breads, soups, meats and fish, salads, etc., but favors categories related to the women's work: "Regional Wire," "Foreign Assignment," and "Original Copy," for example. The actual recipes are embedded in or combined with narratives of the women's work as journalists. The recipe donors are named, and we learn of their work affiliations, too. Thus, through its style, contents, arrangements, illustrations, and recipe attributions, this cook-

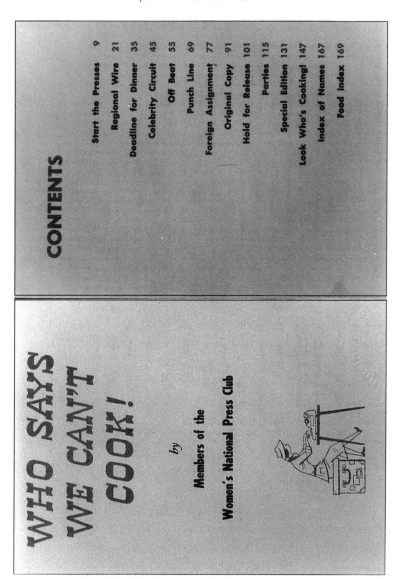

CONTENTS

WHO SAYS WE CAN'T COOK!

by

Members of the

Women's National Press Club

Title and contents pages from *Who Says We Can't Cook!* (1955).
Courtesy Washington Press Club Foundation.

book tells a story of differentiation, of women primarily defining them-selves as journalists but able to accommodate to the domestic role in some way as well.

3. *The plot of moral or religious triumph:* In this plot, found in both the nineteenth and twentieth centuries, the cookbook is used to define woman's role as moral center of the home and / or to demonstrate the ways that food rituals can reinforce religious teachings. This is one of the most consistent and enduring plots in community cookbooks. It coexists com-fortably with both the plot of integration and that of differentiation.

The Center Table, from 1929, is dedicated to recounting a story of the "Jewish home," and that is actually the title of its first chapter.[43] The book is consistently addressed to those within the faith and includes consider-able information about religious ceremonies and food practices. Thus it is the food's religious (and to some extent cultural) associations that form the core of the text's story and of the communal authors' inspiration. Often recipes are selected because of and introduced according to their ceremonial and traditional values; separate chapters are dedicated to the special foods and rituals of Passover and other holidays. The soup chapter is divided into "milk soups" and "meat soups" for the kosher cook. There are also chapters on "The Jewish Home" and "Blessings and Prayers." We can feel, underneath this text, a fear that Jewish "difference" is under threat of assimilation. As Charles Camp has noted, "food is one of the most, if not the single most, visible badges of identity, pushed to the fore by people who believe their culture to be on the wane, their daughters drifting from their heritage."[44]

St. Barnabas Episcopal Church's *Angel Food* is a humble, spiral-bound production, decorated with simple line drawings of angels.[45] The foreword points out that food preparation and food sharing are holy acts, and each food category is introduced with a separator page featuring an angel il-lustration and a biblical quote. Each author's name appears without any qualifications, but her personality often comes through as she credits her source or gives a hint for recipe preparation. "Do your own thing," advises Karyle Chalfant in her "Jazzy Italian Eggplant" recipe. "This is really not my recipe; I got it from a nice Louisiana native one time I was working at the polls during a local election," admits Phyllis Seal about her "Boudin" sausage.[46] For me, this interwoven patter enforces the text's religious ethos of nonexclusivity.

Actually, *A New Daily Food*, to which I referred in discussing the integration plot, also shares many qualities of the religious/moral plot. As its editor, L.S., puts it in the preface, although the book isn't strictly religious instruction, it "tends in that direction." She believes that well-prepared food contributes to our ability to engage in the spiritual life. After all, she asserts, "it is physically impossible for a dyspeptic to be a cheerful Christian and to 'serve the Lord with gladness,' and many a pious man has mourned because he thought himself enveloped in spiritual clouds, when he was only suffering from indigestion."

4. *Historical plot:* Historians construct plots from collected facts, plots which end with the demise or victory of a cause or a group. A few community cookbooks choose this plot, but always with the victorious ending. As far as I can tell, this is strictly a twentieth-century plot form for community cookbooks. Perhaps it is only in our own century that women have grown confident of themselves as constructors of history, entitled to publicly claim their share in the past.

The Historical Cookbook of the American Negro of 1958 privileges history above all else, the history of African Americans.[47] It is arranged according to calendar dates commemorating famous events or persons in "Negro" history or, occasionally, the history of other minority groups. Often the link between history and recipe occurs through famous individuals. For instance, January 5 is marked by a selection of sweet potato and peanut recipes for George Washington Carver (on January 5, 1943, the text tells us, an act of Congress established this date as "Carver Commemoration Day"); Crispus Attucks shows up on March 5 (he led rebels against the British on Boston Commons on March 5, 1770) and Nat Turner in the August section, with a recipe, explanatory text, and two photos to mark the slave insurrection he led in August 1831 (see illustration). Local chapters of the National Council of Negro Women selected the recipes to match these personalities. The book is incredibly educational, and throughout, the individuals or groups contributing recipes are carefully acknowledged—becoming part of the historical record here.

Pots and Politics, subtitled "An Historical Cookbook," incorporates a narrower slice of history than does the text just discussed.[48] This 1976 fund-raiser integrates the 1909 cookbook put out by the Washington Equal Suffrage Association. Part of the plot here is an honoring of a predecessor group of women, a commemoration and preservation and

AUGUST

The above sign stands on U. S. Highway 58, going West from Courtland, Virginia.

Remains of the old plantation house of Nat Turner's master, where the insurrection began.

NAT TURNER CRACKLING BREAD

2 cups corn meal
1/2 cup flour
1 cup fresh cracklings

1 teaspoon salt
1-1/4 cups warm water or
  milk

Mix and sift dry ingredients, add cracklings and stir. Add water or milk and stir until mixture can be handled well. Form into pones and place into baking pan. Bake at 425 degrees F. 25 minutes or until brown.

(THE SOUTHAMPTON COUNCIL)
VIRGINIA

In August 1831, Nat Turner, a Negro slave of Southampton County, Virginia, feeling that he was ordained of God to liberate his people, organized a number of slaves and proceeded to rise against their masters, killing and terrorizing about two hundred whites before being apprehended.

Nat learned to read early, especially the Bible and religious literature. He spent much time fasting and praying and communing with the Spirit. Being abandoned by his chief coworkers in the insurrection, he was forced to go in hiding, in a cave near Cross Keys in Southampton County and emerged only at night. On Oct. 30, 1831, he surrendered, was convicted on the 5th of November and hanged on the 11th, in the courtyard of Jerusalem, the County seat, what is now Courtland, Va.

For the next three decades there was conflict between slavery and antislavery movements, until 1861 when the Civil War itself began. In 1863, Nat Turner's purpose was vindicated by the ultimate triumph of his cause, when Abraham Lincoln declared the freedom of all persons held as slaves. It is said that his favorite dish was known to be crackling bread and sweet potatoes, baked in hot ashes.

Page 74 of *The Historical Cookbook of the American Negro* (1955), showing historical photographs, recipe, and background information relative to Nat Turner. The sign on U.S. Highway 58 reads "Seven miles southwest Nat Turner, a negro, inaugurated, August 21, 1831, a slave insurrection that lasted two days and cost the lives of about sixty whites. The slaves began the massacre near Cross Keys and moved eastward toward Courtland (Jerusalem). On meeting resistance, the insurrection speedily collapsed." Courtesy Bethune Museum and Archives.

duplication of their work. The text reprints a number of important suffragist and feminist documents, from the Seneca Falls "Declaration of Sentiments" to the still unpassed Equal Rights Amendment. An introductory chapter presents information on how the "old" and the "new" groups differ and align, both in politics and in culinary arts. Recipes from both eras are represented, and in both cases names are appended boldly to most recipes.

Canyon Cookery, from 1978, tells its history differently.[49] This complex production of the Bridger Canyon Women's Club announces the link between "Recipes and Recollections" on its title page. It is divided into eras, with extensive text for each section, combining information from various fields (geology, history, photographic records) with recipes to match the factual content. Thus, in the section "Indian and Prehistoric Phase," fry bread, huckleberry tea, and wild rose root tea show up, along with a local contemporary recipe for blood pudding and an 1805 recipe from the Lewis and Clark journals.[50] The section called "The Canyon Today (1959–Present)" includes a wide variety of foods, using modern methods and tools such as the blender ("Nettle Soufflé"). A very careful bibliography documents the historical material.

Books using the history plot often privilege that history above the recipes. Yet the three books I have mentioned also contain elements of the assimilation and differentiation plots in varying degrees. And books that are primarily plotted through some other objective may yet incorporate the history of a region, a city, or a particular group.

My discussion of plot in fund-raising cookbooks has stressed the alignment of people within society—their attempts at differentiation and assimilation and at assertion of spiritual or historical experiences and values. Clearly, such a discussion slides into a thematic approach to texts. My readings engage a process Martin sees in all thematic interpretation: "actively restructuring the past in light of each new bit of information" the text provides. Martin further explains that "theme—the construction of significance backward in time—appears to be as dynamic an element as plot."[51] Indeed, the dynamic of reading makes it difficult to keep these narrative categories separate. However, for my purposes, I think of theme as why plot matters; plot is the particular series or set of events/processes that lead us to grasp theme. . . .

For me, one dominant theme of community cookbooks is the breaking of silence, the coming to public voice of people denied that voice in the past. Deborah Cameron asserts that the "silence of women is above all an absence of female voices and concerns from high culture. If we look at a society's most prestigious linguistic registers—religious ceremonial, political rhetoric, legal discourse, science, poetry—we find women's voices for the most part silent—or rather, *silenced*, for it is not just that women do not speak: often they are explicitly *prevented* from speaking, either by social taboos and restrictions or by the more genteel tyrannies of custom and practice."[52] Community cookbooks are outside "high culture" (usually), and so in them we often find silenced women making a place to express some part of who they are, singly or as part of a group. The texts raise money for the religious, educational, historical, and professional institutions of society, but also provide a space in which women assert their values.

While few women had a public voice in running the major institutions of nineteenth-century society (they were often excluded, for example, from handling church money), their voices were heard, at least to some extent, when they participated in community cookbooks. In later years, women able to give voice to their values and ideas publicly still have found community cookbooks sympathetic venues for expressing certain life values. An interesting example of silence-breaking occurs in the previously discussed *Historical Cookbook of the American Negro.* Contributors to this 1958 text attempt to break the silence of white-written history about the past of African Americans. By commemorating famous people and events of "Negro" history with appropriate recipes, and interweaving in this text famous letters, poems, documents, and photographs, they speak their history beautifully. Just four years after school segregation was outlawed and only three years after the boycott of segregated buses in Montgomery, Alabama, these women claimed their right to have *their* history part of *all* history.

A second theme in charitable cookbooks concerns the importance of woman's domestic role and her power within the home as angel, minister, nutritionist, manager. The women who composed *A New Daily Food* asserted religious values in that book, but another motif in the text is their sense of themselves as "professionals" of domestic work. The introduction asserts that a good housekeeper must be "an expert manager," although women will also, necessarily, find themselves "busy workers." And under the category "Things for a Young Housekeeper to Remember," this book emphasizes that since one person cannot do everything, priorities must be established: "the daily comfort of the family, and the mental and moral training of the children, are of more importance than frosted fruit cake for company. . . . "[53] Later texts, produced by women who worked outside as well as inside the home, maintain an emphasis on the critical importance of woman's work as nurturer, although simultaneously honoring women's nondomestic work.

A third theme, found in many of the cookbooks, is that food is an expression of culture—an art. This is expressed sometimes with verbal exposition, sometimes with artistic presentation, sometimes by interpolating quotations from well-known poems. *The Greek Palette*'s cover features an artist's palette with shrimp, eggplant, artichokes, grapes, etc., in place of pigments; a spoon, mixer, and spatula in place of brushes. The artwork is elaborated in a short introduction, which begins: "Cooking is an ART! Greek cooking is like an artist's palette splattered with a plethora of colors, hues and flavors. Just as an artist dramatically changes a blank canvas into a work of art with a few strokes of his brush and paints, so too, the Greek cook creates beautiful, colorful and flavorful epicurean delights."

The *Legendary Cookbook* compiled by the Llano [Texas] Fine Arts Guild so consistently juxtaposes information about its art exhibits, members' artwork, and history of the Fine Arts Guild itself, that the link between graphic and culinary arts needs no exposition.[54] A number of nineteenth-century cookbooks begin chapters with quotations from well-known writers. Thus, the turn-of-the-century *Stirring Tales Spun by the Fire*[55] heads the bread chapter with the words of Longfellow:

> Behold! A Giant am I!
> Aloft here in my tower,
> With my granite jaws I devour
> The maize, and the wheat, and the rye,
> And grind them into flour.

The chapter devoted to puddings and desserts begins with an excerpt from Charles Dickens's *A Christmas Carol:* "Hallo! A great deal of steam! The pudding was out of the copper. In half a minute Mrs. Cratchit entered— flushed but smiling proudly—with the pudding, like a speckled cannonball, so hard and firm . . . and bedight with Christmas holly stuck into the top." This pattern of using famous writers' words to enmesh the art of cooking with the arts of poetry and fiction was sometimes varied by using poems written by a member of the cookbook community. When Mrs. Eveline F. Riveau contributed her own verses to the 1941 *The Dandy Cook Book*, the link between poetic and culinary arts became part of the text.[56] Presumably both Mrs. Riveau's verses and her recipes (her "Savory Lamb Loaf" among them) gave pleasure to her readers.

Setting, characters, plots, themes—artificial delineations, and yet useful starting terms for pointing out narrative aspects of familiar texts that most people have not read for their narrativity. While the methodical explanation I've undertaken may seem to attempt an objectification of the reading act, in fact, the subjective is an essential part of my approach to reading these texts. The reader's subjectivity, however, can be informed by her knowledge of history, textual conventions, intertextual links, and other backgrounding information. Susan Sniader Lanser comments on this kind of combined subjective / objective textual process in *Fictions of Authority*. She explains that "discursive authority—by which I mean here the intellectual credibility, ideological validity, and aesthetic value claimed by or conferred upon a work, author, narrator, character, or textual practice—is produced interactively; it must therefore be characterized with respect to specific receiving communities."[57] I would add that, relative to fund-raising cookbooks, accessing both the authors and their receiving communities takes a special kind of interactive willingness on the part of the cookbook reader.

My purpose in discussing the literary qualities of community cookbooks is to bring new appreciation to these undervalued texts. Considering the novels of domestic life that she studies, Ann Romines explains that "we have a women's tradition of *writing domestic ritual*, which both inscribes and interrogates women's housekeeping work and art. Such a tradition opposes the confines of essentialism. It implies, instead, that women's traditional lives are worth thinking about, worth writing about, worth reading. It implies that housekeeping may be one of our common human languages, in which we may confront our history and dream our future."[58]

Professional novelists are not the only ones who use the language of domesticity to consider our history, our present lives, and our future. We find the same concerns in nonliterary texts. People have learned recently to appreciate women's letters and diaries. Even more recently, we have realized we could "read" women's quilts as quasi-literary systems. Now I am suggesting that we extend our explorations to community cookbooks. Here we find a bridge between the two kinds of talents Florence Howe perceives in women's traditions: on the one hand, we have the "normative, everyday, talents of women living in a gender-limited world, in a subculture of patriarchy." Here Howe includes the spheres of parenting, friendship, love, community-building, reform work, and domestic arts—the garden, sewing, the kitchen, etc. On the other hand we have the "talents of women writing in a variety of forms, finding the themes and language with which to convey the experience of living in subcultures."[59] This category of "writing" refers to literature, and by literature Howe means the poetic, dramatic, fictional, and essayistic texts we honor as literary. In the many community cookbooks published by women since the Civil War, the boundaries between the two kinds of talents blur, and women from whom we might otherwise never hear tell us their stories.

Claiming a Piece of the Pie: How the Language of Recipes Defines Community

Colleen Cotter

Introduction

Recipes always retain their flavor. Since I started looking at "recipe language" several years ago, I have been enchanted by the many friends and colleagues who continue to pass along personal stories about cookbooks they have just unearthed or great-aunts' recipes they have inherited. They're dimly aware I might be professionally interested (always on the lookout for good "data"), but mostly they want to share a good story, one they know I will understand and appreciate. In a satisfying way, we are all bound by our language, history, family, food, and community. Recipes in many ways can reflect that. Filmmakers know this—witness the many movies in which food preparation and relationships are central themes, from *Tampopo* to *Like Water for Chocolate.*

While Hollywood may not come knocking, almost everybody has a story or two about a cookbook bestowed on them by their grandmother or found at a garage sale. Most often, it's a community cookbook, treasured precisely because its unique tone and style differ from most commercial cookbooks, or because it offers a glimpse into a world that may not be our own. The presentation is often homespun, with insider references, line drawings of muffins, and topics of local interest. It is the language that often delights us; a "tumblerful of flour" seems more evocative than a precise measurement. I propose that we go a few steps past the delight we find in reading our own or others' community cookbooks and set about analyzing the language of recipes, seeking the linguistic components and the structure of recipe texts. The way language is used in the context of recipe discourse shapes our interpretation of many aspects of the cookbook, not only concerning things culinary but also how we view a particular community and its values.

Since the majority of community cookbooks today follow commercial models, I will start with the language of several pie crust recipes from commercial cookbooks. (The immense variation one finds in community cookbooks makes it more difficult to establish the kind of generalizations linguists are trained to look for in linguistic forms.) Once we have a solid sense of how the recipe is put together linguistically, we will look at versions of the same type of recipe from various community cookbooks. One way to look at a recipe is as a form of narrative—a particular kind of storytelling—and viewing it formally and structurally as a narrative enriches our reading of it. To get us into narrative mode, we will see how an existing narrative framework used by discourse analysts can serve as a guide for describing the discourse structure of recipes. Then we'll continue in an even narrower linguistic manner by noting the syntactic and semantic regularities of recipes, using the pie crust recipes for illustration. There are, of course, broader implications in looking at the language of recipes, particularly the way in which language constructs community, establishes personal identity, and tells us who belongs and who is the outsider. This will be touched on in the final section. Political or popular culture texts have long been considered suitable for scrutiny of this nature, and recipes should not be left out of the range of cultural artifacts that give us insight into the world around us, or our place in that world.

By looking at the language and structure of a recipe, we begin to see how a recipe can be viewed as a story, a cultural narrative that can be shared and has been constructed by members of a community. It is no wonder that my grandmother often told me how she could "read a cookbook like a novel,"[1] how she "could get lost in it." I didn't understand it then, but she was a member of a larger community of cooks, with whom she shared implicit alliances and knowledge. Especially when it came to cookbooks put out by her friends in the church parish or by members of various charities in her hometown, this shared alliance was all the more real and immediate. She could "read" her cookbooks because they carried elements that fired her imagination, that drew her in, that caused her to reflect on her own behavior (as a cook), and to construct her identity (as a housewife and mother, which indeed was her occupation) in terms that were readily accessible to her and in relation to her peers. Her cookbooks took her beyond her own kitchen and into her community.

Examining cookbooks at the level of language use gives us many ways in which to investigate a cookbook's content and how it reflects the social mores and expectations of its time. We will see that recipes share common features, as well as exhibit vast differences. Especially as they are recycled over time and through different social contexts, the shared features of recipes can provide, like narrative, a form of cultural cohesion.[2] So, besides the dictionary definition of "recipe" with which we are all familiar, we will see that the humble recipe can be dressed up for scholarly purposes: it can also be viewed as a text form that is "locally situated" as a community practice, and as a text that embodies linguistic relationships and implies within these relationships a number of cultural assumptions and practices.

Toward a Discourse Analysis of the Recipe

Discourse analysis in the manner practiced by many linguists can yield important insights into a text, even when that text is a cookbook. Analysis of this kind can show how the recipe is ordered, the way its small, internal units are related sequentially, and the interpretation that derives from particular sequences. (For example, in a question-answer sequence, a question leads us to expect a response.) The small parts of the discourse—the ingredients—work together to inform our judgments of what the text form "means." Examining a recipe in this way allows us to see what relevance the text form has to the outside world of language users and how it is then used in many social and historical contexts. The recipe provides abundant opportunity to examine the intersection of language and social relationships. Jones and others justify expanding the realm of foodways research in part by citing the essential nature of food preparation in any culture, saying that any society's methods of "preparing . . . food often provide a basis for interaction, serve as a vehicle of communication, and constitute a source of associations and symbolic structures."[3] When this socio-anthropological view is merged with a linguistic approach, the possibilities for additional insight expand yet again, especially through a linguistic evaluation of the symbolic structures that constitute the recipe.

The recipe lends itself naturally to "variationist" study, a theoretical approach in which linguists consider how the same thing is said in many different ways. It is a way of understanding multiple underlying communicative (rather than propositional) messages and answering the question, "Why did she say it like that?" There is no lack of data for qualitative or quantitative analysis in this framework, whether the recipe comes by oral transmission or by written text. If one were to pursue a variationist line of research, one could choose a dish, for example, pie crust (as I do below), and note the potentially limitless ways it is linguistically presented by individuals or in cookbooks. The revelations come in an awareness of the differences.

The recipe can also be examined sociolinguistically, that is, by looking at how language is actually used by real people in real-world contexts. Since the world of cookery divides along professional and domestic lines, often incorporating gender and class distinctions, one could also specify various sociolinguistic variables (gender, age, race, nation or region of country, religion, class, occupation) and observe both similarities and differences based on these constraints. This is relevant in adding "meaning" to a recipe, since personal identity and social context play into what comprises a text or a textual unity, as Schiffrin says.[4]

The pie crust recipes here serve to illustrate how the recipe functions as a narrative form. By breaking the recipes down into their component linguistic and textual parts, we see how the language that describes an identical procedure—making a pie crust—differs radically in many ways. And while recipes may look similar or result in the same product, there is still room for wide interpretation if we also consider the interactional structure inherent in any communicative exchange. The "communicators" involved, the pie crust maker (the cook) and the recipe compiler (the author), bring to the activity of cooking their own assumptions about the background and social identity of the participants. It is this constant mediation of context and text that makes the study of genres such as the community cookbook so rich.

There are other linguistic-based approaches to the texts. While the discussion here is synchronic—the recipes are all roughly from the same span of time—one could look at the material diachronically, cross-generationally, or cross-culturally (as many of the authors in this volume have done). One could also look at handwritten "receipts" handed down within families to determine if those recipe forms show linguistic aspects that reflect an oral tradition rather than linguistic structures that derive from printed, mass-media forms, as the samples here tend to demonstrate. The presentation of recipes on the radio or television also suggests intriguing linguistic possibilities (see Nelljean Rice's essay in this volume) that point to the larger question of the influence of mass media on community assimilation, differentiation, and affiliation.

Distinctive Syntax and Semantics

To consider a broader interpretation of recipes as texts that reflect and affect cultural contexts, we must first examine what characterizes the recipe as a particular form—in other words, its linguistic building blocks. Recipes share a certain distinctiveness in their syntactic forms (the way sentences are structured) and their semantic realizations (what they mean), as well as in their formal discourse features.

The two recipes below demonstrate the language differences between a commercial recipe, in which the author works to engage the largely unknown readership through chatty prose, and a community cookbook recipe, in which the author assumes the background knowledge of her peers, the most likely audience for her recipe. The underlined words are the imperative forms syntactically characteristic of the recipe; the italicized phrases fulfill an evaluative function and vary considerably across similar recipes.

HOT WATER PIE CRUST

Makes pastry for two 8-inch pies with top crusts or two 9- or 10-inch pies without top crusts.

When you mention a hot water pie crust, people look askance, for traditional pie crust recipes always emphasize cold ingredients and ice-cold water. And we're talking about **boiling** water here. But this makes a tender, flaky crust. At one stage, it looks like unappetizing putty, but don't worry about that. I make it in huge amounts, cut it into wedges, and freeze it for nearly instant pies. This is an old, old recipe, and it's been years since I have seen it published.

1 cup lard, very soft	½ cup boiling water
1 teaspoon salt	3 cups all-purpose flour

Place the lard and salt in a large bowl and beat *a bit* with a tablespoon until the lard is *completely softened. You can also do this with an electric hand beater.* Pour boiling water over the lard and blend again. Let this mixture cool to room temperature, but stir often so water and lard won't separate (*although it is not the end of the world if it does*). Stir in the flour, and form the mixture into a ball. *If you use your hands, do it quickly.* Chill for several hours or overnight, then let the cold dough sit out at room temperature for about 30 minutes before rolling out [etc.].[5]

NEVER-FAIL PIE CRUST

3 cups flour	1 tsp. salt
1 cup shortening	1 Tbsp. vinegar
1 beaten egg	7 Tbsp. ice water

Cut lard into flour. Add remaining ingredients and roll out *as regular crust.* Mrs. Norman Bunkleman[6]

The recipe is not an elite text form, so almost any reasonably aware individual could distinguish a recipe from, say, a sonnet or a press release or a legal document. But linguists sort out and name the obvious—especially when it allows a generalization about language that can fit numerous circumstances. In the case of the English-language recipe, the syntax is marked by a series of imperative verb forms that relate to what the recipe is bringing about, for example, "place the lard and salt," "add the remaining ingredients," etc. The imperative verb forms are the recipe's most distinguishing syntactic feature and create internal cohesion between and among the discourse elements. When a *non*-imperative clause or sentence does occur, it plays a role in the narrative as an evaluative or descriptive marker rather than furthering the narrative action as the imperative forms do. Similarly, comments that are not explicitly an integral part of the recipe are typographically or textually set apart, serving as an auxiliary message to the reader. The use of the second-person singular (as in, "if you use your hands . . . ") also fulfills this function; it also reminds us of the pre-literate spoken transmission of recipes through the use of a pronoun (you) that characteristically distinguishes spoken discourse from written prose.

Generally in recipes there is an absence of temporal markers (now, when, as soon as, etc.) or tense shifts, although they can be present (*Laurel's Kitchen* recipes are never without them).[7] Instead, we find that the sequence is relayed by the ordering of elements and is often made explicit with numbers that delimit the particular actions. When recipes deviate from the ordered list of procedural commands, there is a chance that the recipe could be confusing. For example, *Joy of Cooking*[8] often scatters variations on basic recipes elsewhere in a chapter, which is no problem for the expert, of course, but might be confusing for the novice. *Laurel's Kitchen*'s pie crust recipe helpfully mentions what might go wrong during the procedure ("If it should stick to the table, slide a long, sharp knife underneath . . . "). This contingency might be confused with a necessary step, making comprehension of the sequence potentially problematic.

An optional descriptive or prepositional phrase can either follow or precede the imperative sentence, as in the instruction to "Cut half of the shortening into the flour mixture with a pastry blender" found in *Joy of Cooking* or advice such as "On a floured surface, roll out the dough . . . " from *Jane Brody's Good Food Book*.[9] These phrases, which help explain the procedure initiated by the verb, are generally either locative ("on a floured surface"), which expresses the place where action is to take place, or instrumental ("with a pastry blender"), which expresses the means with which something is to be done.

The recipe possesses unique semantic features as well. The recipe's descriptive language—or evaluation clauses, as I call them here—sets similar recipes apart from each other. It also requires a prior knowledge of the genre if these evaluation clauses are to be understood properly. When blending flour and shortening for pie crust dough, one has to know enough about the procedure and outcome to understand what is meant by evaluation clauses such as "the size of peas," "the grain of cornmeal," or "like rolled oats," which refer to the texture of the flour-shortening mixture. How thick is "extra thick" or "desired thickness," and how much is "don't work it in too much"? Much of the description in a recipe is scalar; and knowing where on the scale the meaning of an evaluation falls would indicate the extent of familiarity a recipe user has with the genre. Also, some recipes incorporate more evaluative language than others. So merely counting the evaluative phrases would be another way to describe how different recipes get their point across.

The verbs indicating the actions of a recipe can also be problematic. We all know what "cut" and "clarify" mean, especially in the context of writing, but "cut shortening into flour" or "clarify butter" have meanings very specific to the context of cooking. Besides misinterpreting the semantics, in this case not knowing what action is instantiated by a verb, an inexperienced recipe user might also run into unfamiliar vocabulary, or directions or terminology, that simply cannot be understood unless one is a member of the subculture that knows how to cook.

The Recipe and Its Narrative Components

Beyond its distinctive linguistic features, a recipe is also a narrative, a story that can be shared and has been constructed by members of a community. The recipe narrative not only transmits culture-based meaning, as do more traditional narratives, it can also be viewed as sharing many aspects of the formal structure of basic narratives. The temporal structure and sequential presentation of information in a recipe link it with the more traditional narrative framework as defined by sociolinguist William Labov.[10]

To view a text as mundane as the recipe as akin to the much-studied and much-pondered narrative is not as far-fetched as it might initially sound. Donald Polkinghorne attests to the "almost infinite variety" of stories that the narrative form can "accommodate and generate." Polkinghorne cites French semiologist Roland Barthes's belief that narratives, with their "ordered arrangement of all the ingredients," give cohesion and structure to existence on the individual and on the cultural level, something that comes into play with the recipe, as this chapter and others in the volume attempt to demonstrate. Note that Barthes uses the recipe as a metaphor to describe narrative, which underscores our cultural-cognitive awareness of the recipe as a formal unit.[11]

The recipe form we are most familiar with today—the list of ingredients and instructions on how to compile them—actually was not conventionalized until 1887 with the publication of *The Boston Cookbook*, which "tabulated ingredients at the head of each recipe and offered [details] to guide the housewife who might be confused by the meaning of 'butter the size of an egg.'"[12] Before that, the ingredients would not necessarily be listed separately but mentioned as they became relevant within the narrative, something you'll occasionally still see in recipes today. This "old-fashioned" model caused much chagrin for M. F. K. Fisher, the late celebrated food-and-culture writer, and she railed against it in her essay, "The Anatomy of a Recipe."[13]

Structurally, the recipe can be seen as a narrative form that roughly parallels sociolinguist Labov's classic depiction of a narrative and its composition. Labov's framework is intended to account for the structural similarities in stories. He determined the most narratives contain the following structural components: abstract, orientation clause, actions, evaluations, and coda. We will see how these structural components are realized in the recipe form. The conventional bipartite structure of the modern recipe (a list of ingredients and directions) leads us to add one other bit of narrative "hardware" to the inventory: the "list" (a discourse unit discussed at length by Schiffrin).

Table 1 breaks down the two sample recipes quoted earlier into their structural components. Note how the title (akin to Labov's "abstract") gives key information; the list items relate to procedural order; the orientation components reflect the effort on the author's part to facilitate understanding of the procedure; the actions, in spite of any brevity, are related temporally and sequentially; the evaluative components describe features of the recipe event that relate to identity or action; and the coda provides closure and describes the projected outcome. The community cookbook version of the pie crust recipe, in its brevity, obviously assumes that participants in that cookbook know each other and that it would be condescending to offer more explanation.

The *title* of the recipe is in effect what Labov would call the "abstract" of the narrative, affording the reader a summary of what follows and the proposition that what follows will lead to what is promised in the title. Implied by the title in modern cookbooks is the phrase, "How to make a . . . ," which appears explicitly during the Renaissance in the form,

TABLE I. *Narrative structure of two versions of the pie-crust recipe*

Structural component	Commercial version	Community recipe
Title	*Hot Water Pie Crust*	*Never-Fail Pie Crust*
List	*lard* *salt* *boiling water* *flour*	*flour* *shortening* *beaten egg* *salt* *vinegar* *ice water*
Orientation components	84-word paragraph preceding ingredients list; mention of hand beater	Ø
Actions	*place, beat, pour, blend, let, stir, stir, form, chill, let*	*cut, add, roll*
Evaluations	included in orientation paragraph; marked by italics in (1)	*as regular crust*
Coda	*Makes pastry for two . . .*	Ø

"To Make a. . . . " Earlier recipe titles are less elliptical than today's; take, for example, this one from 1587: "A Tart to Provoke Courage in Either Man or Woman," or this one from 1608: "To Make a Walnut, That When You Cracke It, You Shall Find Biskets, and Carrawayes in It, Or a Prettie Posey Written."[14] Fisher, in her own analysis of the form, insists that the name or title "will perforce give some sort of description: for instance, one does not simply say 'Cake' or 'Bread,' but 'Golden Sponge Cake,' 'Greek Honey Bread.' "[15] Her dictum captures the essence of the narrative abstract, which is to "encapsulate the point of the story."[16]

The *orientation clauses* in a narrative place the actions being described in a particular context, providing information on place and time, the participants, and the nature of the situation. In the recipe, orientation clauses, generally located beneath the title and above the list, appear to be optional; in the pie crust data I describe here, only three of the nine recipes I examined (a mix of community and commercial cookbook recipes) have what could be construed as an "orientation clause." For example, *Jane Brody's* Pumpkin Pie recipe includes this clause (located under the title and above the list): "Although more caloric than the Pumpkin-Orange Chiffon Pie on page 631, this more traditional version still is considerably lower in fat and calories than the standard fare, but it retains the delicious flavoring and texture of a good pumpkin pie."[17] Note that this clause orients us to the health requirements of our diet, something that may be new for many cooks to contemplate, while grounding and reassuring us with references to the "traditional," "standard," and "good."

This orientation function is also fulfilled by many cooks' handwritten notes next to a particular recipe in their cookbook, for instance, "Bill made this for my birthday," or "tasted better with honey," or "yum!" in effect personalizing the recipe and making it part of the cook's personal story. Implicitly, the larger domain of the cookbook orients the reader— for example, I didn't, nor did I expect to, find a pie crust recipe in my Chinese and Italian cookbooks. Also, since *Jane Brody's Good Food Book* is subtitled *Living the High-Carbohydrate Way*, it is no surprise that her orientation clauses throughout the book refer to the recipes' nutritional attributes. Community cookbooks orient readers in this way, too, perhaps indicating that "this is the recipe so-and-so always brings to the annual picnic," or, "Ms. So-and-so won't tell us the secret ingredient in her fudge sauce, but she will share a fantastic recipe for oatmeal cookies."

The orientation clause, especially since it is usually found beneath the title or in accompanying remarks before the recipe, can also function as part of the abstract, indicating for the reader what the implications of following this recipe might be or noting something unusual in the ingredient list or action sequencing that has consequences that may be distinctive or out-of-the-ordinary in the cookery context, as I discovered with pie crust recipes made with whole wheat flour.

The elements of a *list* are "entities" that alone predicate nothing except this existence, as Schiffrin states, although the significance of list elements is relevant to the context in which they are found. Interestingly, in the recipe, the list items' external relationships become apparent in the "narrative" or instruction sequence when their place within the structure of the recipe is revealed. Perhaps this is because the list component is actually a somewhat artificial highlighting of an aspect of the narrative that has become conventionalized in the written recipe format (as we have seen, it is only within the past 100 years that ingredients have been tabulated and listed first). In the recipe, the list items are essentially a collection of entities that bear some inherent relation to each other by dint of their adjacency and subsequent inclusion within a procedure (e.g., sugar and butter are often paired because they become *creamed together*) or within the recipe as a whole (no sugar and butter in a Thai dish, for instance). Sometimes, within the narrative text, there is a specific reference to a list item, often denoted by an asterisk (as in *Betty Crocker's* Standard Pastry recipe),[18] which notes a consequence specific to that ingredient. The recipe list is ordered either in terms of importance of ingredients or order of their use, although most cooks prefer order of use (Fisher finds it essential in a well-formed recipe), which speaks to the salience of list items in relation to the temporal sequences of the recipe narrative structure as a whole.

While the "complicating action" of the narrative—which answers the question, "what happened?"—is defined according to its temporal relation to adjacent clauses, the *instructional actions* of the recipe narrative are defined according to their temporal relation to adjacent elements of procedure. As in the traditional narrative, it is assumed that the elements of the event being described are presented in "proper order" and that temporal adjacency is key in discovering the underlying relationships of the text as a whole. In other words, preparing a dish is in effect moving through event space, the frame in which an event occurs. Each action is predicated on what precedes and follows it. When the order is breached, it undermines the well-formedness of the narrative, leading to possible misunderstandings. (Most cooks have experienced this in some form or other, they've been ready to follow the "next step," only to discover that some crucial other action has not been done because the recipe did not alert them to the necessary timing.) Fisher, approaching the recipe from the user's and critic's viewpoint, testifies eloquently to the significance of order and adjacency in the recipe, underscoring the work many linguists, psychologists, and anthropologists have done in this regard with respect to the traditional narrative. She complains about recipes with the time element "askew," that contain "no time sequence, no logical progression," or that suffer from a "lack of time logic." How can you receive, integrate, and respond to the story being told to you if you can't follow it?

Next to the narrative action clauses, the *evaluation* clauses—*how* the narrator gets her point across—are the most important (according to Labov). In a recipe, most evaluations occur within the instructional narrative sequence and relate to identity (e.g., looks like X or Y) or to action (e.g., beat ingredient X in such and such a way). There are also more macro evaluations in the preliminary description that illustrate some aspect of the outcome of the recipe, such as what other foods would go well with this particular dish or how long the recipe will take to prepare. While there can be some variation in how the recipe's informational actions are presented, the requirements of the particular named activity seriously constrain the options. This is not the case with evaluation clauses, which are the locus for the major differences among recipes and, as such, the components that warrant the most scrutiny. Evaluation clauses differ syntactically and semantically from instructional actions and offer a means by which to compare and interpret the recipe text in its social and historic contexts, especially when we compare the same dish from different sources. Evaluation clauses, in tandem with the list items and instructional actions, combine to offer a subjectivity and objectivity of experience that goes with the transmission of any subtextual messages inherent in the recipe. Because of the subjective nature of evaluation clauses, the reader's own background knowledge or shared or divergent assumptions potently mingle with the narrative evaluation, allowing unconscious judgments to be formed—about herself, her community, and her place in the world.

A sense of completion, psychological as well as literal, accompanies the conclusion of any narrative sequence. In the Labovian narrative, the *coda* ("And that was that") signals the narrative's end.[19] In the recipe, the coda does not have to be made explicit for us to know that we have witnessed the entire cookery event, although it could be argued that a coda-type clause—such as "top with a sprig of parsley and serve," or "serve the oatmeal sprinkled with cinnamon and sugar, if desired"—contributes to maximal well-formedness. It could also be argued, following philosopher H. Paul Grice's Maxim of Quantity (make your utterance as informative as possible), that a coda is necessary. After all, "serves 6" or "makes 3 portions for hungry eaters" is relevant information for enacting a satisfying recipe event. In cases where the coda is absent, we infer (again, in the spirit of Grice's Cooperative Principle, whereby communication is seen as a cooperative occurrence among participants) through the knowledge of our requirements of the procedure, or through the layout and presentation of the cookbook, when the recipe has ended.[20]

A sentence such as "serves 6" still retains its coda function even when it is placed at the beginning of the recipe, as portion amounts frequently are, because we know it refers to the end result of the enacted event.[21] In this case, the reader's attention to the contents of the recipe narrative is informed by the prior knowledge of some significant aspect of "the ending," a foreshadowing technique that we also find in film, literature, and music.

Labov observes that some codas not only conclude the narrative but also "bridg[e] the gap between the moment of time at the end of the narrative proper and the present."[22] The recipe coda, especially when it focuses the cook's attention on the use to which the food will be put, in some sense functions as a bridge, returning the cook to the needs of the present time, the meal at hand and the participants sharing it.

Analyzing Recipes

Breaking down the recipe into its narrative components and noting its syntactic and semantic characteristics is just the first step in analyzing recipes. The data can be evaluated from different perspectives, and it is as important to know the orientation of the research question as it is to find answers. For example, when I examined various pie crust recipes, I looked at them in terms of a certain "efficiency," an admittedly Anglo-American construct. I determined that "efficiency" was a property of both structure and content: how easy was it to follow and understand this recipe; and what amount of evaluation and description would allow a person aware of cooking basics to interpret the instructions and make a creditable pie crust. Table 2, which follows, evaluates seven pie-crust recipes in terms of the narrative framework; my efficiency-oriented research bias and interpretations are reflected explicitly in the comments at the end related to each recipe.

Six of the seven recipes included in table 2 come from commercial sources that vary markedly. Two are from "standard" cookbooks that have long been part of the American cooking heritage (*Betty Crocker's Cookbook*, *Joy of Cooking*); one is from a "standard" cookbook with a contemporary orientation (*Jane Brody's Good Food Book*); two are from "alternative" cookbooks with a nonmainstream message (*Laurel's Kitchen* and *Recipes for a Small Planet*);[23] and one is from a small specialty cookbook intended to transmit certain "ethnic" information (*Pies from Amish Kitchens*).[24] These six cookbooks reflect, to some extent, the range of options available to most cooks from commercial sources. The seventh recipe is from a prototypical community cookbook: *A Garden of Eatin'*, produced by the St. Therese Christian Ladies in Appleton, Wisconsin, and circulated locally in the parish.

Concentrating on recipes from commercial cookbooks was a deliberate decision: it is important, at least for an examination of late-twentieth-century recipes, to be familiar with commercial models, upon which (structurally) most community cookbooks are based. It is relevant to see how community cookbooks compare with their commercial sisters, especially as the latter reflect various standardizing linguistic values of a literacy-based society. A larger awareness of recipes in all contexts, from which we can make generalizations, will give us more insight into a specific category. For example, the one community cookbook pie crust recipe that I include in table 2 and others I refer to later differ markedly from the commercial versions. This uniqueness might have been missed without a wider knowledge base.

Table 2 illustrates some of the differences among these seven pie crust recipes in a very schematic way. The recipes range from the bare-bones Never-Fail Pie Crust with minimal instruction in the community cookbook (*A Garden of Eatin'*) to *Jane Brody's* highly evaluative and descriptive crust accompanying a pumpkin pie recipe. If one is evaluating recipes in terms of efficiency, which Fisher was doing in "Anatomy of a Recipe," then the most effective blueprint for a pie crust may well be *Betty Crocker's* Standard Pastry recipe, which includes thirty-two imperative sentence constructions (representing a great deal of detail) and straightforward descriptive elements. Despite a fairly high number of information elements in *Joy of Cooking's* Basic Pie Dough, there are fewer instructions within the actual recipe, forcing a reader to look elsewhere in the chapter for the needed information, potentially gearing the recipe toward the specialist or someone with a more focused interest in the actual art of cooking who would probably not mind the "inconvenience."

The two recipes that are labeled in table 2 as "regional/community" carry the fewest instructions, thus assuming proficiency on the part of the

TABLE 2.

	(Mid-Am. standard) **Crocker** *Standard Pastry*	(Specialist standard) **Joy** *Basic Pie Dough*	(Regional/community) **Mrs. B** *Never-Fail Pie Crust*	(Regional/community) **Amish** *Never Fail Pie Crust*	(Contemporary standard) **Brody** *Crust*	(Alternative/veggie) **Laurel** *Piecrust*	(Alternative/veggie) **Planet** *PieCrust*
Orientation clause	—	—	—	yes	yes	yes	—
List (in order)	shortening/lard; all-purp. flour; salt; cold water	all-purp. flour; salt; leaf lard/shortening; butter; water	flour; shortening; egg; salt; vinegar; ice water	flour; salt; shortening; egg; cold water; vinegar	all-purp. flour; sugar; salt; shortening; butter; ice water	w. w. flour; wheat germ; margarine; salt; cold water	w. w. flour; salt; shortening; water
Action							
Imperative sentence	32	13	3	6	5	10	9
(Fronted) instr./locative PP	—	—	—	—	3	2	1
Prepositional phrase	—	1	—	—	3	4	1
Infinitival purpose clause	—	—	—	—	2	—	—
Temporal phrase	—	2	—	1	4	2	1
Explicit list reference	x	x	—	—	x	x	x
Meta-message							
Note	x	—	—	—	—	—	—
2nd Person Singular	—	x	—	—	—	x	x
Outside instruction	—	—	—	x	x	—	—
Meta-reference							
See X	2	1	—	—	—	—	—
As shown X	—	1	—	—	—	1	—
Other	—	—	—	—	1	—	—

Evaluation	Crocker	Joy	Mrs. B	Amish	Brody	Laurel	Planet
cut	peas	cornmeal texture; pea size	—	—	criss-cross fashion; uniformly crumbly	rolled oats	not too much
moisten	cleanse bowl	lightly; tidy ball	—	—	just enough water	just enough water; quickly; gently	move gently
roll	—	—	as regular crust	desired thickness	—	thick disc; to size	—
surface	floured	floured	—	floured	floured	floured	—
in pan	firmly	—	—	—	gently; extra thick edges	—	—
bake	light brown	—	—	—	—	so it won't burn	—
Comments	detailed; straightforward; best example	fewer instructions in recipe; can be found elsewhere near text	assumes proficiency, recipe is just a reminder	assumes proficiency (pies only)	descriptive; informational weight	confusing re: narrative structure (see analysis)	insufficient description to enact "event"

Cookbooks

Crocker *Betty Crocker's Cookbook, New and Revised Edition* (1979)
Joy *Joy of Cooking* (30th printing, 1983)
Mrs. B *A Garden of Eatin'*, St. Therese Parish (Appleton, Wisconsin) community cookbook (1971)
Amish *Pies from Amish and Mennonite Kitchens* (1982)
Brody *Jane Brody's Good Food Book* (1985)
Laurel *Laurel's Kitchen: A Handbook for Vegetarian Cookery and Nutrition* (7th printing, 1980)
Planet *Recipes for a Small Planet* (1973)

reader, perhaps because of the readership they are pitched for. The first author is probably aware of the abilities of her fellow cooks within the St. Therese Parish community, knowing that they can function in the kitchen without extensive instruction, while the recipe in *Pies from Amish and Mennonite Kitchens* is found in a collection of pie recipes only. Someone who couldn't already bake a pie would not buy this book, which is fairly small, hand-lettered, and not presented as a comprehensive tome on the pie-making procedure.

The two recipes labeled "alternative" in table 2 specifically call for whole-wheat flour (*Betty Crocker* allows for the variation in a note at the end of the recipe) in their ingredients lists, and their orientation clauses refer directly to possibly problematic properties inherent in the ingredient, suggesting that whole-wheat crusts are "marked" in the foodways context. These recipes also illustrate what happens to narrative continuity and coherence when particular elements of the narrative sequence are faulty. *Laurel's Kitchen*'s Piecrust is confusing because a contingency (nonnarrative) action is inserted in text established for the narrative or instructional actions, and thus can be misconstrued as an actual recipe action. That it is a preemptive statement is not made explicit in the recipe's language. *Recipes for a Small Planet*'s recipe contains insufficient narrative action sequences or evaluative description to enact the "event" of the Whole Wheat Pie Crust, unless the reader has made a pie crust before, knows the procedure well, and is using the recipe as a reminder. Someone "reading" this recipe would be hard-pressed to follow the "plot."

The Role of Audience in Community Cookbook Language

For a reader to follow the "plot" the recipe must be more than merely explicit enough (since, as mentioned earlier, semantic attributes are scalar and their meaning dependent on the extent of the shared background knowledge of participants). This turns the spotlight on the audience and its role in the presentation, linguistic and otherwise, of the cookbook. If we look at a definable genre such as the community cookbook, we see a wide variety in approach and content, despite the shared overt reason for its production: fund-raising. As Charles Goodwin says, this is because the intended audience shapes the outcome.[25] As we begin to look at the broader implications of language use in the community cookbook, as we see how the authors and addressees co-construct an artifact of their community, the role of the audience takes on greater importance in our analysis.

If the audience is a fairly large or generic one and the community cookbook collaborators have the means and interest to produce a volume that is to be seen as serious and comprehensive, then we find a work such as the Junior League of Pasadena's *The California Heritage Cookbook*. Its recipes are very explicit and detailed; its Basic Pie Crust (370) includes as well as explains the consequences of certain optional actions (which are barely if ever mentioned in smaller-scale community cookbooks), such as using dry beans to weight down the bottom crust so it won't puff up while baking, or brushing the crust with egg yolk to prevent sogginess from the filling. The book lacks other features of the genre, such as contributor names for each recipe, as well as linguistic features that mark the discourse as more informal and more personal, as one finds in cookbooks with a narrower distribution.[26]

The *California Heritage Cookbook* stands in contrast to smaller-scale community cookbooks, whose authors and addressees share a more symmetrical, peer-to-peer relationship and do not presume to set themselves apart, either by culinary expertise or editorial control. The audience is a known quantity, which explains certain omissions or inclusions in the text. It has already been suggested that Mrs. Norman Bunkleman's Never-Fail Pie Crust in the St. Therese Christian Ladies' *A Garden of Eatin'* is as abbreviated as it is because she is aware of the abilities of her peers.

A Garden of Eatin' also displays another feature common to smaller-scale community cookbooks; it speaks to the relationships community members share. The *California Heritage Cookbook*, as well as the other commercial cookbooks on which this discussion is based, each include a single recipe for pie crust. However, the *Garden of Eatin'* lists five different pie crust recipes (Never Fail Pie Crust, Pie Crust, Pastry, Pie Crust (very flaky), and Pie Crust, with a separate variation by another member of the community), suggesting an egalitarian approach to the construction of their particular cookbook. No one was in a position to choose which of the five to include, so all were accepted. In all five cases, the recipes are brief, and bear only structural resemblance to the commercial cookbook versions.

Brevity is also a feature in *A Synod of Cooks* from the Chichester (England) Diocesan Association for Family Social Work; there the pie crust gets a one-line mention in the body of a Fluffy Apple Pie recipe: "Rub the butter into the flour, bind with a little water to make the pastry."[27] *Synod* presents itself as a community in a different way than *Garden of Eatin'*. Contributors are not mentioned with their respective recipes but in a general list with thanks at the beginning of the book. The cookbook's diocesan sales distribution is wider than that of the Wisconsin parish and smaller than that of the Pasadena Junior League, which is probably a factor in the design of each cookbook.

In sum, the co-creators of the community cookbook—author and audience—mutually influence each other. Each cookbook, besides sharing common design features, content, and philanthropic goals, is a unique reflection of the community in which it was spawned, a result of the inextricable connection of purpose and text to context and audience. The community cookbook underscores a contention of Alessandro Duranti's: "The recipe for the interpretation of a text is never fully contained in the text."[28] The broader context of which it is part is also relevant.

The Broader Implications

As we communicate through language, we share not only words but parts of our culture, parts of our place and time period. It is important to keep this in mind as we consider the language that structures various forms of spoken discourse or written text. A recipe today, while it shares many features with recipes of the past, not only differs in formal details but also in many of its cultural assumptions. Even if the content is ostensibly the same in its surface form ("take creme of cowe mylke" vs. "take dairy cream . . ."), the apparent similarity does not necessarily imply a unanimity of worldview about either the named ingredients or about the procedures required to produce the end result.[29]

We have already seen that differences in assumptions exist even when formal features of the genre are shared. Nonetheless, the recipe, in the vehicle of the community cookbook, also serves to underscore what is shared and transmitted. In so doing, the recipe provides continuity of form and meaning within the genre, as well as a connection to a situated human activity that has been described and passed along in written and oral form for centuries; this only serves to enhance the recipe's significance as a genre of discourse.[30] Shared structures in food-related behavior have been the basis of much traditional foodways research. Looking at community cookbooks, the genre similarities can provide a basis from which to explore changes over time and through different contexts. Some entire recipes have actually resurfaced in cookbooks in the Western world from the middle ages onward, a recycling over time that can provide, like narrative, a form of cultural cohesion.

Cookbooks have always been repositories for social mores and have offered an often unself-conscious picture of life as it is. That cookbooks reflect social expectations is made especially explicit in cookbooks that predate the twentieth century; there gender and class role behavior is laid out as precisely as a puff pastry recipe. Cookbooks from the Victorian age functioned as mirrors for the times, where "one [could] learn about health concerns, entertaining, fashion, advertising, and economic conditions."[31] It was in that era, during the Civil War, that the first fund-raising cookbooks were compiled, providing another forum for foodways research today.[32]

Behavior and expectations are perhaps not so explicit in contemporary cookbooks (but see Kirshenblatt-Gimblett for a counter-example in the Jewish community), but the question of who contributes to the cookbook is a viable one, as it marks the borders of community and social position in another way. It's no accident that the St. Therese Parish priests contributed a recipe to *A Garden of Eatin'*; after all, they are important members of the community. However, they were the only men to do so, and they cannot be viewed as peers in this context. Similarly, Marilyn Tucker Quayle, Barbara Bush, and other luminaries, whose recipes are accorded their own special section in the *Southwest Seasons Cookbook*, which was put out by the Casa Angelica Auxiliary of Albuquerque, New Mexico, cannot be viewed as "members" of that cookbook's community.

To consider the recipe in the broadest of social senses, it is well to remember that its transmission, as with all forms of exchange, is grounded in social interaction—and as such it is susceptible to social asymmetries and social collaborations that can be made visible through the careful study of language use. If we believe that the recipe is a written reduction of an actual event with social implications (in our context an event largely shared and engineered by women), then we can proceed to explore the sociocultural assumptions that inhere within this tradition and that reveal themselves in the language of the community cookbook.

Part Two

Experiencing Texts

This section of *Recipes for Reading* provides four in-depth analyses of particular community cookbooks, with considerable personal input from each essay writer. The four essays concern books from quite different traditions, and while the essayists express some similar responses or themes within their discussions, each individual brings her own special flavor (yes, it is hard to avoid those cooking metaphors) to the work.

Ann Romines, author of *The Home Plot: Women, Writing and Domestic Ritual* and associate professor of English at The George Washington University, describes the many benefits she derived from a series of Methodist cookbooks and from her relatives' involvement with these books. "Growing Up with the Methodist Cookbooks" also highlights the sense of how communities create and are created through the cookbooks. Ann's second book, *Constructing the Little House: Gender, Culture, and Laura Ingalls Wilder*, will be published by the University of Massachusetts Press in 1997. Her past work includes articles and presentations on Willa Cather, Eudora Welty, and other nineteenth- and twentieth-century women authors.

In "Speaking Sisters: Relief Society Cookbooks and Mormon Culture," Marion Bishop gives us a strong sense of the complex communications strategies at work among twentieth-century Mormon authors of community cookbooks. Marion's Ph.D. dissertation (NYU) explored the rhetoric of women's journals and diaries; and an essay on Anne Frank's diary and *écriture féminine* has been published in Irene Gammel's *The Need to Tell It All.* Marion is assistant professor of English at Bentley College in Waltham, Massachusetts, where she teaches writing and women's studies courses.

With Elizabeth J. McDougall's article, we move to Canada. Her piece, "Voices, Stories, and Recipes in Selected Canadian Community Cookbooks," intertwines literary theory, a wonderful pickle recipe, and observations about particular Canadian fund-raising cookbooks. Elizabeth is completing her dissertation at the University of British Columbia's English department and teaching at Laurentian University in Sudbury, Ontario. Her special interests include women's autobiographies and the influence of gender, class, and race upon the autobiographical form.

The last essay in this section, Sally Bishop Shigley's "Empathy, Energy, and Eating: Politics and Power in *The Black Family Dinner Quilt Cookbook,*" engages in a sensitive, careful, detailed reading of a recent National Council of Negro Women fund-raising cookbook. Of particular value is the way this essay considers the physical design of the book and how its form, content, and values are so beautifully meshed. Sally is associate professor of English at Weber State University and poetry editor for the *Cimmaron Review.* Her areas of special concern in teaching are literary theory and the study of women's fiction and nonfiction writing about gardens; she has a book forthcoming on Elizabeth Bishop.

Growing Up with the Methodist Cookbooks

Ann Romines

They have been there all my life, a dark presence on a shelf, in my mother's kitchen and now in mine. They were not for show, like the bright pottery and the embroidered dishtowels; over the years they grew more shabby, spotted, and worn. But on occasions of ceremony and necessity—Thanksgiving, Christmas, a special dinner, or sometimes a funeral—they were consulted like oracles. Even today, when I want to know how to make the foods that are the most enduring traditions of my family's history, more often than not my mother will tell me: "Look in the Methodist cookbooks." And then she will tell me under whose name to look: Gram's Mustard Pickles, Mrs. Atlanta Pummill's Dutch Apple Pie, Wave's Cookies.

These Methodist cookbooks were published in 1907, 1934, 1941, and 1967 by the women of the Methodist Church of Houston, Missouri, the small Ozark town where I grew up a third-generation Methodist.[1] Like my mother and my sister, I still use them regularly, although I live in a city now, a thousand miles from Houston. More than anything else, they were the authoritative texts of my childhood. Through our Methodist cookbooks, I can access the collective skill and ongoing expertise of women I've known, women I am related to. For these books are not simply records, like the musty local histories or the genealogies written in spidery script in the family Bible. They are *manuals*, as well. When I want to re-create the tastes and the aura of my childhood and of my parents' childhoods, the Methodist cookbooks tell me how, and they evoke the community of cooking women that is my complicated, conflicted domestic heritage, as a woman born and raised in Houston, Missouri.

Growing up with the Methodist cookbooks has made me think hard about the indispensable women who honored, used, and compiled them. They put local cooking into words and into print so that I could carry them with me, wherever I moved, and serve up the tastes of Houston on my own table. I have grown up to be a cook and a daughter, a reader, teacher, and writer of domestic texts. As long as I can remember, the cookbooks have been here, offering their support. They tell me what I have needed to know: for one thing, that women can make their housekeeping into books, books that will endure. (The Methodist cookbooks have probably lasted longer and received harder use than any other texts my family owns.) This essay is an affectionate look at my particular portion of an empowering heritage that many women and men in the United States share: a legacy of community cookbooks.

Poring over the Methodist cookbooks evokes for me—as no other pages can—specific and legendary female figures from my childhood and a cultural heritage that still looms large in my life. Here I have also developed a sense of my home community that extends beyond the boundaries of my own time. Again and again, a question about a name on a recipe has elicited the story of a life. I never knew Atlanta Pummill, an early home economics teacher of my grandparents' generation. But—as my Grandmother Rogers did—I still make her apple pie. Cooking was a common vocabulary for the living or now dead Methodist women who compiled and contributed the cookbooks' recipes. And it was the only commonality of their lives that engendered such enduring, printed texts. As Mrs. Winnie Gladden wrote in her foreword to the 1934 Methodist Cookbook, "We feel under obligation to the friends who have so kindly contributed their recipes and hereby thank them."[2] At their best, the cookbooks evoke a community of mutual acknowledgment and obligation (of which I still consider myself a member). And that community was reconstituted daily, at the kitchen table.

For the members of the Ladies' Aid or Missionary Society or Women's Society of Christian Service, as the Methodist women's organizations have variously been called in this century, putting together a cookbook was often the only experience of their lives with writing and making a book. All four Houston Methodist texts show the attention and skills they brought to their tasks. Each is assembled with logic and meticulous care. In 1941, someone alphabetized with special precision. In 1907, the epigraphs are an especially evocative mix of canonical literary texts (Herrick, Goldsmith, Burns) and nineteenth-century popular songs. And in 1967, the red cardboard covers are hand-decorated with kitchen shapes cut from a favorite sixties product, Con-Tact paper.[3] Recipe styles are sometimes telling; for example, my Grandmother Rogers betrayed her long-past experience with wood-burning cookstoves when, in the sixties, she instructed readers to bake her pineapple pie in a "rather slow oven."[4] Grandmother Romines gave explicit, lucidly detailed instructions for a complicated preparation of Watermelon and Pineapple Pickle, but when she wrote her recipe for Pumpkin Pie, she included only a list of ingredients, apparently assuming (as many of her contemporaries did) that any member of her cooking community would surely know how to assemble and bake them. As recently as 1967, most of these writers were certain that their readers would have mastered a certain body of expertise; in a pickle recipe, for example, "can cold" was considered a sufficient instruction. But, even allowing for such gaps as cold canning in my own domestic education, most of these recipes are still remarkably readable and cookable in 1994. They are laid out in precise, workable formats and framed in clear, economical prose.

The collective voice of these recipes is strong, capable, and assured, so strong that it often almost subsumes the voices of individual cooks. One has to pursue the personalities in these books. My mother, for example, was a married, childless young professional woman in 1941; her three contributions are for fancy "party" foods (ginger ale punch, a whipped cream fruit salad, and apricot candy), typical of an ambitious novice hostess. Only I have noticed, perhaps, that many of her other favorite recipes are also included in the 1941 book (she was on the Cookbook Committee)—but under the names of other women, who had shared their best recipes (a close friend's Lemon Velvet Ice Cream, a great-aunt's reliable Lazy Daisy Cake) with the scrupulous twenty-seven-year-old cook. In the 1967 book, a cache of eight consecutive whole wheat recipes, for everything from waffles to chocolate cake, testifies to the strong personal advocacy of Aline Becker, who eventually wrote her own book on whole grain baking.[5] Sometimes the most obviously personal notes are from very young cooks, in their debut recipes. Sara Hutcheson dutifully reports that her Applesauce Bread Recipe was "given to her by 4-H Leader, Mrs. Norma Troutman"; and Rebecca Jane Brown, in her 1934 debut recipe for Jelly Roll, instructs that the cook may "use any kind of jelly you like, but plum is best."[6] Such frank, overt statements of preference are few; more experienced recipe writers have acquired a language of collective competence that presents a surface of near anonymity and attests to these cooks' confidence that they are members in good standing of a communal domestic culture.

When my mother and grandmothers acquired a new Methodist cookbook, they began the long process of making it truly their own. Spots and stains, creases and burns tell me which recipes they chose to try, which became staples, and which were never attempted. There are cryptic handwritten evaluations and (especially from my experimental, documentarian mother) notes on revisions and emendations. All of the books are crammed with added recipes. The blank pages at the back (a convention of community cookbooks) are filled with closely spaced handwriting. Both my grandmothers recorded Lindberg [sic] Relish—a favorite Missouri tribute to the flight of the Spirit of St. Louis. On another page, in my mother's perfect Spencerian hand, is the recipe she used during World War II for Lye Soap; it is hard for me to imagine this fastidious woman working with lard, borax, lye, ammonia, and gasoline. Nearby, she has penned her recipe for wartime Sugarless Gingerbread. Other recipes are cut from magazines; one (for jelly made from frozen orange juice concentrate) reflects my mother's enthusiasm for combining old processes and new products. (Mercifully, I can't remember the jelly.)

Eventually, Mother made the 1941 cookbook more completely her own by cutting out the pages, punching holes in them, and transferring them to a black loose-leaf binder, into which she also inserted more handwritten recipes and pages from magazines. Like many other women, she was practicing intertextuality, transforming the Methodist cookbook into a testament of her own life as a working American woman. The loose-leaf format made the book almost infinitely expandable; to this day, Mother is adding recipes. The recipe for Wave's Cookies was added back in 1942; one of Mother's oldest friends served these buttery pecan ovals at the baby shower she gave for Mother before I was born. Another telling group of recipes is paperclipped into the pie section. My maternal grandmother always made the Thanksgiving pumpkin pies until she died, at eighty-one, in August of 1967. In November of that year, Mother began devising her own recipe for pumpkin pie. Her precise notes over the next few years, indicating her slight yearly changes in ingredients and oven temperature, indicate how careful and serious she was, in her mid-fifties, about perpetuating her mother's pumpkin pies *and* making the recipe her own. A few years ago, when I decided to attempt the Easter lamb cake I fondly remembered Mother's making in my early childhood, there the recipe was—unused for forty years—clipped into the Methodist cookbook.

Such ongoing intertextuality is one of the most telling intersections of private and public domestic culture, between the collectivity of domestic work and the specificity of particular women's work and lives. For example, when I scrutinize my Grandmother Bess Romines's copy of the 1934 Methodist Cookbook (now mine), I am looking for clues that will help me to read this ancestor, who died when I was five. As a young woman, she tired of teaching in country schools and went to business college; then she took venturesome jobs in the West before coming back to Missouri at thirty-three to marry Frank Romines and bear three sons. Something of this story shows in the angular, legible, practical hand, the # sign she uses decidedly to mark certain recipes (her favorites?), and the penciled notations in the printed text that point to the additional recipes she has penned on the blank final pages. All her handwritten choices are recipes for desserts, breads, or canned goods, and she is forthright with her evaluations, as in "Delicious Rolls" and "*Extra* Good Relish." One title especially touches me—"Apple 'Foo-Foo' (Elmer)." When he was a baby in 1915–16, my father, Elmer Romines, christened this favorite, simple apple dessert "Foo-Foo." My mother still makes the recipe—and my grandmother's penciled notation redeems her from the somewhat stern and decided figure I think I remember, telling me that this woman was fond and observant enough to inscribe the silliest fragment of her youngest son's baby talk.

At the end of this book, I discover my two grandmothers, meeting for the first time after my parents' 1936 elopement and beginning to eat each other's cooking and share each other's children (although they always retained the dignified formality of last names). Here is my maternal grandmother's recipe—Mrs. Rogers' Raisin Pie—inscribed in my paternal grandmother's hand. On this page I read the beginnings of my own story, the complicated mix of genes, history, and cooking that launched my own life as an American woman.

When I was growing up in Houston, I knew of the original 1907 Methodist Cookbook ("Tried Recipes of Various Housekeepers," published by "The Ladies' Aid of M. E. Church, South Houston, Mo.") only as a legend, perpetuated by hagiographic comments and recycled recipes in later editions. Recently I saw this volume for the first time when a Houston cousin obligingly searched her basement and found a copy her late Methodist mother had bought at Mrs. Leona Hiett's sale, after that stalwart Methodist's death. Slender and softcovered, with beautiful typography executed by the local newspaper office, this volume shows the complicated class structure and high aspirations of our Ozark county seat town at the beginning of the twentieth century. Among such practical staples as Lye Hominy, Pickled Pigs' Feet, and Fried Green Tomatoes, I find Watermelon Cake, a trompe l'oeil masterpiece (tri-colored batter, raisin "seeds") worthy of the most elaborate dessert table. And here is a 1907 recipe from the mother of a dear friend (recently dead at eighty-seven) that confirms her hereditary membership in a (putative) Houston "aristocracy" of elegance and means. Mrs. Charles Covert's Christmas Ice implies a family with the money, determination, and artistry to assemble the specialized equipment and the expensive oranges, lemons, and candied cherries necessary to produce a delicate celebratory sorbet in the dead of an Ozark winter. Reading such recipes in the 1907 cookbook, I can glimpse the intricacies of the community my paternal grandparents joined when, in 1910, they married, set up housekeeping, and joined the Methodist Church in Houston.

When I was born in Houston thirty-some years later, their second grandchild, that community had produced a library of three cookbooks. Physically, the pair of 1934 and 1941 volumes was a constant presence of my childhood. The 1934 edition is the first cookbook I remember; with its limp, leathery black cover and gold-stamped lettering, it looked mysteriously like my grandmother's Bible. This book—a 1936 wedding present from her husband's brother—was the first cookbook owned by my mother,

Ruth Rogers Romines. As a bride of twenty-two, she moved to Houston from a smaller village thirty miles away. The Houston Methodist Church became her church, and there she found that her husband's mother was already a formidable institution; even after Grandmother's death in 1948, the Bess Romines Circle kept her name alive for many years. Tentatively at first, Mother began to cook her way into the new church and community, trying her mother-in-law's sanctioned recipes and revising and adding others. For example, in a complicated ritual of rivalry and emulation, Mother adopted her mother-in-law's recipe for strawberry preserves, refining it to lapidary perfection so that each perfect berry hung suspended in transparent ruby syrup.

The 1934 and 1941 Methodist cookbooks became the Old and New kitchen testaments of my childhood. I remember the 1941 volume for the bold mark on its black binding: the spiral imprint of a burner on an electric stove. By now, perhaps the early fifties, my mother was no longer cooking on smelly gas stoves in the tiny apartments where my parents lived as newlyweds, or in the large, drafty Victorian house to which they brought their firstborn (me) in 1942. Instead, upwardly mobile, we were living better with electricity. The burned cover of the Methodist cookbook recalls for me, more than any other single object, the quickness, deftness, and anxiety of my perfectionist mother in the hard-pressed years when she was juggling two young children, an ambitious, distracted husband, and a houseful of proliferating demands—plus, after Grandmother Romines's death, a resident father-in-law. At some moment of frantic overextension, the cookbook met the burner, I imagine (or do I remember?). Under that evocatively marked cover, I still find the recipes for the dishes by which Mother began to make her own cooking reputation: her fragile Cutout Cookies, and the pungent Ham Loaf and impossibly rich Date Pudding that became her perennially popular contributions to Methodist church suppers.

By 1967 there was another Methodist cookbook—the only one printed (so far) in my lifetime. For me, it was a rite of passage. Although by then I was a graduate student in a distant state, I contributed a typical novice recipe—sweet and simple Blonde Brownies—to this volume, the first "real" book in which my name appeared in print. My younger sister contributed a 4-H staple, Banana Bread. Now we were certified members of a cooking community—and published writers.

Already, our mother had taught us that the proper attribution of a recipe was an important moral issue. The foods we ate often bore cooks' names: Leona's Coke Salad, Mrs. Cobb's Lep Cookies, Your Grandmother's Strawberry Preserves. Mother's famous Cutout Cookies, for example, were adapted from Mrs. Sherman Houston's recipe for filled date cookies, leaving out the dates, altering ingredients, rolling the dough thin and baking it crisp. Mother has been baking these cookies her way for more than fifty years. Yet, if you asked her for the recipe today, she would still tell you, conscientiously, that it is Mrs. Sherman Houston's recipe! As Mother has long known, a Methodist Cookbook citation is often the only printed record of a woman's work life in our town. Her scrupulosity acknowledges the importance of such texts and perpetuates memories of specific women. Leona Bennett is ten years dead—but every time I taste the Coke Salad I see her tiny, bent figure and think of her long friendship with our family. The large and heroically complex recipe for Lep Cookies (a half gallon of sorghum, a half gallon of shelled nuts) is a reminder of the Missouri German traditions Mrs. Cobb brought with her to Houston. Thus, when my sister and I arrived at college and were initiated into the elaborate rituals for avoiding plagiarism, they were already familiar; they had been a part of our education from the Methodist cookbooks. When the new 1967 edition arrived, Mother made sure that we knew and remembered whose recipe was *really* whose, even though a less scrupulous cook might have appropriated it and printed it under her own name. For such appropriators, our usually gentle mother has (still) no mercy.

To Mother, the 1967 cookbook was a rite of passage of another sort. For 1967 was the year of her mother's death. Preoccupied with nursing and with grief, she contributed only one recipe, a complicated Lime Pie that demanded skills and precision far beyond her novice daughters. Grandmother Mayme Rogers contributed a recipe too—her favorite Pineapple Pie—although she was dead by the time the cookbook was printed. Thus the 1967 Methodist Cookbook is the only one in which three generations of my family's women appear on adjacent pages. For other families too, it preserves similar chains of collaboration.

In fact, the cookbooks are studded with small memorials, recipes from dead women that preserve someone's craft and an ongoing domestic tradition. One such recipe was a rare male contribution in 1934; C. E. (Deacon) Elmore submitted "Extra Delicious Apple Custard Pie" as a

"Recipe Used by Aunt Matilda Elmore, Deceased. . . . In Memoriam."[7] Similarly, in 1967, Cynthia Christie honored her dead mother-in-law and acknowledged that recipes were community property, prefacing a recipe with this note: "Since a number of people have requested Grandma Christie's recipe for strawberry preserves, on which she won blue ribbons every time she entered them in the Texas County Fair, I am copying it herewith."[8] Soon after she shared this recipe, Cynthia Christie herself died of cancer.

A food historian could reconstruct much of the texture of my small town's culture in this century from the Methodist cookbooks, and the spots and stains on pages are clues as to which (unused) recipes reflect our food pretensions and which (used) recipes reflect our constant fare. Staple Ozark foods recur over sixty years: sorghum, blackberries, black walnuts. There are hints of political allegiances—Mrs. Lyles's Confederate Jeff Davis Pudding has appeared in every edition since 1907. After World War I, a few timid international notes begin to appear; there is a 1934 Roman Holiday (spaghetti baked in tomato sauce), 1967 Spanish Sauerkraut and Zucchini Parmesan. Perhaps most amazing is 1934 Shanghai Chicken, which calls for cheese, noodles and "1 can pati-fois-de-gras (American brand)."[9] For the most part, however, the books inscribe fairly standard Midwestern/Southern fare: Wilted Lettuce, Tamale Pie, Tuna Casserole (with potato chips), and Three Bean Salad. The acknowledged cooks are almost exclusively women; in four volumes and hundreds of recipes, there are only four contributions from men.

As the abundance of recipes for preserves, pickles, and relishes testifies, most people had gardens or access to them, and they liked some variety in the way they prepared their produce. (Grandmother Romines's markings indicate that, in one book alone, she tried at least a dozen recipes for cucumber pickles.) And the market successes of processed foods have left their marks, as in the Jello recipes that multiply from volume to volume, showing that refrigeration is no longer a luxury but a standard kitchen convenience. Other convenience items show up too, as in a Junket Ice Cream, and an Eagle Brand Salad Dressing. (For this last innovation, Mrs. C. M. McCaskill added salt, egg, vinegar, and mustard to sweetened condensed milk, a product that had become a Southern staple during Reconstruction.)

In addition to this mine of food history, the cookbooks' advertisements, interspersed with the recipes, offer a commercial history of my town. My father, a local banker for fifty years, reads these advertisements—the closest thing to a commercial directory in a town as small as Houston—with close attention. He does not miss the implications of a particular name on a board of directors in 1934 or of a car dealership's changing names in 1941. In these pages, the mostly male business community is bound together with women's recipes, all in the context of a powerfully sanctioned institution, the Methodist Church. Through such fund-raising projects, women's organizations tapped male enterprises (as well as women's businesses) for financial support, and they commodified their own domestic processes and products, selling their recipes and then feeding the profits back into the Methodist Church. Often the cookbooks were produced in years when the church's financial needs were unusually pressing. In the deep depression of 1934, for example, the Methodist congregation was so strapped by a large mortgage that it could no longer pay a minister's salary; the minister was forced to ride a circuit to three other towns. And in 1967, cookbook funds went toward an ambitious new church building, proudly illustrated on the volume's title page (although it was not yet built).

Cookbook advertising also provides a covert glimpse of the importance of women to the economy of Houston. Many of the advertisements, solicited by Methodist women, make at least mild obeisance to the importance of women consumers. In 1907, Houston Roller Mills' advertising copy evoked women's competitive pride in their domestic expertise with this brief local scenario:

> What a Delicious Cake!
> How Good Your Bread Is!
> That is what one Houston housewife said to another. Here is the
> secret: They were made from
> GILT EDGE FLOUR.[10]

In 1941, Watson Hardware Company proclaimed, "WE HAVE WHAT YOU NEED," and then went on to specify just *what* they imagined their readers needed: "Enamelware, Chinaware, Aluminum, Pressure Cookers [which had recently been introduced at the 1939 World's Fair], Canner Sets"—all kitchen equipment that cooks might use in preparing and serving recipes they found in the Methodist cookbook.[11] One of the two local weeklies, *The Houston Republican*, suggested that the newspaper was essential for keeping "a thrifty Housewife" up to date on "Grocery Specials." Even Lay's Pool Parlor, an establishment patronized exclusively by men, advertised only properties that would appeal to the Methodist wives and mothers of their male clientele: "Good Order—Clean Amusement."[12]

As counterpoint to such tributes to female domesticity, West's Variety proposed an astringently antidomestic 1941 "Recipe for Slimness: Buy your Foundation Garment, Silk Undies, Hosiery, Dresses, Hats, Shoes and coats, all slenderizing styles—and do not cook."[13] This singular ad (for a business run jointly by a wife and husband) indicates a powerful undercurrent that seldom comes to the surface of these domestic texts: the competing demands of a slender and glamorously packaged public persona and the constant practice of a cook's craft. Another such note is sounded by a recurrent recipe for sugarless Saccharine Pickles. Later, my mother—with two chubby daughters—inserted a notecard with her handwritten instructions for converting her mother's Mustard Pickle recipe to a "slenderizing" version with "6 packets of Equal" substituted for the sugar.

Among these advertisements I also find discreet evidence that women who work outside their homes have always been part of the Houston community. Even in 1907, Mrs. Lillie Huckshorn and Miss Verde Sutton are cited as joint proprietors of the Ozark Confectionery and Restaurant, offering "ICE DRINKS" and "SHORT ORDER MEALS AT ALL HOURS."[14] Miss Sutton is also a recipe contributor— as is a mysterious personage who has left no other mark on the collective memory of Houston, as far as I've been able to determine: a woman physician, Dr. Nettie B. Shanks, who contributed her recipes for Pickled Beets and Chipped Pears (a confection) in 1907. Businesswomen are also in evidence in 1934—for example, Mrs. Alice Rutherford's Ozark Grocery advertises "We Have Everything That the Recipe Calls For" and Faye's Beauty Shop forthrightly offers "All Kinds of Hair Work" and "Permanent Waving."[15] When indoor running water came to small Ozark towns like Houston in the thirties and forties, hairdressing became a more feasible career for women, as the cookbook ads indicate. By 1967, Betty's Beauty Salon (where my mother was a satisfied customer for more than thirty years) had a full-page ad that emphasized professionalism: "Our hair stylists are all members of the National Hairdressers and Cosmetologists' Assn." Also in 1967, a realty company advertisement signalled another career, real estate sales, that was increasingly attracting small-town women;

it featured a woman, "Wave Akins, Sales Manager." Wave Akins and Betty Dunn (of the Beauty Salon) are also family friends, and their recipes, printed and handwritten in the Methodist cookbooks, are among the treasures of Mother's repertoire. We still make Wave's pecan cookies and Betty's sour cream coffeecake.

Undeniably, the official culture of Houston prescribed a restrictively domestic agenda for girls. (Typically, in a precollege curriculum at Houston High School, I was advised to take three years of home economics and no foreign languages.) Nevertheless, as the central domestic texts of our household, the Methodist cookbooks encouraged my sister and me to recognize that domesticity and professionalism were not necessarily mutually exclusive. Thus, I grew up knowing (although often unconsciously) that these cookbooks were texts that empowered women and made their work—domestic and otherwise—an important, acknowledged resource of our community. The bright covers and color photographs of my mother's other mass-market cookbooks—the Betty Crocker, the James Beard— spoke the same fashionable language as the glossy girls' and women's magazines we read. Those books and magazines were powerfully attractive, but they infected me with longings that were hopeless and abject. Nothing I cooked and nothing I did to myself was going to resemble the flawless photographs in *Seventeen* and *House Beautiful.* But the black-bound Methodist cookbooks of my childhood were something else. Serious, unillustrated and enduring, they printed and preserved the names and the cooking of women I knew, whose food I had seen and eaten and might reproduce— women who had managed to survive and even to thrive in Houston, Missouri.

My adult life, as a university professor, has been spent in cities far from Houston. Yet the heritage of the Methodist cookbooks is clearly one of the reasons that my own scholarship has come to focus, again and again, on domestic texts and on U.S. women's complex relations to a history and heritage of housekeeping. I've written often about this subject. But nothing I've published has come closer to the bone for me than this present essay. Sitting at my computer and handling the stained, brittle, infinitely evocative pages of these borrowed and inherited texts, I also touch—with my fingers, with my words—the most precious and painful dynamics of my life as a daughter and an inheritor of a domestic culture. Normally I keep my books separate: theory, fiction, poetry, and painting on the book-shelves and the desk; cookbooks in the kitchen. But as I've been writing this essay, the books have moved again and again. Today the 1934 cook-book is here on my desk, propped by the computer. Yesterday it was propped in the kitchen, as I followed a recipe (Eggplant Casserole). As I try to meld these kitchen staples into a text that will be printed in a scholarly book, some of the (protective? preventive?) boundaries of my life seem to be dissolving. Thus, as I seldom have before, I worry about how my mother will read this essay. Although I have not lived in Houston for thirty years, I also worry about other possible readers, my old friends in the Houston Methodist Church.

When I first began to study the cookbooks, I bridled at their impas-sive, collective language, looking for any small rents in these near-seamless texts where individual preference and particularity showed through. Now I recognize that such language is a credential, a validation as important and necessary as the professional argot I use in my own scholarship. In these community cookbooks, the daily texture of private kitchen life is brought to the page with an almost formulaic anonymity, the language of the recipe. That dignified, standardized language seems to have been impor-tant and validating to the women who employed it. It confirmed their unwritten community, the body of skill and knowledge they shared but did not include on the page (for everyone, of course, knew what it meant to "can cold").

Writing this essay, I feel that I've blown my cover in two different communities. Clearly, I've betrayed my limits as a traditional cook (what *does* it mean to "can cold"?). Also, although I've drawn heavily on my own research in domestic culture for my reading of the cookbooks, I've pro-duced a very questionable piece of scholarship—the only books I cite are four small-town cookbooks! Nevertheless, this latest engagement with the Methodist cookbooks has, yet again, taught me a great deal. First, I've realized that I needn't be torn between two communities—one for scholar-ship, one for cooking. Most women and some men have allegiances and at least rudimentary vocabularies in both. Thus, the texts that interest me most now are the mobile ones, those that can move from desk, shelf, computer to kitchen table. Texts like the Methodist cookbooks that are, in the best and fullest senses of the term, *community cookbooks*. By their very existence, these books keep community alive and cooking. They celebrate continuities that women have labored to maintain. I'm grateful to have inherited a portion of that labor—in the Houston Methodist cookbooks.

So, in the spirit of community cookbooks, I'm going to end this essay with a recipe. Perhaps you'll read it, try it, revise it, write it in *your* book. Here, from the 1934 Houston Methodist Cookbook, is a very good recipe for Cutout Cookies. Contributed by Mrs. Sherman Houston, revised by Ruth Rogers Romines, and made for the past twenty-five years by her daughter, me, Ann Romines.

CUTOUT COOKIES

⅔ cup light brown sugar	⅔ cup white sugar
2 teaspoons cream of tartar	pinch salt
2 eggs	¾ cup softened butter
3 cups flour	1 teaspoon baking soda
1 teaspoon vanilla	

Cream sugar and butter. Beat in eggs and vanilla. Sift dry ingredients together and combine well with butter mixture. Divide dough into two portions, wrap each in waxed paper, and chill, preferably overnight. Roll thin (about ⅛ inch) on a floured pastry cloth and cut into shapes; decorate with colored sugar as desired. Bake on a lightly greased sheet at 375 degrees for 4–5 minutes until very lightly browned. Cool and store in tins.

Speaking Sisters:
Relief Society Cookbooks
and Mormon Culture

Marion Bishop

Joyce Eck died in 1987. She was fifty-three years old and had intestinal cancer. Randy Eck, her son, was my best friend in the small neighborhood in northern Utah where I grew up; his older sister, Tammy, was the best baby-sitter my brothers and I ever had. I haven't seen either of them since their mother's funeral, but I think of Joyce often. Every time I roll tangy, cream-of-tartar cookie dough in sugar and cinnamon to bake her Snicker Doodles, or press whole Hershey's chocolate kisses into the center of cooling, round peanut-butter cookies for Peanut Blossoms, I remember her sun-browned skin, the way her chewing gum snapped when she talked, and how one summer she let us paste up construction paper signs in her kitchen that said things like "Welcome to Randy's Cafe," and "Thank You for your Patronage." Her memory, her presence and her recipes are preserved for me in *Joyful Cooking*, a community cookbook published by Mormon women in Providence, Utah, in 1963.

Joyful Cooking, Millville Favorites (1987), and *Country Thyme Flavors* (1986),[1] are all books I cook from frequently. All three are "Relief Society" cookbooks, compiled by the Relief Society (the women's service organization) in three different Mormon (The Church of Jesus Christ of Latter Day Saints) congregations or "wards." *Joyful Cooking* and my mother taught me to cook; *Millville Favorites* reminds me of Millville, Utah, the town where I lived as a teenager; and *Country Thyme Flavors* connects me to my sister-in-law, a busy young mother, and her Lakeside, California, ward. Stained with margarine and brown sugar, flour and Campbell's cream of mushroom soup, each page and each recipe bears at least one woman's name. These women and the way they use recipes to speak, building a female sense of community, are the subjects of this chapter.

I am an insider/outsider. I have been nurtured and fed by the rich food in these books, but I have also learned to ask questions about ingredients, culture, and practice. In many ways, these are questions these women taught me to ask. As I watched them compose meals, substitute for missing ingredients, and pay careful attention to detail, I realized they were communicating two decidedly different messages in their cookbooks: in a patriarchal religious culture, where the most frequently heard public voices belong to men, Relief Society cookbooks provide their contributors with a way to affirm their religious faith, yet also to speak and be heard as individuals. Like a woman singing the melody of a familiar song, but composing her very own words, these cookbooks sustain the Mormon traditional religious value of family, along with woman's role in the home and in the church community, while at the same time articulating and validating more individualized ideas.

Cooking Community

All three Relief Society cookbooks are directed to readers who cook for families. Recipes are for casseroles, pasta salads, and quick desserts. Ingredients lists are relatively short, but the amounts they call for are usually large and followed by notes that say things like "feeds 12" or "leftovers freeze well." As a child I learned to "double" recipes from the back of a package of Nestle's toll house morsels, or Quaker oats—something I rarely had to do for a recipe in *Joyful Cooking*. The cultural norm that taught me bigger was better—reflected in ingredient amounts and recipe notes—is fueled by the necessity of cooking for a growing family and cooking often. The picture implicit in the kinds of recipes the books contain is one of a busy homemaker using staple ingredients to make wholesome, easy-to-prepare meals that can cook alone in the oven while she spends time with her children or throws another quick load of laundry in the washing machine. Hence, there are no gourmet recipes for intimate dinners for two, and both the 1986 and 1987 books include chapters on microwave cooking. The busy-family-around-the-dinner-table lifestyle these recipes reflect is articulated by an anonymous author in the following poem from *Joyful Cooking* (48), tellingly titled "Happiness Recipe":

> Combine one husband and one wife and add, for sheer delight,
> Assorted children, any size, and mix with all your might.
> Now add a pinch of helpfulness and loyalty galore.
> A dash of patience and a smile—and faith and stire [*sic*] some more.
> Now sprinkle kindness over all for happiness and health,
> Garnish it with love supreme and what you have is wealth.

As this poem and my use of the word "she" in the previous paragraph suggest, the books make it difficult to separate family references from the role of woman, and from her responsibility as spiritual home and community maker. Woman-as-homemaker is clearly the implied audience of these books, and actual references to women's roles are abundant. *Country Thyme Flavors'* "Expression of Appreciation" confirms that this is a women's book, about women's work: "Also many thanks to all of the *sisters* in the Lakeside Relief Society who so generously shared *their* favorite recipes for this book" (italics mine); and *Joyful Cooking* openly assigns gender to role when it explains that "an ideal homemaker plans a program or a schedule for each day so that she is the master [sic] rather than the victim of her work" (386). *Joyful Cooking's* dedication further illustrates this interweaving of family and women's roles:

> This book is dedicated to the Modern Homemaker. Our Mormon Doctrine ascribes a spiritual as well as a physical importance to all things. The human body is regarded as the tabernacle wherein is housed the spirit of man. It is God's will to conserve health, intel-

ligence and spirituality. Therefore, when assuming the responsibility of feeding a family one takes on not only a physical task but a spiritual one as well.

God grant us the wisdom and love to make meal-time, not only a time of filling our stomachs, but also, one of thanksgiving and of re-fueling our emotional and spiritual needs as well.

Reading this passage in 1995, I am initially concerned that human bodies are for "spirits of men" and that women cooks disappear into the generic term "one," but I trust that in 1963, the plucky women who compiled *Joyful Cooking* were only concerned with being grammatically and stylistically correct. More pertinent to the cookbooks' dual role of sustaining religious culture and carving out a place for women to speak is the way this dedication links day-to-day work with spiritual responsibility, imbuing homemaking with power and importance. This set of values dominates nineteenth-century community cookbooks of all Protestant denominations, and has also shown up in the domestic science movement. But references to this "Cult of Domesticity" in my Mormon cookbooks are particularly noteworthy, because the books were published so recently: the linking of day-to-day work with spiritual and religious responsibility is an important part of Mormon tradition from pioneer times *to the present.* In fact, the importance of woman's role in the home was articulated as recently as 1987 in a statement from Ezra Taft Benson, past president of the church: "Wives, come home from the typewriter, the laundry, the nursing, come home from the factory, the cafe. No career approaches in importance that of wife, homemaker, mother—cooking meals, washing dishes, making beds for one's precious husband and children."[2]

This delineation of women's roles is part of a larger definition of male and female responsibility. Every worthy male over age twelve is ordained to the Mormon priesthood and given its corresponding authority and responsibility. In a church that has no paid clergy and is run entirely by its members, priesthood is a prerequisite for most leadership roles. Men preside over and run church meetings, while women usually perform more supportive roles. Hence, the public domain comes to belong mostly to men, and women exercise their authority in the more private sphere of the home. As an exception to this, Relief Society, the women's service organization, is staffed and run by women and conducts its own meetings each Sunday in tandem with men's priesthood meetings. Further, it is important to note that outside of church service, many Mormon women have successful careers, others delight in their choice to work in the home, and still others perform some combination of both. My point is simply that this doubling of day-to-day work with divine responsibility is evidenced in the cookbooks: it creates an arena where women's voices are both expected and encouraged, but it is also part of a larger definition of male and female roles that reserves certain kinds of speaking and authority for men. This accounts for the two messages I hear Mormon women speaking in the cookbooks.

In addition to illustrating women's roles and responsibilities within the home, the cookbooks also support other Mormon values. The third page of *Country Thyme Flavors* reads: "All proceeds from the sale of this cookbook go toward building the San Diego Temple. We sincerely thank you for purchasing this cookbook and helping to make a temple in San Diego a reality." A temple is a sacred meeting place for Mormons, and this small passage from the opening of a book filled with recipes for taco casserole and chicken enchiladas demonstrates the way a Relief Society cookbook builds community and at the same time affirms religious beliefs (and raises money!). Another way the books sustain the spiritual community is through the recipes' adherence to the "Word of Wisdom," a dietary code which prohibits tobacco, alcohol, coffee and tea. Like other religious groups, Mormons set themselves apart and create community through their dietary habits. With one exception, none of the prohibited ingredients appears in my three cookbooks, and the deviant recipe, one for Pecan Stuffed Mushrooms that calls for "2 Tbsp. sherry," lists the item as "optional."[3]

The cookbooks show that women also build community and articulate church principles through the theme of thrift. There is a doctrinal precedent for this, namely the counsel of church leaders that each family have a year's supply of food and household items in storage for times of economic difficulty. Leonard J. Arrington and Davis Bitton explain that "it is improbable that most Mormon families have sufficient reserves for an entire year, but many have substantial quantities of canned fruit and vegetables, tins of flour and honey, and other commodities that could provide sustenance for several months in case of emergency. The practical reasons for this particular program . . . are a combination of sheer prudence, [and] the experience of scarcity and near-starvation in pioneer times."[4]

All three of my Relief Society cookbooks reflect this mandate to store food. There are many recipes for items that can be stored for long periods of time, and other recipes have been adapted to include items—such as wheat and beans—that are commonly in storage. Wheat finds its way into not only plain breads, or items like Whole Wheat Banana Nut Bread, but even into chili in a recipe that boils "2 ½ c. dry wheat" in five cups of water for twenty minutes before adding a pound of browned hamburger and other traditional chili ingredients.[5] Additionally, all three books anticipate shortages of staple foods and include lists of substitutions for missing ingredients. A cook without access to baking powder will learn, on page 57 of *Millville Favorites*, that she can substitute "¼ teaspoon baking soda plus ½ teaspoon cream of tartar" for each required teaspoon of baking powder. And the Lakeside, California, book even gives directions for mashing boiled potatoes, flour, and sugar for Sourdough Starter, explaining that "Homesteaders used to call this 'Cellar Bread.'"[6] The books are also full of recipes for preserves, relishes, and even vegetable soups and salsas that can be bottled in a cold pack or a pressure cooker and eaten at a later date. *Joyful Cooking* has a recipe for Fruit Cake that calls for two cups of "Tomato juice or soup,"[7] items commonly canned from garden produce. Additionally, because part of the food storage program is the encouragement to grow a garden, the books are full of recipes for fresh produce. In August, a basket of zucchini left on the front porch by a neighbor is seen more as a prank than a gift, but a family weary of Zucchini Stir Fry might be fooled into eating Apple Zucchini Cake, or tolerate the green vegetable in November in Zucchini Pineapple preserves or on a hot-dog with lots of mustard and ketchup in Zucchini Pickle Relish.[8] With these clever recipes for garden produce, Mormon women are doing more than finding uses for an over-abundant zucchini crop: they are also writing Mormon culture into the recipes of their cookbooks. But these women also infuse the culture-sustaining melody of the cookbooks' traditional values with messages about their own personal lyrics, words, and worth.

Counting Connections

When I married and moved away from Utah, I received the three books I am writing about as wedding presents. I also received a small wooden box from my paternal grandmother with thirty-five of her favorite recipes typed neatly on four-by-six cards. At the end of each recipe that was her own, my grandmother signed her name; if the recipe had come from a friend or neighbor—often women in her ward—their typed names were included next to the title. For a time, I was very possessive of these recipes, not sharing them, and clutching them close to me as substitution for my grandmother and the warm meals that were half a country away. Then my grandmother became ill. I realized that after her death, I wanted to eat her rolls at my sister-in-law's home on Thanksgiving, her Texas Cake at friends' birthday parties, and I began sharing her recipes—always taking care to write her name across the top of each copy. When she is gone, her recipes will give many of us access to her, through aroma, taste, and texture. This connection between a recipe, a woman's name and the validation of her life is at the heart of the personalized messages of the cookbooks and is the focus of the rest of the essay.

I once saw a woman doing needlepoint while wearing a T-shirt silk-screened with a counted cross-stitch motif and the phrase "I count." The words of this shirt and the way their message equates a traditional form of woman's work with validation of her existence resound throughout my three Mormon cookbooks. Unlike the cookbooks' first message, with its validation of community and shared roles and values, the second message is based on individuality and personal worth. At the most basic level, this message of "I count" is actually played out through numbers: the texts were contributed by 480 women and 19 men. *Joyful Cooking* is the largest book with 317 contributors; *Country Thyme Flavors* and *Millville Favorites* come in second and third with 122 and 60 contributors, respectively. Together, the books contain 1,719 recipes, a number that indicates multiple submissions from individual cooks were common. In reality, the number of recipes individual women contributed varies widely: many women did contribute just one recipe; others, like Joyce Eck, whose story begins this essay and who has 11 recipes in *Joyful Cooking*, shared quite a few; and some contributed substantially, as in the case of one woman in *Millville Favorites*, given credit for 37 recipes.

As I counted the recipes, attributing them to different cooks in tally columns next to each woman's name, I felt like I was working with a culinary book of life. I realized that for many women, a Relief Society cookbook was the only place they would ever see their names in print. If this is the reality, Shirley Biorn's recipe for Oatmeal Crispies[9]—her only entry—or Cheryl Johnson's thirty-seven contributions to *Millville Favorites* begin to resonate with special meaning. So does *Joyful Cooking*'s mention that in 1963 the Relief Society canned "1987 cans" of sauerkraut, "totaling 43 cases and weighing nearly two tons,"[10] a report with numbers so specific it seems to be counting and measuring more than just the sauerkraut the Swiss immigrants of Providence were famous for.

In her article "Recipes for Reading," Susan J. Leonardi explores the connection between recipes, food, and woman's worth by arguing that a recipe is a piece of discourse that invites response: the recipe's implied audience, the "you" the cooking directions are given to, is invited to respond to the speaker by following the directions and cooking the dish, by revising it to suit personal taste, or by speaking—by saying "I baked your apple pie and my family loved it."[11] Ultimately, these responses make the writer of the recipe count, and in the case of my Relief Society cookbooks, spoken responses—comments, questions and compliments—are especially important. In the close-knit wards my books come from, to have a recipe included in a Relief Society cookbook is to open conversation about it—at least with the other cooking women in the community. Each contributor's symbolic attempt, through the recipe, to say "I count" is rendered real with a response, with someone saying "that's right, your Chinese Noodle Casserole was great, and you do count." Women's use of language in this way—to create their own texts as well as a responsive audience around them—is particularly significant, because in Mormon communities, men usually have authority over the word—both written and spoken. By contributing to the cookbooks, Mormon women create a rhetorical situation that calls for affirmation and perpetuation of their worth: a woman's word—her name and her recipe—is made concrete in cooking, eating, and talking about the recipe, and to compliment a woman on a particularly tasty dish is to acknowledge and verify her life.

Mary Field Belenky and her coauthors explain in *Women's Ways of Knowing* that the importance of such a supportive, responsive audience cannot be overstated. They suggest that an attentive audience is essential for the development of a woman's own voice—so important that they call the women who have not had such a response "silent."[12] This idea is especially applicable to my cookbooks, because a recipe, with its giving of directions and taking charge of procedure, is historically one of the few places Mormon women can speak with authority. If a woman's assertive voice of authority is heard, responded to, and perhaps even respected, a recipe becomes a powerful piece of discourse—an opportunity for women to speak and be heard based on an economy of food. The long-term popularity of Dianna Sutherland's Icebox Muffins—a recipe for "six dozen large" bran muffins made from batter that can be stored in the refrigerator for "up to six weeks"[13]—indicates more than just a community interest in healthful eating and time-saving recipes. It also configures Sutherland as a strong speaker, and the baking of muffins as ongoing dialogue about women's lives and work.

The life-validating second message of the cookbooks that connects speaker to responder, recipe-writer to cook, is also heard in the recipes named for women and the inclusion of recipes from multiple contributors. A telling 47 of the 445 recipes in *Country Thyme Flavors* have a woman's name in their titles, an occurrence which is common in the other books, too. Some women name their recipes for themselves: Karen Drake contributes a recipe for Karen's Salad Dressing, and Mikki Mastellar shares one for Mikki's Pecan Pie,[14] references I read as a woman's double use of her name to insure that her recipe and the life and work it represents are taken seriously. Other titles like Olive's Oatmeal Cake or Sis. Brickley's Fruit Salad, contributed respectively by Jeanine Hanet and Carol Lindquist,[15] seem to indicate something more than just courteous acknowledgment of the cook they originally came from. Implicit in these titles is an affirmation of the contributors' existence by drawing on the value and life of another woman, in a she-exists-so-I-do-too kind of equation. In this regard, it is telling that there are many recipes with the words "mother" and "grandmother" in their titles. When a woman contributes a recipe with this kind of title and adds her name at the bottom, she confirms women's domestic tradition and her line of ancestry within it. Although the loss of full names in recipes like Mom's Spanish Rice or Grandmother Moore's Oatmeal Cake[16] objectifies the namesakes in a significant way and echoes the community values of the cookbooks' first message, the titles also affirm and honor a grandmother-mother-daughter matriarchy—a naming and placing of the self within a female, family tradition.

Recipes like *Joyful Cooking*'s Fast Rising Rolls or Scones,[17] where five separate cooks are listed as contributors, show women capitalizing on yet another form of counting. When the compilers of each book received the same recipe from more than one cook, they chose to list every contributor of the recipe rather than selecting just one woman as the source. This practice creates a reverse on the male norm that equates autonomy with power: each of the contributors draws credibility from the other cooks she is listed with. Five women's names banded together at the bottom of a recipe usually guarantees that the dish is a particularly tasty one, but it also demands a certain kind of respect for the individual women who submitted it. In recipes throughout the books, groups of women bear out the theory, articulated in Lyn Mikel Brown and Carol Gilligan's *Meeting at the Crossroads,* that women often establish identity and make meaning through connection and relationship.[18] Sharing credit for a recipe with other women validates not only one's tastes, preferences, and cooking style, but also one's credibility and esteem within the community. I learned a practical application of this idea as a child, tracking certain names through *Joyful Cooking,* knowing that when they appeared together, the recipe was a real winner. On a more theoretical level, I see now that I was learning that my identity exists in relationship with other women: by connecting myself with women in my community whose cooking—and hence speaking—was respected, my own speaking and living were affirmed.

Finally, contributors to the cookbooks also articulate their message of individual worth in the way they use recipes to tell stories. In some ways, a recipe works like a journal, where it is difficult to deny the existence of days and events that are recorded and assigned a specific date. Whereas in a journal the date functions as the signifier, in my cookbooks, the recipe titles serve that function: a journal needs a hundred entries to validate a hundred days, but in the writing of one recipe, a woman may validate and tell the story of hundreds of meals or days. What is lost in specificity is gained in depth: an individual recipe's title implies all the various settings and circumstances in which it was served. A good example of this is the way stories are sometimes encoded in recipe names. A title like Christmas Spritz Cookies has the ability to recall all the Christmases when it was prepared and served. Stories are also embedded in ordinary recipes like Busy Day Roast, Left-Over Meat Pie and Eat 'n' Run Breakfast,[19] whose titles carry with them the memories and resonance of countless days and meals. When a woman contributes a recipe for Busy Day Roast to a Relief

Society cookbook, her rhetoric embeds the stories of all the busy days she cooked that dish into its title, knowing that those implied stories will speak to other cooks.

At other times stories—or parts of stories—are written into the texts of individual recipes. Kelly's Taco Filling, a recipe that mixes together ground beef with refried beans, carries the explanation: "This original recipe, Mom thought up so our meat wouldn't drop out of the [taco] shell. Other examples of this story-telling include a recipe for Spaghetti Sauce that explains: "This is an excellent dish to put in a crock-pot or other slow cooker during church," and one for Tuna Casserole that ends by saying, "Makes enough for 4 to 6 hearty appetites."[20] By including such story-telling phrases in their recipes, Mormon women reveal information about their personal practices and preferences. Then too, for the reader-user of these cookbooks, a recipe may serve as a token or symbol of memories and stories: the recipes in *Millville Favorites* from the mother of one of my high school friends always reminds me both of my friend and the stories he told about his mother; and when I cook from *Country Thyme Flavors* I always remember which women in that California community have been particularly kind to my sister-in-law. In this way, oral histories and the recipes work together to breathe life into the women whose names accompany the recipes.

In their effort to document and value their daily work, Mormon women articulate the Relief Society cookbooks' second message—one that is sung to the melody of the first but that affirms individual worth instead of traditional, religious values. Yet the nourishing food, the rich aromas and the sense of something solid sitting in my stomach lead me to ask how this happened—and *if* it happened—or if with ears so eager to hear women from my culture speaking, I have heard their cooking instructions and recipe titles say something they never intended at all. Additionally, because I understand that Mormon women both use and are used by Relief Society cookbooks—that the texts serve as a vehicle for women to speak but still support traditional cultural expectations of women—I wonder if any aspect of the cookbooks transcends such discouraging circularity. To answer these questions, I must add a few additional ingredients to this essay. Drawing attention to the connection between the words of a recipe and a woman's bodily-based life experience, these ingredients work like freshly ground spices, enhancing and heightening ideas already covered, and cementing the bond between a woman and her word(s) in a recipe.

Writing Recipes

In her "Eating Patterns as a Reflection of Women's Development," psychologist Janet L. Surrey focuses on the connections between food, eating, and a woman's ability to hear her own voice. She describes a woman's distancing herself from her own voice as characteristic of eating disorders. What interests me particularly is the *function* she assigns food and eating. She begins by explaining that "inner sensations and perceptions . . . are the basis of self-knowledge and healthy self-expression." She continues this idea by arguing that the "ability to feel 'alive' inside, to feel connected to oneself, is important in all human functioning. . . . Further, the ability to feel 'connected' in this way, to feel and enjoy bodily pleasure, may be partially a function of healthy enjoyment of food, since food is so basic to life."[21]

Surrey's research provides a way to push each previous argument I've made a bit further and suggests that woman are speaking through food in even more powerful and specific ways than have been explored so far. By tying food so closely to a woman's ability to stay connected with her inner feelings and sensations, Surrey's research helps us understand that the writing, sharing, and cooking of a recipe constitute more than just meal preparation. These tasks can also be understood as rituals that keep a woman in touch with her inner desire and the voice of her body; and recipes can also be read as texts that connect a woman's outer and inner worlds. In fact, recipe writing is a discursive act that requires a woman to rely on her connection with her own voice—with what brings her pleasure and satisfaction. When a woman writes a recipe and then signs her name to it, she establishes a connection to her inner world and maintains the kind of internal awareness Surrey believes is essential for mental health, personal knowledge, and self-expression.

Research by French feminist theorist Luce Irigaray works nicely in tandem with Surrey's assertions to flesh-out the connection between the body and the word and how it is embedded in the writing and cooking of a recipe. Whereas Surrey's emphasis is on the way food provides a woman with a connection to her inner world, Irigaray focuses on the voice of that inner world—the voice of a woman's body—how to access it, and what it might say. In "The Bodily Encounter with the Mother," Irigaray urges: "We must give her [woman] the right to pleasure, to *jouissance*, to passion, restore her right to speech, and sometimes to cries and anger. . . . We have to discover a language [*langage*] which does not replace the bodily en-counter, as paternal language [*langue*] attempts to do, but which can go along with it, words which do not bar the corporeal, but which speak corporeal."[22]

Essentially, Irigaray is calling for the discovery of a new language—one founded on a woman's bodily-based connection to the word. As she explores ways to uncover such a corporeal language, Irigaray suggests that it is good to speak while feeding children so they can come to associate words with their inner sensations of hunger and desire. It is this suggestion that comes to bear most directly on my three Relief Society cookbooks: the same triad of food, hunger, and words that Irigaray believes will give children access to the voices of their bodies exists in recipes. In short, recipes are texts written full of the bodily encounter. The writing of a recipe, or the work required to gain the bodily-based knowledge intrinsic in a phrase like "I'm hungry for [a specific food]," begins to bridge the chasm between the world of the felt—the sensed, the lived—and the world of the word. The text of each recipe represents an effort to assign measure-ment to the immeasurable—to render hunger, pleasure, and desire into language. In other words, ingredient amounts and cooking directions are linguistic indicators of how the recipe-writer and responding cook define the bodily sensations of pleasure and hunger. Bound to the recipes in my Relief Society cookbooks is the idea Irigaray and her colleagues label *écriture féminine:* as recipes move from hunger, to food, to writing about the body, to writing-the-body, they provide language for woman to give voice to her most corporeal feelings and desires. Phrases like "Very Good!" and "Out of this world"[23] at the end of recipes signify more than just good-tasting food—they also indicate that the recipe writer has made the con-nection from unwritten inner desire, to the symbolic word, and ultimately, to physical satisfaction of the desire. Indeed, it only seems appropriate that my early, anonymous author chose the recipe as the genre for her "Happiness Poem," and that women in a culture that has traditionally provided them with limited opportunities to speak find a measure of solace, power and connected speech in Relief Society cookbooks.

And I believe these women also find each other—that in making the journey to their own bodies they connect themselves with the bodies of other women. I am referring here to the idea of a feminine culinary genealogy—a matri-lineage based not just on a woman's name but also on her kitchen, her act of cooking, and her body. Irigaray defines and explains the importance of the term "feminine genealogy" in "The Bodily Encounter with the Mother." She believes that establishing such a genealogy is necessary for women to own and understand their identities. In advising women to discover their heritage, the following passage begins to explain the power of the matri-lineage that is also a part of my cookbooks: "It is necessary . . . for us to assert that there is a genealogy of women. There is a genealogy of women within our family: on our mothers' side we have mothers, grandmothers and great-grandmothers, and daughters. . . . Let us try to situate ourselves within this female genealogy so as to conquer and keep our identity. Nor let us forget that we already have a history, that certain women have, *even if it was culturally difficult*, left their mark on history and that all too often we do not know them. (Emphasis added.)[24]

Among all the other services they provide, Relief Society cookbooks also allow women to leave their mark on history. The cookbooks record women's names, cooking styles and preferences, and often their relationships. Because of *Joyful Cooking*, my children and I will always have access to certain kinds of information about Joyce Eck. We will always know and remember her. On an absolutely practical level, because I have her recipes, I also know her name and have many of her stories. In publishing and sharing women's recipes and names, Relief Society cookbooks preserve a portion of women's histories and identities. Although I do not know all of the women in my three cookbooks, or all of their stories, that is not the point—neither do any of the readers. But because I have their recipes, I can ascribe a genealogy to the women I do know, passing on their names and their stories. The intestinal cancer that killed Joyce Eck need not silence her voice, and the whole community of women who joined her in *Joyful Cooking*—many of whom are now gone or retired to nursing homes— continues to speak of Providence, Utah, and of women's lives in 1963.

In part, this is a definition of genealogy that defies the patriarchal notion that it exists only through lineage. Although some specific references to lineage exist in the books, and certain recipes like Mom's Sugar Cookies[25] remind me of three generations of related women—the woman who contributed the recipe, her mother that it is named for, and her daughter who was my teenage friend—a definition of genealogy based only on lineage belies the depth of the books. Not only are women creating and affirming identity through connection, they are fostering new kinds of connections that suggest altogether new ways to configure community and family: for me to remember a recipe is to remember the woman it came from, how it was passed on to her, and where I can situate myself within my culinary female family.

Finally, I can add the word "culinary" to my discussion of a feminine genealogy and explain how Relief Society cookbooks infuse what would ordinarily be just a linguistic genealogy with the aromas, flavors, and bodily pleasures associated with cooking and eating. Marrying the cookbooks' recipe titles, contributor credits, and all of the tools that provide a feminine genealogy to a recipe's ability to write the body creates something very powerful indeed. It generates not just a woman's name, statistics, and origin, but nearly her presence as well. For in baking Joyce Eck's Snicker Doodles[26] I am taken into the inner world of her desire, pleasure, and hunger—immeasurable bodily sensations, articulated in a recipe and made real for me in my own kitchen in the form of texture, taste, and smell. As a young girl, I visited her kitchen; through her recipes, I now invite her into mine. Perhaps this entirely sensual connection, based on a body's response to stimulus and written into the text of a recipe, is what Irigaray intended when she wrote: "We must also find, find anew, invent the words, the sentences that speak to the most archaic and most contemporary relationship with the body of the mother, with our bodies, the sentences that translate the bond between her body, ours and that of our daughters."[27]

Joyce Eck is not my biological mother, but her food connected me to a bodily based sense of the maternal in the community where I grew up. Today, her recipes provide me with both a linguistic and corporeally based knowledge of my culture and roots. It is this ability of a recipe to bind the experience of the body, the unwritten, into measurable amounts that can be replicated, that makes the idea of a feminine culinary genealogy not just about cataloging names, but about literally preserving the *sense* of a woman's life. Each recipe serves as a textual token—something a woman can hold in her hands that speaks of and connects her to wor(l)ds both linguistic and corporeal. Because of this, my Relief Society cookbooks provide a way for a contributing cook to connect her word—her name— and her body, to powerful bodies of women, stretching across both culture and time.

It is October 1972 and I am eight years old. Apples from my family's orchard huddle in boxes in the garage and spread out in bushel baskets across the back porch. In the kitchen I wash Ball and Mason quart bottles in hot soapy water, while my mother, grandmother, and Joyce Eck fill them first with quartered apples, and then, following traditional recipes, with apple pie filling and smooth, thick applesauce. From time to time we stumble over the bushel of apples in the middle of the kitchen floor, and I listen carefully as the women share child-rearing stories and discuss favorite canning techniques. Toward the end of the day, I curl into a corner where two kitchen cupboards meet. The women begin counting backwards, remembering details of each apple harvest. About the time they reach the year I was born, my head falls on my shoulder and I'm asleep.

Voices, Stories, and Recipes in Selected Canadian Community Cookbooks

Elizabeth J. McDougall

I love the long drawn-out process of making pickles. Carole Frook's recipe, Best Ever Eleven Day Pickles is the one that I use.[1] I have eaten hundreds of Carole's pickles over the years at different community events. She is a friend of my mother, and her son, Brian, and I went to high school together. Her pickles really are the best ever. The recipe calls for *a six quart basket of cucumbers that are not too big—no larger than those used for large dills. You prepare the cucumbers by washing them and slicing them into ½ to ¾ inch thick pieces.* Washing cucumbers is one of my least favorite chores because the spines get stuck in your skin. Since your skin is wet and the spines are wet too, it is impossible to get them out right away. It's not excruciatingly painful, but it is bothersome.

These pickles are so good, the labor is worth it. I am glad that Carole included her recipe in the curling club's cookbook. The women in our community usually publish a cookbook as a fund-raiser every few years;

my family owns most of them. The recipes in these cookbooks are failsafe, "tried and true," family favorites that find their way into the community through social events and through these books. Because I grew up in a very small community, Chatsworth, Ontario, population 500, the contributors are all people I know. When I read through these cookbooks, memories of eating resurface as I remember all the get-togethers in the church basement, at the community center, or at the curling club. Cooking is a big part of my relationship to these people.

Although cookbooks are a form of expository writing to be used for and when cooking, they are also a good read. I enjoy reading cookbooks, looking at the ingredients, and imagining the food coming together. A good cookbook is not just about food; it is about the expression, the presentation, and representation of food in textual form. My main interest in reading cookbooks is the food, but I am also intrigued by the processes through which food is transformed into text. The use of literary theories of language in the exploration of the reading and writing of these texts uncovers the history and art of cooking—the way language works within a cookbook for both reader and writer—and the future possibilities of the text as food. Both literary theory and community cookbooks emphasize the relationships between reader, writer, and text; both the language of recipes and the very food we eat derive from personal and cultural beliefs. I consider recipes and cookbooks to be part of an alternative field of literature, important in part because they are texts associated with the women who read them, buy them, and write them, especially community cookbooks that are more often written by women and their organizations. A consideration of literary theories of language in relation to these texts reveals their complexity.

The presence of the cook is in the food, coming out in the creation of the food as a result of the interactions between text and reader/writer and between food and reader/writer. Cooking, like no other activity, reveals the lack of power and authority people have over food and language. My mother, my aunt, and I all use the same recipe for bread, we use the same ingredients and follow it to a T, but you would never know it by tasting our bread—each cook's bread is noticeably different. We may knead the bread differently or maybe our ovens are not exact in their temperature—who knows? All we know is that the recipe is the same and the bread is different.

Just as the cook's presence is apparent in the food, the presence of the recipe writer is in the text along with recipe writers of the past. A recipe is never totally new; it is based on recipes and procedures of the past, reflecting the communal sense of cooking and the long tradition behind it. Creating a "new" recipe involves combining, changing, and adding to old recipes. The "new" recipe will probably be further revised by its readers, continuing the process. Writers of recipes have little "authority" over the reception of their texts because reading a recipe is an active process, be it reading and choosing recipes to make in the future or reading the recipe as you cook, turning the words on the page into action. Reading recipes is an interpretive process as well: cooks change a recipe at will, leaving out ingredients that they don't have or that they don't want or adding ingredients that seem to fit. Every interaction with food and with text is specific, subjective, and creative.

The subjective nature of food makes it more than just daily sustenance and nutrition; it also possesses meaning for people—traditional foods are appreciated because of their association with holidays and ceremonies, everyday foods are familiar and comforting, and unusual foods may be shunned or searched out, depending on the cook and the audience. Women participate in the creation of meaning in food, especially for foods and meals that are of great cultural significance, such as those for Christmas, New Year's festivities, Yom Kippur, and so on. Since women are the primary cooks in most societies and because much of their time is taken up with the demands of cooking, it is a major aspect of female cultural heritage. Women make time to read cookbooks because these texts relate to the daily tasks of cooking; consequently, cookbooks are a form of writing familiar to and associated with women. Since women, in the past, were not encouraged to write literature or supported in their literary endeavors, their writing often appears in less traditional forms. The recovery of women's writing, women's history, and women's lives involves a consideration of many alternative materials such as cookbooks, letters, diaries and so on. Recipes convey information, but they also record the history of recipes, of food, of women cooking, and of women writing.

After washing the cucumbers, add 2 cups of coarse pickling salt and cover with boiling water. Let stand four days, stirring every day. My favorite part of cooking is stirring because it is so quiet and calm, perfect for thinking, dreaming, and imagining.

Stirring is not one simple motion. Different foods are stirred in different ways. For example, stirring soup involves a completely different process than stirring pudding, salad dressing, or pickling cucumbers. When I stir soup, I stir slowly, languidly, allowing the vegetables to swim in the broth, mingling with the spices in a leisurely way. When I stir pudding, I become a little bit stressed out because I am continually worrying that the pudding might stick to the bottom of the pot and burn. I overreact to this threat by trying to keep the pudding from having any contact with the bottom of the pot, an obviously impossible task. However, I have developed a technique of stirring that allows me to come close to my objective: I stir in a figure eight, manipulating the spoon so that the largest possible portion of the bottom surface of the spoon comes between the liquid and the pot. I also swing the pot back and forth in the hope that the spoon will cover the whole area of the pot bottom with the combination of moving both the pot and the spoon.

When I stir salad dressing, I am hysterical. This hysteria results from trying to combine the salad oil and the vinegar. From a scientific standpoint, vinegar and oil will never mix permanently and on an intellectual level, I know this; however, on an emotional level, I need the two to combine before I can pour it on my salad. So I stir in a frantic way, moving a fork back and forth in a jar, making a tinkling noise. As soon as I stop, the dressing separates. So I hold the jar over the salad, stirring madly, and then I quickly turn the jar over and dump it on the salad, defying all laws of science.

When I stir the pickling mixture, I have to be careful not to bruise the cucumbers. So I move my spoon from the outside of the bowl down and up through the middle, slowly moving the cucumbers through various positions, turning the bowl as I stir to further movement. Because I have eleven days of stirring, I feel confident that each cucumber will occupy multiple positions, achieving the right amount of texture and taste.

On the fifth day, you must drain the juice off; cover with boiling water again, stir and let stand for 24 hours.

Recipes do not discuss the intricacies of stirring because it is assumed to be a skill the reader already possesses, one learned through watching others cook. In the past, watching and listening to others was the method of transferring skills from one person to another, from one generation to another, in a communal oral setting. Recipes have not always been written down but have been passed on through speech and demonstration as women cook together. There are still some recipes in my family that are remembered rather than read: my grandmother's biscuits and lemon squares, my aunt's cabbage rolls, my mother's soft ginger cookies. The community cookbook maintains the sense of a sharing of ideas, but because recipes cannot duplicate the personal, oral relationships between cook, text, and food of the past, gaps in communication arise between the reader and the text.

The translation of an oral form into written discourse results in a form and style that reflects orality. Although recipes appear in textual form, the recipe is presented to the reader through a speaking voice, the "I" of the cook, with the reader occupying the position of listener or follower of instructions and guidelines. The language has the attributes of spoken speech or dialogue, with the "you" or "one" being understood: "Sift dry ingredients together and add to wet mixture"; "Cook for one hour," and so on. Although the implied subject is the reader, the text is ambiguous, revealing the fluidity of the relationship between writer and reader. "You" could refer to the writer as she or he cooks, creating new recipes and translating the process of cooking into textual form. The identities of writer and reader merge together in the role of the cook and consequently, the subject "we" is also a possibility as reader and writer work together to decode the language of food.

Recipes adhere to specific codes between reader and writer concerning their form, style, and content. Roland Barthes sees all texts as functioning "according to certain rules" and as a "process of demonstration."[2] The expected form of a recipe begins with a list of ingredients followed by several short statements of instruction. The text is as minimal as possible, revealing a need for brevity and concision and resulting in a specialized language in which certain words represent a concept or series of actions, for example:

Baste: to moisten meat or other foods with pan drippings, fruit juice or sauce, preventing drying of food surface and adding taste.

Braise: to cook slowly in a small amount of liquid in a covered pan.

Julienne: to cut meat, vegetables, or fruit into long, matchlike strips.

Knead: to manipulate with a pressing motion accompanied by folding and stretching. For yeast bread: fold dough toward you, push dough away using the heel of your hand, rotate ¼ turn and repeat. For tea biscuits, kneading process is much less vigorous and requires less time.[3]

To include these definitions within the text of every recipe would not only lengthen the text, but would also make the cookbook extremely repetitious; however, for the less experienced cook or reader, cooking terms are baffling because of their foreign nature. These words seem foreign because they are ancient, dating back centuries in some instances: "knead" first appears in old English texts as *cnedan*, and it is surmised to be older as an oral form evident in consistent sound patterns across different languages, for example, Dutch *knedan*, German *kneten*.[4] The alien nature of these words stresses their location in the specialized field of cooking, encouraging the formation of an image. Mikhail Bakhtin describes the appearance of a specialized language in texts as "an object of representation."[5] In recipes, these words serve as signs, indicating the long and continually changing history of cooking, recipes, and cookbooks.

These words assume a position of authority not only because they are old, but also because of their foreign character, just as Latin words function in medical discourse or Italian words in musical discourse. Words like "sauté" and phrases like "à la mode" have become a part of our cultural heritage and a part of the English language, but they maintain the flair of a different language in their spelling and pronunciation. They also highlight the series of actions they represent as particular to recipes and the cooking experience. This language of cooking corresponds to Bakhtin's notion that "language is structured and perceived in the light of another language, and in some instances not only the accents but also the syntactical forms." The syntactical forms of recipes reveal the traditions of cooking, displaying its oral roots, communal atmosphere, and antiquity. Through a combination of the word, the definition, and the recipe, the cookbook reader is connected to the text; this process is similar to Bakhtin's view of language, in which author and text act as variables that "mutually and ideologically [interanimate] each other."[6] The specialized language that could be a barrier to understanding for a reader unfamiliar with cooking terms is also a path to understanding, transforming the text into a dynamic object of communication.

On the sixth day, drain and add 1 tablespoon alum and cover with boiling water. Stir. Let stand.

The connection between language and food, between the recipe writer and the reader, is not simple, direct, or unified. Language is a variable not a constant. For Bakhtin, certain texts are written with not one language but with many "intersecting" languages or planes of language.[7] Cooking involves texts consisting of the many languages generated from a mixing of times, countries, and cultures. Alongside words like "kneading" from long ago are new words that enter the discourse of cooking as new technology and different ingredients affect the cooking process. Many recipes add instructions for the cook who has special machines and devices, for example, Shortbread Cookies "(made in blender)" and Microwave Cheesecake.[8] Then too, as the language of the cookbook evolves, it encompasses other languages; words like "julienne," "sauté," "salsa," and "pesto" become commonplace. Julienne and sauté evoke the qualities of French cuisine, while salsa has Latin American connotations and pesto has Italian roots. These terms are indicative of more than just language; they also illustrate a whole culture of cooking and the way it changes through time. Pesto initially referred to the act of grinding food with a mortar and pestle; now it is used specifically to describe the garlic, basil, and pinenuts concoction that is currently so trendy. Salsa has also acquired a narrow meaning—although it loosely translates into a sauce or condiment; North Americans associate salsa with tomatoes, cilantro, garlic, onions, and jalapeno peppers. In recipes as in other texts, language proves to be continually mutating, acquiring a plethora of meanings and applications through time.

On the seventh day, stir and let stand.

The language of food possesses meanings beyond taste as readers associate recipes with remembered experiences and with cultural norms. Food signifies a lifetime of memories, as evident in a Georgian Bay community cookbook that emphasizes the link between recipes, certain times of the year, and special places:

> Spring is a lovely time of year . . . but the best part about it is that summer is right around the corner. Those lazy, hazy, crazy days of summer. You can't beat them. But before you enjoy them, there's work to be done in the home, in the garden, at the cottage.
>
> A sure sign of spring on Georgian Bay is "break-up" time. The great blanket of ice which covers the water for those long winter months first turns "black," then begins to crack and break up. Slowly it moves out with the help of a good south-east wind. Great hunks of

ice have been noticed out in the gap as late as mid-May—which usually disturbs the swimming enthusiast who likes to take his first dip of the year on the May 24th weekend!

Whatever your springtime activities, be sure they are accompanied by good food. This chapter provides you with lots of ideas—a brunch, a hearty dinner for hard workers, a last-minute meal when you are forced indoors because of rain, and much more.

Finally, celebrate the Spring with our delightful "Sniff and Cook" section—unusual recipes which utilize flowers and blossoms characteristic of this wonderful time of year.

Try them? You may find you can have your flowers and eat them too![9]

This cookbook introduces the notion of "break-up" time to illustrate the mental, emotional, and spiritual elements of spring, especially in the sense of freedom from winter imaged in the cracking and disappearance of the black ice. Although this change in seasons is dramatically titled "break-up" time, it is actually a slow transformation of nature from winter to summer that requires effort, time, and complex processes. Similarly, people expend many kinds of effort in their preparation for summer, and the food reflects the activity of the season: "a hearty dinner for hard workers." The food suits not only the demands of work and the inconsistencies of the weather, it also suits the desires of an audience yearning for the colors, smells, warmth, and life of spring. The addition of the flowers to the menu works to celebrate this season of hope and inspiration.

As well as actual felt experience, certain foods receive meaning from cultural assumptions about exotic places and peoples. For instance, curry tends to be a spice infused with cultural meaning. During a cooking demonstration on *Regis and Kathie Lee*,[10] a caterer vigorously encouraged viewers not to exclude the curry from her fried chicken recipe, suggesting that people avoid curry for reasons other than its flavor. Curry is a spice to which people react strongly, not necessarily because of the flavor, but because of the "idea" of curry or preconceptions about curry. According to Bakhtin, "images of language are inseparable from images of various world views and from the living beings who are their agents."[11] The North American reader traditionally considers curry as solely an Indian spice, which causes certain expectations—food spiced with curry may be prejudicially rejected because it is Indian and therefore strange and distasteful. In this instance, curry represents an ethnicity, not a spice with multiple uses. The writing of recipes is situated within this myriad of beliefs and ideas about food and its peoples, cultures, and languages.

The reader of a cookbook brings past experiences of and cultural influences on cooking and eating to the reading process. Working with a recipe involves a dynamic response—not just in terms of the physical activity of cooking but also in terms of reading. Barthes defines text as process, with the reader acting as a "coauthor" of the text, generating meaning and subsequently "completing it rather than giving it expression." In addition, he states that "the text itself plays and the reader plays twice over, playing the text as one plays a game, looking for a practice which reproduces it."[12] Reading a cookbook requires active participation, be it in the form of cooking or in the form of responding to the text before beginning to cook. For example, how does the reader decide that the words on the page could be transformed into something that tastes good? Recipes stimulate the reader to imagine a world of cooking and eating. Iser believes "the creation of illusion" to be a part of any reading: "The reader constantly has to lift the restrictions he places on the 'meaning' of the text. Since it is he who builds the illusions, he oscillates between involvement in and observation of those illusions, he opens himself to the unfamiliar world without being imprisoned in it. Through this process, the reader moves into the presence of the fictional world and so experiences the realities of the text as they happen."[13] Recipes are not so formulaic as to deny escapism; they, too, involve creating images of foods, tastes, and smells that take the reader into a fantasy world of eating and cooking.

With any text, the title is of prime importance in attracting readers and in encouraging them to continue reading. Intriguing titles may promise a brand new recipe or dish: Pumpkin Dazzle, Tipsy Tomato Soup, and Rising Sun Salad. Or they may tempt the reader by inviting a twist on an old favorite, as do Cranberry Coffee Ring and Raspberry Sour Cream Pie. Variations of a known food are both intriguing and pleasing to the mind's stomach, evoking an image of taste, texture, or process: a coffee cake ring with a new element—cranberries; or raspberry pie with a swirl of sour cream. Many titles reflect time factors and level of difficulty, conditions crucial to incorporating cooking into a busy life: Fast Cinnamon Buns,

Quick Carrot Cake, Quick and Easy Chocolate Cake.[14] Such titles suggest a known food achievable in a short time and with minimal difficulty, a pleasing option to most people.

On the eighth day, drain juice again. In large pot, add vinegar, eight cups sugar, 3 tablespoons of cassia buds and 3 tablespoons whole allspice; bring to a boil; pour over cucumbers, stir and let set 1 day.

When reading through a cookbook, we bring expectations with us to the cooking experience, wanting a recipe to fulfill our needs and capabilities. According to Stanley Fish, the "efforts of readers are always efforts to discern and therefore to realize . . . an author's intention."[15] With regard to a cookbook, the author's intention is to enable the reader to prepare a specific dish; but following a recipe is so much more complicated than "realizing" the author's intention. Our intentions are equally important and we, as cooks, as consumers of food, and as readers of cookbooks, are affected by our past experiences and approaches to food and to cooking. This in turn influences our choice of recipes and our ways of cooking. For example, I never use salt when cooking, and I actually make a point of striking it from the recipe. The reason I do this is because my mother does this. The reason my mother does this is because her mother did this. The reason her mother did this is that three of her nine children had kidney disease and could not ingest salt without dire consequences. Hence, Grandma struck the salt from recipes so that no one would mistakenly put it in the food. My mother and I do it out of habit, and since we have become accustomed to this practice, any added salt makes the food distasteful to us. I was not aware of my grandmother's role in my cooking habits until recently; before that, I was just following my mother's example of the "correct" way to cook. When we read, we often do not recognize the effect our family, our education, or our culture has on our interaction with a text, demonstrating that when reading, as Iser says, "we bring to the fore an element of our being of which we are not directly conscious."[16] Making food is not solving the puzzle of the recipe, it is the intersection of a text with a reader that leads to an understanding and a finished product specific to that reader.

On the ninth day, drain syrup into large pot and add two cups sugar; reheat; pour over cucumbers. Stir and let stand.

The reader's creative impulses bring endless plurality to texts, a plurality derived from the multiple meanings inherent in words and language.

Bakhtin terms a text with a plurality of meaning a "polyglossia"; such a text demonstrates the role of language in generating multiple meanings.[17] Multiplicity is a quality both satisfying and frustrating to the reader, who brings to the recipe and to the cooking process multiple options: ingredients can be substituted or added at whim, measurements can be estimated, and directions can be changed. To many, this is the joy of cooking, granting freedom from the restrictions of a recipe and making the reader aware of the act of creation in cooking.

However, multiplicity is not all joy; it brings responsibility alongside freedom—responsibility for the resulting success or failure of a changed recipe. Foucault states that for both writer and reader, "writing unfolds like a game (*jeu*) that invariably goes beyond its own rules and transgresses its limits."[18] Precise measurements and cooking instructions are a form of control, crediting all creativity to the writer of the recipe and locking the cook into a preset formula. Bakhtin would call this a monoglossia,[19] a text that denies plurality to the reader, a concept seemingly applicable to all recipes with their exacting requirements of measurement, timing, and temperature. Some cooks want or need this amount of direction, feeling a sense of control over the food, while others take control of the recipe by changing it and making it their own. Regardless of the amount of control the recipe attempts to exert, the cook has the power to modify the cooking process.

Some recipes release control to the reader by using language that suggests less exacting attitudes toward the measuring of food, using terms that depend on the judgment of the cook: instead of cup measurements, jellies are called for by the jar and juices by the glass; butter is measured according to the size of an egg, a walnut, or in curls; spoon measurements are not divided into quarters, eighths, or sixteenths but defined as a pinch or a dash; a measurement is left to personal judgment as is sometimes the case with a flavoring like vanilla; or an ingredient is called "optional," for example, nuts.[20] This type of measurement has an accuracy that varies with each cook. This dependence on the cook recognizes creative license in recipes and in cooking and in the total process of making food.

On the tenth day, drain syrup into large pot and add two more cups sugar; reheat; pour over cucumbers. Stir and let stand.

Because the cookbook reader may change the text by suggesting alternatives and variations and experimentation, the mental picture or mental taste of the food twists and turns as each option is considered and judged. Similar to the reading of any text, the reading of a recipe becomes not "a fulfilment of the expectation so much as a continual modification of it." By turning to the reader for interpretation and meaning, the writer presents a text that possesses "something beyond what it actually says," a "something" that comes from the hints of the writer, the expectations of the reader, or a combination of both.[21] For example, the recipe for Ship-wrecked, a meat casserole, states that "any vegetable may be used instead of carrots."[22] Adding a different vegetable has the potential to revise Ship-wrecked into a different recipe—one that has different ingredients and maybe even a new title to accommodate the changes. Although the revision is not a totally new creation, it does demonstrate the creative process of working with a recipe and the potential new recipes within old ones. The revision is a product of two recipe writers whose voices intermingle, influencing both the recipe created and its readers.

On the eleventh day, drain syrup into large pot and add two more cups sugar; reheat; pour over cucumbers. Stir and bottle.

Recipes like My Mother's Really Old Raisin Pie Filling[23] express a connection to and a dependence on the past and the communal tradition of cooking through the voices of the women who taught us to cook. Often this voice comes through as a drone of ingredients, measurements, and instructions; but sometimes a character rises up to greet us. Recipe writers give advice, preventing a mistake that has been experienced by the writer from being passed on to the reader—"if necessary, add a little water or stock, to avoid sticking."[24] Writers express the joy of cooking in the text, too, a joy that takes many forms. Writers share their amazement at the ease of a recipe, thrilling to a quick taste fix—"so easy and so good," or gushing over the pleasures of eating a certain dish: "these are easy, sticky, juicy and yummy."[25] The reader of a recipe is affected by the writer's commentary on the recipe, avoiding problems or choosing a recipe because it sounds good. Many literary critics believe that the author plays no role in the reception of the text and is in effect "dead" in terms of the life of a text, which then rests solely with the reader. Contrary to this opinion, Iser writes, "the author himself takes part in the narrative, thus establishing perspectives which would not have arisen out of the mere narration of the events de-scribed."[26] Although the reader has control over the interpretation of the text, making the meaning of the text, the narrative voice is not silent and often speaks directly to the reader of the text, as evident in some recipes.

Ultimately, for the writers of recipes, the outcome of the recipe rests in the hands of others—not only in the form of food but also in the form of language. Recipes are revised continually in the kitchen and then again in language when a community cookbook's revised edition appears. Because a recipe belongs to its readers, it is the reader who determines the future of the recipe, immortalizing it by passing it on or rewriting it to accommodate a food processor, a low fat diet, or time restrictions. Recipes that become legends for a community of people gain their status not simply through the writing of a good recipe but through the veneration of others who retell the recipe, promoting a knowledge of it and its popularity. Susan Winnett sees the "retelling" of legends as "beyond our control"; they become the possession of the community, not the writer, subject to multiple manipulations over time.[27] Some recipe writers credit the author of a recipe, as in Mary Jane's Dip, Larry's Caesar Salad Dressing, Eileen Hill's Cucumber Salad, Zucchini and Leek Bisque—Mom's Recipe;[28] but are these people the creators of these recipes? Determining the founding legend of a specific recipe is impossible because authorization is unattainable. Recipes, like legends, are "unauthorized," belonging to the community.[29] Who discovered or created kneading? And who invented the Best Ever Eleven Day Pickles? Did Carole create this recipe, or did she revise a recipe of her mother or of a friend? Is this recipe a product of one person or of a community of women sharing their ideas about food? The stories of cooking and of recipes lie on a continuum of knowledge and language, established by a community and by the retelling of these stories over and over again.

On the twelfth day, rest.

Empathy, Energy, and Eating: Politics and Power in *The Black Family Dinner Quilt Cookbook*

Sally Bishop Shigley

When freshman composition papers become too much for me, I read cookbooks. Instead of flinging marginal barbs that are more a product of my own impatience than a student's ineptitude, I put down my pencil and retreat to my chaise longue with a collection of culinary wisdom. My tastes are eclectic: when I want to be seriously distracted, I open *Joy of Cooking* and wade into the exhaustive, often wickedly witty instructions. For duck: "unless you choke your duck, pluck the down on its breast immediately afterward and cook it within 24 hours, you cannot lay claim to having produced an authentic Rouen duck. . . . If, as is likely, duck strangling would bring you into local disrepute, you may waive the sturdy peasant preliminaries and serve a modified version, garnished with quotation marks."[1] When in a page-turning mode, I scan the quaint illustrations of the *Moosewood Cookbook* or the rapid-fire presentation of *365 Ways to Cook Pasta*. When the thermal inversions of a Utah January leave me longing for the sun, I dream of sunlit verandas and *melanzane filanti con mozzarella* (eggplant and mozzarella fritters from Luigi Carnacina's tomelike *Great Italian Cooking*), or of the beaches of Ixtapa and tart *cebiche* from Diana Kennedy's *The Cuisines of Mexico*. Margaret Atwood confesses a similar passion. She says: "I'm one of those people who read cookbooks the way other people read travel writing: I may not ever make the recipe, but it's fun to read about it, and to speculate on what kind of people would. One man's cookbook is another woman's soft porn; there's a certain sybaritic voyeurism involved, an indulgence by proxy. . . . Any cookbook, read in its entirety, creates its own imagined view of the world."[2]

Atwood's equation of cookbooks with a reality outside the realm of mere instructions is essential and is nowhere more evident than in a cookbook I have read with keen interest: the National Council of Negro Women's *The Black Family Dinner Quilt Cookbook* (1993).[3] Like any good book, this one takes the reader to different times and places: recipes for pinto bean pie and hoe cakes look back to the struggles of slavery, while strawberry tea cake and salmon lasagna remind us of happier, more comfortable times. Like any good cookbook, it contains detailed, well-organized instructions and, like a timely 1990s cookbook, it includes nutritional and caloric information for each recipe—yet the tone and the focus of this book/cookbook are different from those of its contemporaries.

This difference can best be explained if we start with the literal beginnings of the book: the title and the introductory material. The full title reads *The Black Family Dinner Quilt Cookbook: Health Conscious Recipes and Food Memories*. The purpose of this volume is twofold: to raise funds for the National Council of Negro Women's National Center for African American Women, and to pay tribute to Dr. Dorothy I. Height, civil rights leader and president of the NCNW. Anyone who regularly browses in bookstores has seen an ethnic cookbook, a family cookbook, a health-conscious cookbook, or a cookbook in memory of some great cook. This book combines them all and adds quilting to the mix as well. The metaphor of quilting holds the text together in a narrative that pieces together the history of the NCNW, food traditions, and shared meals. The NCNW as an organization is a kind of patchwork since it was formed initially to "harness" diverse black women's clubs and groups into one, more efficient whole. This book illustrates with wit and humor how these empowered, interesting women from a variety of backgrounds conduct important business across a dinner table as effectively as they do over a conference table. More importantly, through its narratives, its "food memories," and its connecting of domestic and public worlds, it offers hope and a sense of continuity to a wide spectrum of women.

Each word of this book's title forms a mini-patchwork: the varied histories and ancestral nationalities of African Americans combine with the panoplies of family and the dizzying variation that is dinner. In addition, the book itself is part of a very small patchwork. Preceding this volume, the NCNW sponsored *The Black Family Reunion Cookbook* (1991) and dedicated it to Mary McLeod Bethune, a former slave who later became both a cabinet member in the Roosevelt administration and the founder of the NCNW.[4] This book contained recipes, food memories, and section dividers made from photocopies of batiks, kentes, dashiki prints, and other African fabrics. The more recent volume differs from its predecessor not in subject and focus but in its intricacy and organization. *The Black Family Dinner Quilt Cookbook* takes the ideas of textiles, cooking, nutrition and health, and the reality of women's lives and creates a richer, different kind of patchwork.

Appropriately, this book about cooking appears initially as a kind of metaphorical sandwich, as both the front and back covers show pictures of the quilts promised in the title. On the front cover, we see a quilt called "Mealtime Dialogue" by artist Faith Ringgold; it depicts Mrs. Bethune and Dr. Height in their Sunday clothes having tea together. In the background, other NCNW members create quilts. Near the edge of the quilt, the words of Bethune, her legacy, charge the viewer with hope, harmony, and the responsibility for future generations. The quilt on the back cover depicts Harriet Tubman, famous "conductor" in the Underground Railroad. This tapestry quilt was made by the History Quilt Clubs of Sausalito and Marin City, California, and was designed by architect Ben Irvin. It depicts Tubman standing against a midnight blue background and flanked by both an owl, symbolizing her wisdom and unerring night vision, and the North Star, which she used to navigate on her treacherous journeys. These two images of quilts serve as a distilled version of the narrative of this book. The modern women on the front join with the women of history to model the power of perseverance and hope despite difficult and dangerous odds. The woman opening this book holds in her hands a literal representation of what women could and can do.

Once opened, the book continues this message of optimism. "Women," a poem by Alice Walker, begins the dedication as we see

They were women then
My mama's generation
Husky of voice—Stout of
Step
With fists as well as
Hands.[5]

These women and others like them, the dedication tells us, showed Dorothy Height and the women who followed her how to survive and succeed in a world where gender and color are the first elements by which people are evaluated.[6] It is to women who still struggle with these prejudices, as well as Dr. Height, that this book most directly sends its messages. Part of the power of this book, however, is that it speaks to me, a middle-class, white, academic woman as well. The weaving of hope and despair, oppression and opportunity form a text that can transcend racial, ethnic, and class boundaries.

These ideas are conveyed through language, through pictures, and through recipes for both modern foods and traditional, "heritage" foods that were cooked during the bondage of slavery. The book is divided into six recipe sections (soups, salads, main dishes, side dishes, baked goods, desserts) with a facsimile of a quilt by or depicting African American women, in shades of black, white, and gray, introducing each section. On the reverse of each photocopied quilt is a history of how the quilt came into being and what inspired its subject. "Grandma's Porch," a quilt by Michael Cummings, depicts his grandmother standing on her porch and waving goodbye to him. The fabric clothing the figure in the quilt is the actual fabric he took from one of his grandmother's housedresses. "Reprise," by Marie Wilson, presents a patchwork of influential women, while "The Oldham Family Quilt," by Carolyn Mazloomi, represents the life and work of the family of Bettye Torrey Oldham.[7] Not all of the quilted images represent positive memories, however, as "Meredith" by Sandra German was conceived in the emergency room of a hospital where the child of the title was taken after being cruelly assaulted by an acquaintance; "I'll Fly Away," also by Michael Cummings, shows the early American icon of "an African American woman caught in the forced labor system of slavery."[8]

Nestled between each of these quilts are the recipes, complete with nutritional information on calories, sodium content, number of grams of fat, percentage of calories from fat, and cholesterol and protein amounts. On the literal margins of these recipes lie memories of food and history and leadership from famous political and social leaders and ordinary women. An irony too pointed to be accidental places the comments of these brave, insightful women and men in the margins, the edges, the outside. Yet as the reader opens the book, these margins face each other over nutritious and nurturing recipes—just like the women of the NCNW faced each other over the dinner table to work out the problems and opportunities in being "marginal." And when the book is closed, these margins come together to form sheet after shaded sheet of wisdom and solidarity. An anonymous woman relates how Dr. Height was forced to eat fried chicken and boiled eggs from a shoe box on a civil rights mission to the South because she could not be served in the restaurants.[9] Beverly Coleman describes with delight how Dr. Height met with Malcolm X, Lorraine Hansberry, and other black leaders to try to form a united front among black groups. Ms. Coleman's favorite part of the story, however, is how Dr. Height was taken to the meeting by Sidney Poitier in his brand new sports car.[10] Jason Crump tells of how an impressive young man was invited to dinner with Dr. Height. This delightful young man made a lasting impression on the older woman—his name was Martin Luther King, Jr.[11] On the leadership qualities of Dr. Height, whom she refers to as "the Godmother," the Honorable Eleanor Holmes Norton, member of the House of Representatives, comments: "Just as no man would submerge any vital part of his identity, his blackness or his maleness, Dorothy has taught us that integrity lies in being whole. She has taught us to be proud African-American women. The Godmother continues to watch over us. We know that we are safe."[12]

The integrated wholeness that Congresswoman Norton speaks of is composed of the parts that make up all women, and in the final "memory," Dr. Height includes all women in her call for women to speak their valuable voices and refuse, no matter what their position, to remain in silence.[13] The words of these exceptional people nourish the soul of the reader in a way that even the "soul food" recipes cannot. This book stands as a model

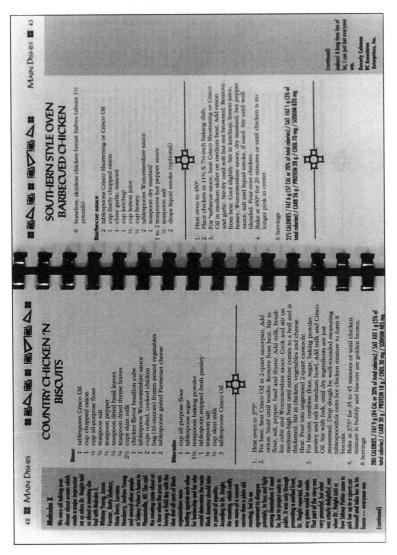

Pages 42 and 43 of *The Black Family Dinner Quilt Cookbook,* showing visual relationship of sidebar (anecdote about Dr. Dorothy Height and Malcolm X by Beverly Coleman) to recipes. Courtesy Simon and Schuster.

of how Dr. Height and women like her have used their entire selves to succeed. The same hearts and hands and heads that quilt and cook can forge civil rights legislation and provide safe havens for women in danger. In this nexus of recipes and quilts and memories and nutrition sits a reminder that possibility and hope and power lie within the patchwork of mind, body, heart, and head that makes up all women.

As I have described this book, I have mentally stumbled trying to decide what to call it: it is filled with recipes, so is it a cookbook? It possesses a narrative, so is it a story? It has a persuasive intent to raise money, so is it rhetoric? The question becomes complicated because a hierarchy exists in our culture, especially academic culture, that divides "serious" books from all other kinds of written texts between covers. "Real" books, be they artistic or informative texts, possess automatic authority: the writer is an expert about something or an inspired creator, and the result is something that is approached reverently, read in a linear fashion, studied. Cookbooks, and especially community cookbooks, are not seen in this way. One may approach Julia Child's *The Way to Cook* with deference, but that is hardly the mood in which we traditionally approach a work such as *Let's Eat!* a fund-raising effort for the senior citizen's center of Brigham City, Utah. Most people scan commercial and fund-raising cookbooks for ideas when they are stumped about what to cook for dinner, or they go to them when they are faced with an unfamiliar or difficult culinary situation: the zucchini have come on and need disguising, or an intrepid shopper discovers couscous on sale and doesn't know what to do with it. Most cooks don't approach cookbooks for stories or support or feelings of solidarity. In fact, I doubt if many people consider what they do with these books to be *reading*.

Susan J. Leonardi tries to dismantle this hierarchy between books and cookbooks when she notes that "a cookbook which consisted of nothing but rules for various dishes would be an unpopular cookbook indeed. A recipe needs a recommendation, a context, a point, a reason-to-be." She adds that, through asides and evaluations at the beginning of recipes, the author becomes "an identifiable persona with whom the reader not only can agree or argue but is encouraged to agree or argue . . . each recipe thus comments on every other recipe in the section."[14] Leonardi sees cookbooks as implicit dialogues between individual recipe texts and between women, not as "how to" manuals. She notes that even in communities of women of different class or race or age, the sharing of recipes can go on. She calls it an "almost prototypical female activity."[15] As I write this statement, I can immediately think of several women who don't cook and who would find this remark sexist. I don't think that it was meant in this spirit, nor that it needs to be. Leonardi and other feminists, including myself, do not explore "traditional" activities in order to reify stereotypes or prove that women are limited. On the contrary, examination of cookbooks or quilts or other "female" domains illustrates how women have used the discourses available to them to make profound and effective statements.

In fact, it is just such a hierarchical disjunction between "domestic" and "professional" women, or between public and private spheres, that *The Black Family Dinner Quilt Cookbook* tries to undo. Laura Esquivel illustrates the dangers of this potentially oppressive binary division in her cookbook / novel *Like Water for Chocolate*: "the joy of living was wrapped up in the delights of food. It wasn't easy for a person whose knowledge of life was based on the kitchen to comprehend the outside world. That world was an endless expanse that began at the door between the kitchen and the rest of the house, whereas everything on the kitchen side of that door, on through the door leading to the patio and the kitchen and her gardens was completely hers."[16] The danger of all that lies outside the kitchen does not materialize in its feared form as the novel progresses. In fact, the protagonist's influence reaches far beyond the kitchen as her cooking influences the lives and loves and fates of everyone who eats it—and that is precisely the point that the NCNW wants to make with their book. The four women and one man who put together this book are not editors or compilers or co-chairs or any of the other designations that one usually sees at the beginning of community or fund-raising cookbooks. These people are talented professionals who find nothing remotely disjunctive in their interest in cooking and quilting and "domestic" art. Faith Ringgold is an artist. Brenda Rhodes Cooper is a novelist. Carolyn L. Mazloomi is a fiber artist and historian. Lonnie Robinson is a graphic designer. Lauren Swann is a nutritionist. The people writing the "marginal" food memories include members of congress and judges, community leaders, college professors, and clergypeople.

Foodways scholar Charles Camp supports this "intersection of food and culture" as an important part of community mythmaking. He argues that "ordinary people understand and employ the symbolic and cultural dimensions of food in their everyday affairs," adding that "what most people learn at home is a mix of information, skill, judgement, and meaning that recapitulates family, ethnic, religious, and social values." In Camp's mind, and in the judgment of sociologist Jack Goody, the so-called lines between the domestic and the professional, the private and the philosophic, are rather blurred.[17]

It seems no small coincidence then that, aside from the cover, everything that is not written "text" in this book exists in shades of gray. The quilts take their hues from the charcoals and lead tones of photocopying, and the marginal memories are highlighted in gray bands on the edge of each page. Black and white dichotomies of all kinds lose their centrality in this work as the focus shifts significantly to the gray and to the margins. This is not to suggest, however, that this book is in any way "color blind"; it is a work inspired by exceptional black women to raise funds for less fortunate black women, but it invites all women to accept the empowering message that it offers.

This cookbook avoids the worst pitfalls of the genre. Ethnic foodway scholars Linda Keller Brown and Kay Mussell note that in many instances "cookbooks and restaurants convey relatively static concepts of a subculture and reinforce stereotypical assumptions that are further diluted by the imperative of the marketplace."[18] The rich spices and traditions of the Mexican mole sauce, through a strange commercial metamorphosis, become the bland tomato sauce and hamburger concoctions at the local fast food taco stand. Americans can, in a sense, have their tortillas and their familiar tastes, too. The authors of *The Black Family Dinner Quilt Cookbook* have avoided this potential error by mixing recipes for the traditional food of African American culture with recipes that contemporary African Americans are cooking. The soul food or heritage recipes are not homogenized and made mainstream but are complemented with more updated dishes: both are essential components in the "canon" of African American cooking. The power of this text lies both in its refusal to accept the divisive power of cultural or racial binaries and in the individual, the distinctive, the potentially unfamiliar: in the memories that line each page, the shared meals, and the sense of community that knits the women of the NCNW together. Their power and spirit rests in the very diversity of background and experience that each woman brings to the organization. The difference, the blending, the "grayness" is key.

The importance of the gray marginalia deepens if we consider the history of cookbooks in general with reference to the idea of hierarchies. Food historian Reay Tannahill notes that as early as the "self-assured days of Pericles," food has been used as a marker of social and economic standing or class."[19] Tannahill names the ancient Greek writer "Archestratus . . . [as] the first in that long line of gastronomic pedants who have guided the world ever since. The style remains familiar today. While most Athenians who liked tuna had to make due with the dried or salted variety from the Black Sea, Archestratus laid down that none but the fresh kind from Byzantium would suffice, and that it should be eaten only in autumn."[20] Every cook, experienced or novice, recognizes this tone, usually accompanied by a disgusted sniff of some kind, that suggests that anything less than an impossible to find and obscenely expensive ingredient is not worth considering, let alone eating. Barbarians, these recipes suggest, and others who don't keep kilos of saffron and pounds of paté in their pantries need not even attempt to cook.

The Black Family Dinner Quilt Cookbook rejects such culinary ultimatums. It not only illustrates the "domestic" activities of "professional" women, and encourages "cooks" and others to expand their horizons, but achieves this blending of skill and possibility in a genre that has traditionally been used to establish hierarchies, not to dismantle them. This book refuses to be the kind of work in which the sheer number of imported dried mushrooms, hard-to-get spices, and incomprehensible cooking terms marginalizes all but the most courageous chef. But that does not mean that it is unimaginative. Cheesy Tomato and Beef Casserole and Wilma's Skillet Hash offer quick, nutritious alternatives to the after work cook, while Pizza Garden Style offers a low fat alternative of home-made dough, herb sauce, and fresca toppings so appetizing that you'll never miss the artery-clogging pepperoni. Festive occasions merit the Chicken Jerusalem with sherry and artichokes followed by Saucy Vanilla Rum Bread Pudding. Eschewing culinary snobbery in favor of exuberant eclecticism, this work invites all women—and men too—to partake of both its recipes and its implicit model of hope and possibility.

Scholars writing about African American quilters make a similar point as they speak of the "creolization" of this form. Maude Southwell Wahlman notes that "Afro-American quilts mirror the diverse influences that shape the lives of black women in the United States," and she adds that "Afro-American artists maintaining this creolized aesthetic demonstrate the power and vision of African cultural traditions in contemporary American society."[21] The blend of recipes and diverse women's voices in the NCNW's work achieves much the same end.

The creolized gray margins of the book graphically mimic the goals of the NCNW: to include all women in their quest for equality. The black and white print of the recipes exists in "community" with the grayness of the margins. This point is made both within the cookbook and by another quilt and craft scholar, William Ferris. He notes that "quilts are a salvage art in which quilt makers recycle scraps of cloth into new shapes and color combinations. They select colors and pattern designs which are easily distinguished from white traditions in Amish and Appalachian communities."[22] The dedication of this book invites all women to explore the possibilities within the pages: women of color, "skin in shades of the rural Pennsylvania autumns [the authors] knew as a child"; "immigrant women, new to this country . . . women who made their own chewy breads, their own spicy sausages"; even "patrician" women, who helped the careers of women such as Dr. Height.[23] In this creolized ideal the roots of difference in black women's struggles cannot be forgotten. Lauren Swann, the book's nutritional consultant, provides both a "History of Soul Food," detailing the legacy of the "heritage" foods included in the book, and a section on nutritional, satisfying menu planning. In her history she notes that soul food "evolved from the rich heritage of African customs, was shaped by Southern cookery practices, expanded by the similarly tribal habits of Native Americans, and [was] regionally influenced by West Indian, Caribbean, and French cooking."[24] Swann adds that "as slaves, African Americans were not permitted to learn how to read or write, so they cooked not from recipes but by 'knowing,' giving strong credence to the essence of 'soul food.' Slaves had virtually no control or choice in life. So cooking became a way to express feeling, share love, and nurture family and friends. Meals were time for sharing common feelings of happiness and sorrow. Food was comfort while in bondage, and because they could control cooking, it was one of their few real pleasures, a way to feel free."[25] Cooking equals freedom in this book. Cooking also serves as a model for the dismantling of hierarchies both external and internal. *The Black Family Dinner Quilt Cookbook* allows all women to see how other women have overcome personal and political obstacles and achieved the freedom to move and act—that is cook—as they chose. The same Dorothy Height that ate chicken out of a shoe box, this narrative implies, ate and eats with presidents.

Twenty-five years before *The Black Family Dinner Quilt Cookbook* emerged, Ruth Gaskins published a small cookbook entitled *Every Good Negro Cook Starts with Two Basic Ingredients: A Good Heart and a Light Hand* (1968).[26] Gaskins says she wrote this book because there was not one like it available, and she felt that it was important that these recipes be recorded. Both this work and the more recent one contain a history of soul food, traditional and modern recipes, and commentary on the lives of African Americans; yet Gaskins's book is very much a product of its time. Like Swann, Gaskins sees food in the lives of slaves as a metaphor for control; and like the contemporary authors, she discusses the importance of food in ceremonies and community events. The important difference lies in the audience addressed and the use of pronouns. When Swann discusses the nutritional choices of modern African Americans, she uses just that term: "Homecooked meals begin with food selection, and African-Americans have come a long way from having no choice but to accept pig parts and corn meal."[27] Gaskins, on the other hand, seems to be writing to an audience outside her cultural and ethnic group. When referring to the recipes and habits of African American cooks, she consistently uses the pronoun "we": "we cook for the friend who might drop by. They are our family, and we consider our family numberless," or "we rarely serve separate courses at our meals. Having it all on the table makes us feel good."[28] In the context of the painful and violent racial turmoil of the sixties, this unifying rhetorical gesture is understandable. Swann and the other authors chose the third person not to somehow ignore difference and suggest a resolved conflict, but to recognize diversity and invite dialogue. Brenda Rhodes Cooper writers: "The lives of Mary McLeod Bethune, Eleanor Roosevelt, Dorothy Height, and all the people who have come in contact with Dr. Height form a marvelous fabric that is not seamless, but is quilted together by threads of shared experiences. The quilt, made up of these lives, is varied and colorful. Pieced together out of scraps . . . moments of conversation during meals eaten in places high and low push open a door to the past."[29]

These scraps also provide keys to the doors of the present and future for all the various textures and patterns of women who make up the feminine patchwork. Ann Romines explains how this works when she argues that housekeeping and, we can assume, cooking, should be seen as more than a domestic, mundane activity: "If housekeeping can be inscribed, if the home plot can appear on the page, then it is acknowledged as continuing fact, problem, and resource of our common life. Such writing may postulate a life in which boundaries between public and private spheres and between male and female spheres become elastic, permeable, or perhaps even nonexistent."[30] By working through what Tannahill has defined as a potentially hierarchical and limiting genre, the writers of this cookbook have made a move to dissolve these binaries by illustrating that there is nothing anachronistic or compromising in the image of a professional woman in the kitchen, nor need anything prevent the so-called "domestic" woman from venturing outside that realm. Literary theorists Patricia Yeager and Andrea Nye make similar points. Yeager suggests that the possibility of only two poles or two extremes of women's discourse is overly limiting. She argues that we must find a mean between strictly women's writing and the marginalized silence that comes from trying to write against or within a patriarchal structure.[31] Nye expands on this idea as she adds that women must create a balance between claiming and honoring that which is inherently female and recognizing that they must utilize linear, "patriarchal" language in at least a limited way to interrogate that language.[32]

In writing their cookbook/narrative, the authors of *The Black Family Dinner Quilt Cookbook* have done just that. They have, in the words of Hélène Cixous, found the "two, as well as both, the ensemble of the one and the other."[33] They have presented the lives of these women as they are—very complex—instead of dividing their worlds artificially between their professional lives and the rest of their lives. Within this full depiction of women's lives, food is as important as philosophy—perhaps more important. Mary Anne Schofield eloquently argues that "food cooked, eaten, and thought about provides a metaphoric matrix, a language that allows us a way to get at the uncertainty, the ineffable qualities of life . . . to write about food is to deal with the most important and the most basic human needs and desires."[34] In real women's worlds, food and life exist simultaneously, and, as this book has shown, in complement to one another.

Discussing the history of recipes, Susan Leonardi tells us that " 'rule' used to be a synonym for recipe—a kind of archetypal and model rule, which allows for infinite variations while still maintaining almost complete reproductability and literality."[35] Instead of standing above their audience and lecturing to them about life or roles or recipes, the editors and contributors who created *The Black Family Dinner Quilt Cookbook* offer models that inspire hope but encourage as many variations as there are women. Without moralizing or telling women to "have it all," this book shows how many women have dissolved the hierarchies in their own lives and minds and integrated all of the facets of themselves. Their stories list essential ingredients and do-able, if not "easy-to-follow" instructions for the women inspired to follow them.

Part Three

Community Cookbooks in Context

Building on part 1, with its theoretical and historical focus, and part 2, with its concentration on discrete community cookbooks, part 3 explores published, unpublished, radio-transmitted, and fictional community cookbooks in a variety of contexts. Here we see the many ways in which an understanding of community cookbooks furthers a variety of research interests. The six essays in this section cover two centuries and include work originating in three different countries. The values inscribed in the community cookbook form, whether nationalist, regionalist, feminist, sociopolitical, racial, or religious, whether self-serving or altruistic, may emerge in a number of related texts.

For Barbara Kirshenblatt-Gimblett, professor of performance studies and Hebrew and Judaic studies at New York University, it is important to see the relationship between an older Jewish community cookbook and the fund-raising fair where it would originally have been sold. Her essay,

"The Moral Sublime: The Temple Emanuel Fair and Its Cookbook, Denver, 1888," takes great care to see both fair and cookbook within a distinct society: late nineteenth-century Denver, and situates both efforts within the larger picture of women's philanthropic work. Barbara has published many articles and books on Jewish culture as performance, including *Authoring Lives,* and the extensive article, "Kitchen Judaism," which appeared in *Getting Comfortable in New York.*

Alice Ross, author of "Ella Smith's Unfinished Community Cookbook: A Social History of Women and Work in Smithtown, New York, 1884–1922," is a culinary historian based in Smithtown. Alice uses her extensive research into the personal and work lives of Smithtown, Long Island, women to elaborate on Ella Smith's attempt at a fund-raising cookbook; in the process we discover how valuable a manuscript cookbook can be within the context of other research materials (diaries, letters, church and business records). Alice has published in *Historical Archaeology, Bulletin of Primitive Technology,* and other journals; is an adjunct instructor at Queen's College, Department of Home Economics; performs research, consultation, and demonstrations at numerous museums using her extensive collection of antique cookware and cookbooks to explore early ethnic foodways, Native American cookery, as well as seasonal and holiday foodways. She also directs Hearth Studio hands-on cooking workshops at her home on Long Island.

"A Tale of Three Cakes: On the Air and in the Books," by Nelljean M. Rice, introduces a completely new conception of the community cookbook—the radio homemakers' creation of an unbound community and unbound text. This essay uses information from a variety of radio homemakers, particularly Evelyn Birkby, along with scholarly research and interviews. Nelljean has a Ph.D. from the University of South Carolina and an M.F.A. from the University of Arkansas; she teaches English at Coastal Carolina University and has published poetry, reviews, and articles in *Women Poets: The South* (an anthology), *Calyx, Arkansas Times, The Arts Journal, The Beloit Poetry Journal,* and others.

Nina M. Scott, professor of Spanish at the University of Massachusetts, Amherst, takes us to Argentina to investigate the relationships between the life and social milieu of an accomplished famous nineteenth-century writer and her work as a cookbook author. In "Juana Manuela Gorriti's *Cocina ecléctica:* Recipes as Feminine Discourse," Nina creates a lively mixture of local history, textual analysis, and feminist exploration. Besides having written numerous articles, Nina is coeditor of *Breaking Boundaries: Latina Writing and Critical Readings* and *Coded Encounters: Writing, Gender and Ethnicity in Colonial Latin America.*

Next, historian Jeffrey M. Pilcher takes us into nineteenth-century Mexico, looking at the role of community cookbooks in helping to forge a national identity. "Recipes for *Patria:* Cuisine, Gender, and Nation in Nineteenth-Century Mexico" uses a historical contextualization, seamlessly showing the relationship between culinary customs and transformations and the changing political scene. Jeffrey, assistant professor of history at The Citadel, has published articles on Mexican culinary history in *The Americas* and *Studies in Latin American Popular Culture.*

To close this section and also close *Recipes for Reading,* Cecelia Lawless provides an essay that asks us to consider a recent popular work of fiction from Mexico as a kind of community cookbook. In "Cooking, Community, Culture: A Reading of *Like Water for Chocolate (Como agua para chocolate)*" she sees Tita, the heroine, as creator of both narrative and food, simultaneously offering sustenance to others and being consumed. Cecelia, who completed this essay while on a Fulbright Fellowship in Venezuela, has taught Spanish language and literature courses at Hamilton College (New York) and is currently teaching at Ithaca College. Her Ph.D. in comparative literature is from Cornell University.

The Moral Sublime:
The Temple Emanuel Fair and
Its Cookbook, Denver, 1888

Barbara Kirshenblatt-Gimblett

The Fair Cook Book, published in 1888, is the earliest known Jewish fund-raising cookbook in America. Jewish charity cookbooks were appearing with greater frequency by the first years of the twentieth century, and examples are extant from Omaha, Milwaukee, Houston, New York, San Francisco, Portland, Pittsburgh, Seattle, and other locations. In most ways *The Fair Cook Book* is not very different from the many other cookbooks that would follow. What makes it quite exceptional is how much we know about the circumstances of its production—the women who provided the recipes and the occasion of its publication. *The Fair Cook Book*, published by the Ladies of Temple Emanuel, was sold at the fair that Jewish women organized in 1888 to raise money to pay off the mortgage on Denver's Temple Emanuel.[1]

Cookbooks were one of many devices for raising money at these fairs, and they continue to function in this way today. Some fund-raiser cookbooks have gone on to earn millions of dollars in their own right, the most famous being *The Settlement Cook Book*, which first appeared in 1901. Though Jewish fund-raiser cookbooks are more profuse than ever, they have never been accorded much importance by scholars. Libraries do not collect them. Bibliographers are inclined to ignore them. Even cookbook collectors look askance at them—not all recipes have been tested; the volumes are repetitive; the recipes of even poor cooks make their way into their pages; and the borscht jello rings and gefilte fish quiche of yesteryear hold little interest for those seeking gourmet cuisine or traditional Jewish dishes. Little is known about the exact circumstances of the books' production, and the older the book, the less likely it is such information will be recovered. For all these reasons, *The Fair Cook Book* is a precious opening into the lives of Jewish women and their efficacy in the public sphere.

Fairs like the one mentioned in the volume's title have their own history both in the Jewish community and in the wider American context, from church fairs during the first half of the nineteenth century to the Sanitary Fairs during the Civil War. These events show women actively producing a distinctive public sphere, one that is heterosocial and predicated on a gift economy. *The Fair Cook Book* offers an unusual opportunity to analyze American Jewish women in public, and their instruments, including food and its inscription, for mobilizing the local community and sustaining its institutions. The Temple Emanuel Fair and its cookbook— the work of German Jewish women in the western United States—offer a fresh angle of vision on a subject that has been studied as a largely Protestant phenomenon during the Civil War period and the decades immediately following.

The Fair Cook Book is a modest volume of forty-nine small pages. That it survives and has recently come to the Rocky Mountain Jewish Historical Society says something about the historical consciousness of the German Jewish family and the Denver Jewish community from which it comes. This little book bears the name of its original owner, Mrs. Celestine Wisebart. The Wisebarts were a prominent family in Denver and active in the Jewish community. Celestine's husband, B. W. Wisebart, was elected mayor of Central City in 1876 and was also a trustee of Temple Emanuel. Celestine's sister-in-law, Frances Wisebart Jacobs, was known as the Mother of Charities for her pioneering work in creating the Community Chest, a federated, citywide charity organization in 1887. Frances was also a founding member of the Hebrew Ladies Benevolent Society in 1871. Born in Kentucky—her family had come to the United States from Bavaria—Frances died in 1892. Her funeral, attended by 4,000 people, was one of the largest the city had seen.

Kept in the family all this time, Celestine's copy of the cookbook was found by her grandchild Emmett Louis, now living in Cortland, New York, when he was cleaning out a cupboard in the basement of his home. He sent it to his cousin Jean Morris, also one of Celestine's grandchildren. Thanks to the good offices of Jean's husband, Milton, both of them devoted supporters of the Rocky Mountain Historical Society, this cookbook is now part of the collection.

As in later Jewish fund-raising cookbooks, most of the women who contributed recipes identified themselves. From their names we know that some of them were married to prominent members of the congregation and the larger Denver community. Women not only contributed recipes but also worked at the fair itself. The cookbook compilers also prevailed on local businesses to buy full-page advertisements, many of them similar if not identical to their announcements in the *Rocky Mountain News*. Some of the women were married to the proprietors of these businesses—they were de facto appealing to their own husbands—and several of the proprietors were also trustees of the Temple.

The recipes themselves are divided into thirteen sections: breads and biscuits; soups; fish; meats; salads; pies; oysters; puddings; fruit cakes; cookies; cakes; pickles, sauces, and catsups; and miscellaneous. Recipes are loosely classified and do not always belong in the sections where they appear. The cuisine is diverse. American favorites include corn bread or Johnny Cake, white muffins, graham gems, okra gumbo, and specially oysters, which were very popular in this period. Though not kosher, oysters figure prominently in cookbooks addressed to Reform Jewish readers in the nineteenth century. *The Fair Cook Book* is distinguished by the prominence of Central European and some Anglo-Jewish dishes.

Mrs. Adler contributed recipes for what we would recognize as *kreplakh* (what she calls forcemeat) and matzoh balls, both of them for soup. Her matzoh balls call for ginger, and her potato soup uses mace. These aromatic touches are characteristic of Central European Jewish cuisine. There are thirteen recipes in the fish section, several of them for boiled or stewed fish, served with a golden sauce thickened with egg yolks and seasoned with lemon, parsley, cayenne, mace, and ginger. Some are served cold. Mrs. L. B. Weil, whose husband was a trustee of the Temple at the time, contributes a recipe for sweet-and-sour fish that is prepared with raisins, ginger snaps or *lebkuchen*, vinegar, and molasses. In her Fish Chowder recipe, salmon, tomatoes, and potatoes are layered in a deep dish and baked. Mrs. S. Landman's Entree Fish surrounds fish croquettes with mushrooms or truffles. Such fish dishes play a prominent role in Jewish cuisine, particularly as one of the courses of a Sabbath or festival meal. Cold fish is specially important in meals for holy days when cooking is prohibited.[2]

The meat section includes four recipes for tongue. Fresh tongue is boiled with pickling spices (mace, cloves, cinnamon, allspice, nutmeg, cayenne). Or the tongue is pickled, baked, and served cold. Pressed beef is made by tying an eight-pound brisket "tightly in a cloth with some marjoram, cayenne pepper, salt and ginger." After two weeks in brine and four hours of boiling, the brisket is allowed to cool, pressed with a heavy weight, and eaten cold. Of the four recipes for salad, one is for potato salad and the other three for chicken salad.

About half the cookbook is devoted to desserts, which is not uncommon. Several factors have contributed to the preponderance of recipes for baked goods in cookery books of the period, including changes in the technology of stoves; introduction of new ingredients (hydrogenated oils and baking powder, for example); the importance of exact ingredients, temperature, and timing in baking; and the elaboration and complexity of pastries and confectionary. These are often the show pieces of the kitchen and reserved for special occasions.

Three of the five pie recipes are for lemon meringue pie. There are eighteen pudding recipes. Mrs. H. Goldsmith's Rich Purim Pudding is to all intents and purposes a plum pudding. Passover recipes also turn up in this section, as with Mrs. Decker's Matsos Charlotte, a kind of sweet matzoh lasagna—three whole matzohs are soaked and drained, layered with butter, raisins, lemon peel, nutmeg, cinnamon, and sugar, and covered with a rich milk and egg custard. Mrs. H. Goldsmith also provided a recipe for Grimslechs for Passover, a pudding made by boiling together raisins, almonds, apples, currants, brown sugar, matzoh, and lemon, and then adding wine and eggs. The fruit cake section includes seven fruit cakes and four tortes (almond, poppy seed, apple, and bread). In addition to Molasses Cookies and three recipes for cream puffs, the cookie section provides instructions for Almond Cakes (another word for cookies in this context), Poppy Cookies, *Lebkuchen*, and Almond Kifels, which are a kind of almond macaroon. There are also eighteen cake recipes, ranging from pound cake to Bund Kuchen, Pepper Nuts (there is a second recipe for pepper nuts in the section on fruit cakes), and a citron cake.

The pickle and catsup section includes Mrs. S. E. Cohn's Deutsche Senf Gurken, which calls for cucumbers to be packed in salt and later removed from the salt and treated with vinegar, horseradish, mustard seeds, and peppers. (Cohn's husband had been a trustee of Temple Emanuel some ten years earlier.) This section also includes Mrs. B. M. Emanuel's Grape Catsup. Highlights in the miscellaneous section are the Tutti Frutti, fruit and sugar soaked in alcohol for a long time; and Heavenly Hash, oranges, stuffed with chopped mixed fruit, and then frozen and "tied with narrow ribbons"; Sweet Pickle Peaches; and Potatoes [*sic*] Pancakes.

By taking a not strictly orthodox approach to ritual law, by affirming philanthropy, and by cultivating a distinctive cuisine, *The Fair Cook Book* is a characteristic expression of German Reform Jews in America in this period. First, it is an example of the *treyf* (in violation of ritual purity) cookbook. The inclusion of oysters, lard (which may refer to hydrogenated cottonseed oil rather than pork fat), and suet, and the mixing of milk and meat, indicate that *kashruth*, while rarely violated in the volume, was not scrupulously adhered to. In the Reform movement, the rejection of *kashruth* was a matter of principle, rather than indifference.[3] This cookbook reflects the more moderate Reform stance of Temple Emanuel.

Incorporated in 1874, the Temple was the only synagogue in Denver at the time and it served the small Jewish community—as late as 1885, there were fewer than 500 Jews in town. Most of them were from Germany (especially Bavaria and Prussia), a good number from Russia and Poland, and a few from France, the Austro-Hungarian Empire, England, and Canada. Less than 25 percent were born in the United States, coming mainly from New York, Missouri, Ohio, and Illinois.[4]

Second, the cookbook is an affirmative instrument of philanthropy. Philanthropy was one of the most powerful ways in which German Jews expressed their Jewishness, but philanthropy was also an acceptable way for women to participate in the public culture of the Jewish community and of the city more generally. They were expert orchestrators of the gift economy at the heart of fund-raising enterprises like the fair and its cookbook.

Third, as in other Reform Jewish cookbooks, we find a diversified Jewish cuisine. The repertoire is eclectic, drawing from Anglo-American and regional American cuisines, from the Anglo-Jewish kitchen, and most important, from the Western Ashkenazi table—and in the Denver case, more specifically from the Jewish culinary traditions of Bavaria and Prussia. This is flavorful cuisine—aromatic, spicy, sweet and sour. It is also a bourgeois cuisine.

The cookbook was one element in a larger fund-raising project, the Temple Emanuel Fair. According to the announcement in the *Rocky Mountain News* on October 21, 1888, the fair was "given by the Ladies' Fair Association." It was held at the Armory on Champa and Fifteenth Street from Monday, October 22, through Saturday, October 28. The purpose of the fair was to raise a substantial amount of money to pay off the Temple's debt. In this it succeeded, and two weeks after the fair, the trustees turned over $12,315 to pay off the principal and interest. A substantial portion of this sum came from fair proceeds, which totaled more than $4,000. The minutes of the Trustees of the Temple indicate that the women were asked to provide an exact financial reckoning, but no details are there recorded.

One of the sixteen booths at the fair (No. 7) "was designated as the Cook Book and stationery stand." It was here that *The Fair Cook Book* was sold. The cookbook figured in other ways as well. Because of services at the Temple on Friday evening, the Fair closed early that day. But it did feature a merchant's lunch from noon to 2:00 P.M. The *Rocky Mountain News* announced that the lunch would be "served under the capable direction of Mrs. Dr. Eisner. All the pretty young ladies will be present to wait on the tables, and the lunch will be prepared from the receipts in the cook book compiled by the ladies of the fair. All the delicacies of the season will be served, and we can safely advise anyone wishing something good to eat to attend to-day." The press characterized the cuisine as the "good old-fashioned German style of cooking," noted the ample portions, and declared the venture a success: "Quite a large sum was realized from this lunch, and the ladies added to their already well-known fame as caterers." The lunch would have appealed to the largely German population of Denver.

Mrs. Dr. Eisner, who was in charge of the restaurant for the duration of the fair, is reported to have said that the merchant's lunch "will be the finest lunch ever served in this city." As a prominent socialite who entertained visiting luminaries, for example, Oscar Wilde, Mrs. Eisner was famous for her hospitality and for her table. Clearly, the women had confidence and pride in their cooking skills and some even had good reputations as caterers. Mrs. Dr. Eisner was assisted by Mrs. Goldberg, Mrs. Emanuel, Mrs. D. Cohen, and Mrs. Heitler. Presumably those who tasted the food would want the recipes and the merchants' lunch would not only generate income in its own right but also stimulate sales of the cookbook. Though the fair closed the day after the lunch, the cookbook was presumably for sale until the stock was exhausted.

This fair was like the many Jewish fairs mounted in the United States at the time to raise money for synagogues, hospitals, orphanages, homes for the aged, and other Jewish institutions, especially the large sums necessary to pay for new buildings. When there was a financial crisis, such as imminent foreclosure on a mortgage, it was imperative to raise a large sum of money very quickly. The crisis was often not just financial but also one of leadership and congregational or community morale. As American women learned during the Civil War, nothing could generate more money faster than a fair and, as it turned out later, than a cookbook. The fair had the added benefit of pulling people together around a common cause in a way that was immensely pleasurable. This is what one observer of the period, writing about the great Sanitary Fairs during the Civil War, called "the moral sublime."

Women were largely responsible for organizing and running these fairs, which bore the imprint of their sensibility. Within the space and time of the fair, women created a distinctive public sphere for the whole community. Indeed, their presence at the fair was perhaps its greatest attraction, for beautifully outfitted respectable women en masse in public was a "brilliant spectacle," as the male reporters of the period were fond of writing.

The Temple Emanuel Fair is firmly in this tradition. Indeed, it was neither the first nor the only such fair organized by Temple Emanuel. The ladies of the Temple had organized an earlier one, from September 11–16, 1876, to raise money to offset the debt on what was then the new synagogue building. The 1876 fair featured a ball, raffles, prizes, a "Tabernacle Illustrative of Old Jewish Ceremonials; [and] an art gallery, original and attractive." The ladies also ran a Strawberry Festival in 1884 and various other fund-raising events, including charity balls.

The 1888 fair ran for a week—in bigger cities with larger Jewish populations, fairs might run for two weeks. Usually these events took place in major public spaces—typically, as in Denver, in the Armory. The space was often lavishly decorated with evergreens, bunting, flags and banners, and gas lights. Predicated on a gift economy, these events used various devices to separate visitors from their money.

First, there were goods for sale—most of it outright, some of it by raffle, lottery, or auction. Local merchants contributed from their stock, members of the community brought in items from their homes, including furniture, jewelry, a fancy pipe or walking stick, and women made things for the fair, often fancy work that showed off their needlework skills. On the opening day of the 1888 Temple Emanuel Fair, the press reported that the beautiful and symmetrically arranged booths would "contain everything in the bric-a-brac line imaginable and will be presided over by a bevy of beautiful ladies."[5] Some stands were thematically decorated. The Turkish booth (No. 1) was outfitted "in Oriental style" and featured cigars and coffee served by Mrs. Loeb, Mrs. Tischler, and Mrs. Shandal. While some stands sold a particular kind of merchandise—confectionery (No. 6) and crockery (No. 16)—others offered miscellaneous goods. Several stands were the responsibility of Jewish organizations, such as the Young Ladies' Aid, which sold embroidery and fancy articles at their booth (No. 4).

Second, there were standard fixtures—the art gallery, post office, lemonade stand, floral bower, restaurant, voting contests, and the fair newspaper. An art gallery was featured at both Temple Emanuel fairs. Since it was customary at other fairs to charge admission to the art gallery, I would assume that to be the case here too, although sometimes the price of admission to the fair itself included entrance to special exhibitions. At the fair post office, "letters were given to the young men from their sweethearts by Mrs. Auerbach and Miss Maud," an indication that for a good cause, young women could be quite forward in public. Clearly the fair was also a courtship ritual. The flower booth was the centerpiece of the mise-en-scène. No man without a flower on his lapel could escape being pressed to buy a boutonnière from the women responsible for this booth. The beverage stand was usually billed as Rebecca at the Well (sometimes as Isaac's Well) and the Temple Emanuel Fair was no exception. Miss Esther

Franklin, "attired in Oriental costume, is a very charming impersonation of Rebecca at the well, and is kept busy all evening slaking the thirst of the dry people with lemonade." The fair restaurant might be run by the women themselves or, in the case of very large events, by a professional caterer.

At the political booth, people voted for the most popular candidate for governor by paying ten cents for each vote, there being no limit on the number of times one person could vote. This was one of the most popular attractions at the fair. The advertisement for the closing event especially noted the "final vote on silk flag for governor," the silk American flag going to the winner. A total of 8,245 votes were cast, netting $824, which was more than the fair had earned in an entire day earlier that week. Political booths and other types of voting contests were standard features of such fairs.

In this way the entire event reversed the logic governing business to produce the distinctive gift economy of the fair. Merchants gave goods away and sellers did not keep the money they earned. People were encouraged to speculate in the irrational sphere of raffles and lotteries and fortune-telling. Reversing the crime of buying votes, they paid to vote and to vote as many times as they wished, whether for most popular political candidate or for most popular little girl, who at this fair received a doll. They were encouraged to have their fortunes told at No. 9, "the fortune teller tent, at which two beautiful young ladies, Miss Maud Miller and Miss Ryan, dressed in fantastic Gypsy costumes, revealed the past, present and future for the small sum of 25 cents."[6]

The reversals of this gift economy gave to the fair some of the features of carnival associated with the fancy dress and masked Purim balls so popular in this period. This is especially apparent in the thematic booths, not only the Turkish and fortune-telling booths and Rebecca at the Well, but also No. 12, which was "a pretty illustration of 'The old woman who lived in a shoe,' whose children were waited upon by Misses Rothschild, Weill and Silverman." From the press, we know that in several cases the women were in costume. So too were the children who performed dances as part of the entertainment programs at the fair—Chinese, Japanese, and Gypsy dances, and the dances of all nations. The good cause sanctioned the spectacular presence of women in public and gave to such Jewish public culture a particularly performative quality.

Formal performances were a featured part of the fair and a way to get visitors to return night after night. Entertainment was provided by professional musicians, the Koenigsberg–Lewis Orchestra, well-known elocutionist Miss Josephine Beemer, and the choral society of the Trinity Methodist church, which performed sections from the oratorio "Joan of Arc." The press billed the Children's Carnival as the highlight of the event: "nearly sixty children, from 4 to 16 years of age, will execute a number of fancy dances under the direction of Professor Louis Mahler, who has been drilling the little ones for nearly six weeks past" and in appropriate dress. Their performances each evening and at the Friday matinee were warmly received. Indeed, having children perform was a sure way to draw adults to the event, at the very least their families and friends.

The fair opened with grand ceremony and ended with an auction, dancing, and at midnight, the announcement of the winner of the political contest. The opening started with an overture performed by Mr. S. Koenigsberg's orchestra. Then Dr. DeSolla offered a prayer, Dr. Donald Fletcher, president of the Chamber of Commerce, delivered an address, and Miss Clara Bernetta recited a passage from "Lucretia Borgia." About thirty children performed a dance, after which the sale of raffle tickets began.

Dr. Fletcher's speech suggests the larger importance of the fair to the Denver Jewish community. First, he aligned himself with women's rights and praised "the woman of the Israelitish church from the dawn of history" for her role "in the home, the church and the state." Lauding the work of women in raising money for worthy causes and volunteering their own time and labor to help the less fortunate, Fletcher argued that the social welfare provided thereby "prevents more wrong than the court house cures" and urged those assembled to give generously to the cause. He then compared this fair with church fairs, denomination by denomination, praising Jews and Judaism as the "tap root of Christianity." Condemning the humiliations that Jews have suffered, Fletcher listed illustrious Jewish statesmen and artists and noted "the patriotism of the race" and the aristocracy of Jewish blood.

He prevailed on the fairgoers to give generously because, "Let me remind you, there is not, I believe, a single church, charitable institution, or building of a benevolent institution in this city, but that it is partly paid for by contributions from our Hebrew fellow citizens. Now let us all reciprocate." (Just the previous year Frances Wisebart Jacobs had established a city-wide charity organization.) Fletcher went on to suggest that the synagogue is "a financial barometer." He explained that where there is a synagogue, there are Jews, and where there are Jews, there is prosperity. He asked what would happen if Denver allowed Temple Emanuel to foreclose on its mortgage and the Jews of Denver were to move to Pueblo or Cheyenne: "where is the bottom of your real estate prices gone to?"

Fletcher appealed simultaneously to the self-interest of Denverites—Jews are an asset to the city's economy—and to their moral superiority in transcending sectarian differences, putting aside bigotry, and "with enthusiasm, appreciating the model home life, the loyalty to home and state institutions and the good citizenship of the people who attend the Temple Emanuel." "In one short week," he explained, "all creeds and no creeds, could wipe out the debt in the midst of general good feeling." He then declared the fair open. Indeed, Jews were among the first to settle in Denver and they were prominent in Denver politics, government, and business. This fair offered the larger Denver community an opportunity to show their ecumenical spirit by supporting the effort to put Temple Emanuel on a secure financial footing. Fletcher's speech is a prime example of the moral sublime.

While it is believed that fund-raiser cookbooks like *The Fair Cook Book* date from the Civil War, the fairs themselves are older—and possibly the cookbooks, too. Because they are so ephemeral, we cannot assume that the earliest extant volumes are the first to have been published. The immediate model for the many Jewish fairs that were held across the country during and after the Civil War are the Sanitary Fairs, which also prompted the publication of cookbooks to raise money for the cause. Cookbooks were but one of many types of publications occasioned by such fairs, which might include collections of poetry, limericks, or songs, albums of signatures of distinguished fair visitors, addresses and memorials, programs, guides, and art catalogs, daily fair newspapers, souvenir albums, and reports of various kinds.

During the Civil War, more men were dying in infirmaries than on the battle field due to unsanitary conditions and inadequate medical supplies. Many women lost husbands, fiances, brothers, fathers, and other loved ones. Widows were left without support, many of them with children. Compassion for the men on the field and for the women and children they left behind prompted women to lobby the government to form the Sanitary Commission. Women then set about raising millions of dollars through Sanitary Fairs that they organized in many parts of the country. Many features of the Temple Emanuel Fair can be found in those earlier events. Indeed, these fairs had become so popular that *Our Daily Fair,* the newspaper published daily at the Philadelphia Sanitary Fair in 1864, could refer to the "fair movement in the United States" and trace its history "in other countries and former wars," including the French Revolution, the Prussian uprising against the French in 1813, and the revolutionary movements in Europe in 1848. But, *Our Daily Fair* continues, despite the popular enthusiasm and patriotism expressed in the prior examples, they were "short-lived and spasmodic" in comparison with the Sanitary Fairs.[7]

Though they were the largest events of their kind at the time, the Sanitary Fairs were elaborations of earlier church fairs, ladies' fairs, and fancy fairs popular in New England since the 1830s and modeled on even earlier English fairs. As Beverly Gordon has suggested, these events—and their economic, social, and political importance—have been underestimated by later scholars (although their importance was certainly appreciated at the time). She attributes later dismissals of these events to the stereotype that they were run by housewives with time on their hands who made useless things for sale, like fancy work, or who supplied equally superficial bric-a-brac and other novelties.[8]

Two principles governed the organization of fairs: type of merchandise and institutional sponsor. To achieve greater coherence, fair organizers arranged merchandise by category and created a temporary department store. To express their solidarity, organizations also set up their own booths. At the Sanitary Fair in Cincinnati, the Jewish community set up four stands: "one each by the Allemania Club, the Phoenix, a group calling themselves the 'Independent Ladies,' and the Broadway Synagogue."[9] The Jewish stands are estimated to have contributed about a third of the proceeds generated by the Fair. However, Jews were not in accord on the question of group participation. Some felt that Jews should participate as citizens and should not label "Jewish participation as Jewish."[10] Nor did they want to be the only ones to establish "denominational stands."

The Sanitary Fairs, as well as the Jewish charity fairs that followed, drew on world's fairs, the first of which took place in London in 1851. Not only did various states of the Union take part in Sanitary Fairs, there was also some international participation. England, for example, showed support for the Sanitary Commission's compassionate efforts to care for war sufferers on both sides of the conflict.[11] Even the exhibits and entertainments owed something to world's fairs, for example, the Indian Department and the performance of "War Dances" at the Metropolitan Fair in Manhattan in 1864.

The Sanitary Fairs also built on the custom of using admission to specially organized art exhibitions. As early as the 1790s in France, such exhibitions were used to raise money to help destitute workers. Indeed, as Bertram W. Korn notes in his study of American Jews and the Civil War, "August Belmont [a Jew] . . . opened his art collections to the public eye and swelled the coffer of the Sanitary Commission with the proceeds from admission fees."[12] Art exhibitions were a regular feature of world's fairs, Jewish charity fairs, and Sanitary Fairs, and the Jewish press reported extensively on them. With respect to the Metropolitan Fair, for example, the *Jewish Messenger* recommended the art collection there to "those who never have been among the wondering visitors to the *Louvre* or the *Munich Gallery*" and went on to say that "the Gallery at the 14th Street building will compare more than favorably" to the painting and statuary at the Crystal Palace. This statement is clear evidence that world's fairs were a point of reference for these events.[13]

Jewish women had participated in Sanitary Fairs and in other fundraising efforts for the Sanitary Commission. As already noted, many members of Temple Emanuel's Ladies Fair Association had come to Denver, established only in 1859, from New York, Missouri, Ohio, Illinois, and other states. No doubt some of Denver's Jewish women had visited and possibly even participated in Sanitary Fairs held in Manhattan, Brooklyn, Philadelphia, Baltimore, Chicago, Pittsburgh, New Orleans, and San Francisco, among others.

Moreover, Jewish women had established their own charitable societies even before the Civil War and were already very experienced at fundraising for various causes. According to Korn, "In 1860 there were thirty-five permanently organized charitable societies in New York City" and many of them were not associated with a synagogue.[14] New York City Jews formed a large community, with over twenty different German congregations, at the time.[15] In the case of Denver, where the Jewish community was smaller, it was harder to raise large sums of money. A similar fair in New York in the 1880s could yield more than $100,000.

This was a point of considerable pride. In a little "history of Jewish fairs," the *Jewish Messenger* started its account with the fair organized in 1860 by the ladies of the Portuguese Synagogue in New York. The article then declared that in "picturesque appearance, elegance and perfection of detail, and substantial promise," the Hebrew Charity Fair of 1870, which prompted this historical account, would have "no rival since the Great Sanitary Fair seven years earlier, not alone in pecuniary results, but in character as spectacle."[16] With the following words, the reporter captured the moral sublime: "A more lovely spectacle can scarcely be imagined— glowing with bright colors, brilliant with light, gay and glorious in the noble assemblage of 'fair women and brave men.' "[17]

During the Civil War, already existing Jewish women's organizations redirected their efforts to wartime needs by collecting supplies or providing personal service or by directing the proceeds of their fund-raising efforts to the Sanitary Commission. Jewish women also formed new organizations expressly for this purpose. Some Jewish women and their organizations found that participation in the large metropolitan Sanitary Fairs offered them an unparalleled opportunity to take part in a spectacular local event that had high national visibility.[18] In the case of New York, the organizers of the 1864 Metropolitan Fair, as it was called, included Jewish representatives on the various committees, "undoubtedly to assure the cooperation of all the Jewish organizations."[19] Jewish participation in these activities was a mark of patriotism and good citizenship and let Jews show that they were not parochial.

Women were the impresarios of some of the largest philanthropic social events in their communities. In conceiving, organizing, and managing these events, they not only raised large amounts of money in a very short time but also helped create the public culture of their communities. A round of philanthropic activities gave form to social life—from the Purim balls and Hanukkah pageants so popular during the latter half of the nineteenth century, both largely organized by men, to the Purim Kettle Drums and charity fairs, which were mainly in the hands of women. Among German Jews, social events with a charitable objective became an important way of dealing with the Jewish holidays. Families rented boxes at the opera house where Purim balls were held and received visitors there, instead of at home. Special Purim quadrilles were composed for the occasion.[20]

Supplementing the studies of how women organized events by and for themselves, Mary Ryan has analyzed how women participated in community-wide civic events.[21] My concern is their role in organizing events for the whole community. With the exception of Gordon's pioneering work, these events have received little if any attention. One reason may be the tendency to view instruments like cookbooks and charity fairs as trivial means to consequential ends. As I have tried to show, the ends are also the means, and these events are worthy of analysis in their own right. Fairs were, among other things, experiments in a heterosocial public culture managed by women.

Listen to an observer complain in 1864 of the limited range of places that respectable women could visit: "There is one thing that always strikes us with wonder in the amusement world of New York, which is the want of matinees or afternoon entertainments. There are thousands of ladies and children, those who perhaps have not attendants even for evening amusements, who would be glad to patronize an afternoon performance if they had reliance on its perfect order and respectability. These are confined to the Museum, the Stereoscopticon and the Menagerie. Why some of our first-class theatres should not give an occasional matinee we do not know. Certainly there can be no better time for the experiment than during the Sanitary Fair, when the city will be full of strangers only in for the day, or citizens out for a day's pleasure."[22] In no small measure, the fairs addressed a felt need for a public social place in which women would be comfortable and in which they could act.

The apparent frivolity of these events, according to Gordon, was carefully staged by the women who organized them, to display "the powerful playing at being powerless."[23] It was as if by magic that these women worked their wonders in the fairyland they deliberately contrived. Magic removed the aura of work from the arduous efforts to organize and run these events, though the women who ran the Sanitary Fair were faulted for tiring of "the daily routine of amateur shopkeeping and dickering" and sometimes sending "clerks and subordinates" to fill in for them.[24] Cultivated and strategic, the aura of frivolity made the display of entrepreneurial women less threatening.

These fairs were an artform in their own right, as Gordon rightly claims. So dizzying was the spectacle that one observer referred to the Sanitary Fair as the "Insanity Fair," while others spoke of fair mania.[25] Like the cookbooks, the fairs operated within a gift economy and valorized financial transactions that in other contexts would be considered irrational if not illegal. As for the cookbooks, they formalized the informal exchange of recipes among women. They moved the culinary expertise of women from private interpersonal transactions into a coordinated collective enterprise, whereby accumulated kitchen wisdom sustained large community organizations.

While most of today's fairs are a pale shadow of the nineteenth-century extravaganzas, the cookbooks have enjoyed an efflorescence. By the end of the century, the fairs had become so big and so arduous—and repetitious—that people became ambivalent about this way of raising money. There was even the feeling that the very idea of a fair was worn out. At the same time, fairs like the one mounted by the Educational Alliance at Madison Square Garden in 1895 became even more "sophisticated and professionally run events," as Gordon notes, to the point that magazines published articles on how to administer them and even encouraged women to buy exotic goods wholesale and sell them at a profit at the fair, as was being done in England.[26]

By the 1930s, these affairs had diminished to the small ventures organized by a local school or church that are familiar to us today. Several factors are at work here, perhaps most important, the professionalization of philanthropy—both the raising of money and the uses of it for social welfare—and the emphasis upon a more rational, if not scientific, basis for these activities.[27] Women made careers for themselves in the helping professions. There arose new media and genres for mobilizing personal giving: the mega-media events of our own time, from Hands Across America and Live Aid to telethons and marathons. At the same time, changes in public culture and the roles of women have affected the demise of the great charity fairs.

How is it that the cookbook should have had the opposite fate?[28] *The Settlement Cookbook* has gone through more than forty editions and sold over 1,500,000 copies, continuing to generate revenues for charitable causes for almost a century. By 1970, the sheer volume of charity cookbooks in the United States discouraged some groups from reprinting their cookbooks.

After selling 2,000 copies of a cookbook first published in 1978, one organization reported that "our area now has many Temple cookbooks, and we
feel sales would be too slow to warrant the expense to our sisterhood."
Others continue to do brisk sales, notably *Second Helpings Please*, which has
gone through more than nine printings and 125,000 copies since 1968.
Some congregations give a copy to each bride married in their synagogue.[29]

A survey that I made during the 1980s reveals that Jewish organizations are producing fund-raiser cookbooks in editions as small as 250 and
as large as 25,000. Some cookbooks have stayed in print for over sixty-five
years. Many, but by no means all, are kosher, not necessarily by conviction,
but in deference to kosher coreligionists. Some volumes are highly
profitable—a single edition of *Second Helpings Please* could gross half a million dollars in three to seven years, before being replaced by a new edition.

Other cookbooks offer modest financial rewards but rich social satisfaction. Women report wanting to issue another edition to include the
recipes of new members of the community, or to celebrate the merging of
two congregations. One woman explained that it was important that everyone be represented in the cookbook, and another pointed out that
including many people would increase the market and sales. An Alaska
volume has an editorial policy of no rejections. Some volumes grow out of
cooking classes at the synagogue or Jewish community center, while others, like *Waiting for Sunset*, the Chabad cookbook published in California
(1984), are created "to show it's possible to keep kosher in Santa Barbara."

A Canadian volume was undertaken with the goal of interesting new
and younger members in joining the auxiliary. One editor complained that
the response of the women to requests for recipes had been so poor that
she and her coeditor ended up contributing most of the recipes under the
names of various family members. One of the Sephardic cookbooks began
as the independent project of one woman, who, when she could not find a
publisher, offered to split expenses and profits with the congregation. In
another case, a terminally ill member appealed to the women to finish the
cookbook as her legacy to the Temple.

Jewish charity cookbooks persist today in a space between personal
giving, where each donor is identified by written and culinary signature,
and collective effort. Profitability aside, this type of cookbook offers
women a vehicle for activating a distinctive gift economy predicated on
culinary knowledge and its exchange. The book itself is a vehicle for their

coming together. It makes tangible and visible their connections with one another and their mobilization. Not only are recipes contributed and distributed, they are also performed each time someone cooks from the book. Presented at the table, these dishes enable a kind of virtual commensality. Authors absent from the table, but present in the book, make their appearance. They sign the meal, so to speak. They are made tangible from the archive, from the collective culinary memory that the cookbook represents. Perhaps this is why *The Fair Cook Book* survived the hundred years since its appearance and so many others have followed in its wake, even as the fairs themselves have faded.

Ella Smith's Unfinished Community Cookbook: A Social History of Women and Work in Smithtown, New York, 1884–1922

Alice Ross

Ella Smith (1849–1922) was a serious recipe collector. By 1905, after decades of recording, soliciting, clipping, and saving, she had gathered well over one thousand recipes, copied into pads and notebooks, filed in manila envelopes, or simply dropped unsorted into a large box. Many survived as they had been given to her, written on odd bits of paper and signed by their donors, occasionally embedded in an accompanying note that wished her well with her cookbook. And write the cookbook she did. The Herculean task of sorting, editing, organizing, and composing 750 chosen recipes into a coherent manuscript (by hand) was completed, and two abortive attempts at typing a final copy were begun. At this point the work faltered and was never resumed, to present knowledge. No title page had been composed, and her records contained no identification of the cause her intended book would have supported.[1]

Fortunately, Ella's collected materials were not thrown away; they now make possible the reconstruction of complex social issues. On the simplest level, the manuscript fits the configuration of a charitable cookbook; in light of information from associated Suffolk County papers, diaries, letters, and church records, the probable beneficiary appears to be the First Presbyterian Church of Smithtown. The puzzle pieces combine to give a picture of the dynamics that produced such projects, the kinds of people involved, and the challenges faced. Ultimately, Ella's story can be linked to the larger issues of women and work at the turn of the century.

Identifying the genre of the book was a simple matter. Manuscript recipes were signed by their donors (predominantly local women of the Smithtown Presbyterian Church community), organized loosely into chapters, and copied as given into a coherent manuscript. Unedited for style and preserved in the loose and variable paragraphs form that predated exact measurements and instruction, the recipes themselves carried nothing of Ella. Her contribution was faceless but nevertheless well based in family background, social position, and commitment to the church.

Ella's Credentials: Family, Church, and Leisure

Ella's family background and personality were such that she could only have undertaken an extended effort of this type as an act of service. Ella Mathilda (Smith) Smith was in many ways typical of other Suffolk County philanthropists in that she was born to local "aristocracy" and married to a thriving businessman.[2] To the extent that the small village of Smithtown offered silver spoons, she had one. Ella and her husband (Mr. and Mrs. Theodore Willis Smith) were each descended directly from Smithtown's Patentee, Richard Smith (1613–1691). Endowed with land and local authority, their families claimed local judges, superintendents, assessors, and committee chairs, and were comfortable with leadership.[3]

Ella grew up on the family homestead, a small farm near the hamlet of Smithtown Branch. Hers was an area in which everyone was a Smith by birth or marriage and traditionally tied to local, long-established churches. One can read the origins of her essentially Protestant identity in her family's close association with the Beechers; her father, Lyman Beecher Smith, had been named for and christened by the noted Reverend Beecher, a Presbyterian leader of the nineteenth-century Second Awakening. Most likely, his accomplished daughters, Catharine Beecher and Harriet Beecher

Stowe, each a prolific writer and early proponent of women's power within the domestic sphere, had influenced Ella's fusion of religion, women's pre-scribed roles, and home cookery.[4]

After their marriage (1879), Ella and Theo (as he was called) lived near his farms in neighboring St. Johnland (now Kings Park), where their only daughter, Faith, was born (1885). In 1892–94 they built a new home within easy walking distance of the Presbyterian Church in Smithtown Branch, where Theo developed thriving businesses, Faith attended school, and the entire family threw themselves into church work.

Following their family traditions, Ella and Theo served in positions of leadership for over thirty years. Although they worked for such civic philanthropies as the new town library and firehouse, their chief commu-nity effort was directed toward the church. Theo was a trustee, and Ella served repeatedly as an officer on the boards and committees of the church's Ladies' Aid Society and Women's Missionary Society; guided the Young People's Christian Endeavor; sat on regional Presbyterian boards; and was often a delegate to synodal conventions. Between regular services and prayer meetings, the Smiths attended church several times a week. Ella regularly chaired fund-raising events centered on food (church suppers, festival and fair food tables, and income-generating convention meals).[5] If anyone was to do a church cookbook in Smithtown, the logical candidate was Ella, a food-oriented leader whose central focus was service to her church.

Despite her strong sense of duty, Ella could not have undertaken the effort demanded by the cookbook without long stretches of discretionary time. Compared with many other middle-class village women, her domes-tic responsibilities were relatively light. Faith, her only child (1885–1977), was born when Ella was thirty-six years old and well established. From age twelve to twenty-two, Faith was away at boarding and professional schools and then working in New York City. During these years she spent weekends in Smithtown, where she assumed her own regular church re-sponsibilities, helped her parents with occasional projects, and kept up friendships.[6]

Despite her relatively simple household, Ella struggled with "the servant problem," as did her more privileged peers; free time for her volun-teer work was a strong priority. Whenever possible, the Smiths hired part-time local help to relieve Ella of the heavier aspects of Theo's business, the gardens, and the household (cleaning, cooking, and laundry). In critical situations, Ella called on her older sister, Phebe Smith, who was unmarried and living next door. Phebe was often a willing adjunct to Ella's larger projects and chores; during three days in December (1903), she wrote: "14 Mon. PM, I went over to help Ella cut up 90 lb pig for sausage. . . . 15 Tues. Went over to help grind sausage meat, gave *me* some. . . . 21 Mon. I kept house for Ella and Theo to go to Riverhead as witnesses. . . ."[7] The sisters' bond was such that Phebe helped Ella with large church projects, even though she was personally disinclined to public committee work and preferred anonymity.[8] Thus, Phebe bought, boiled, and carved hams, and sometimes boned chickens for quantities of salad for suppers and socials. When Ella worked on the cookbook, in place of signed recipes Phebe offered a series of rhymed couplets for the chapter headings.[9]

All things considered, Ella had enough time for an array of interests and hobbies that secondarily nourished her cookbook. For example, in the manner of many nineteenth-century, middle-class women, she was a reader of such home-oriented magazines as *Ladies' Home Journal, What to Eat, Greens Fruit Grower, Nature Study, C. E. World, Sunshine Bulletin,* and *Rural New-Yorker.* From these she clipped and saved articles, sorting and pasting them into scrapbooks by subject. Collecting itself was a popular passion; Ella's many scrap books were variously devoted to autographs, religious sayings, poems and mottoes, travel records and general information, postcards, trees, stamps, and, of course, recipes.[10] In fact, her stylish inclination to self-education through scrapbook-keeping provided (coincidentally) the tools, structures, and experiences with which to organize a cookbook.

Ella also enjoyed travel, sometimes in the company of a family member but most often alone. She visited Faith for shopping and theater dates, attended distant church conferences, and took annual summer vacations at church-associated boarding houses in scenic or historic areas of New York, Pennsylvania, and New England. Wherever she went she took copious notes on her experiences and described in great detail everything from the boardinghouse accommodations and guests to the details of her locale.[11] A perpetual researcher, whenever she encountered others who were sympathetic to her church project, she borrowed their cookbooks and recipes.[12]

It would seem, from her leisure and activities, that Ella's social identity was entirely based on privilege and authority; however, another facet of her life was deeply rooted in the mundane, daily concerns of semirural village life. Like other women in her position, she performed a steady round of food production and home cooking, preserving, cleaning, wallpapering and painting, and contributing to the family business. Her food activities were often the same as those of her less well-to-do neighbors, although her kitchen may have been more fully equipped. Her farm childhood had familiarized her with the physical work of food production, preservation, and preparation; and she raised, killed and dressed her own chickens, and maintained a large garden and orchard for home, extended family, and occasionally market use. Ella's grounding in village life also kept her in daily contact with a cross section of women in the area, many of whom would be her recipe donors. Thus, she was in a position to gather recipes from the same women who sold her groceries, milk, butter, or cakes, and was able to achieve a blending of rural and village subcultures.[13]

Ella's credentials as church worker and collector are readily documented; but could she cook? She certainly had the basic ability to handle the endless round of family meals, church suppers, and recipes, but there is little evidence that she was adventurous. Neither Phebe nor Ella recorded instances of experimentation with new dishes, and in the many public accolades Ella inspired, cooking was never mentioned. Even Phebe's compliments were rare. Once, in a letter to young Faith, she wrote: "Tell your mama that her sausage is ahead of Mrs Dunham's I think." And once, after dining at Ella's, a diary entry commented that the beans "tasted good."[14]

Instead, the sisters' foods were the plain essentials of home cooking that did not require special training or skill: boiled dinners, hominy, preserved and canned garden produce, simple puddings, and pumpkin pie. Chocolate cake (filled and iced) may have been the most demanding of such staples. Relatively few of Ella's recipes appeared in her manuscript; she signed her name to "Soft Molasses Cake (an old recipe)," but its qualifying reference to tradition suggests that she was not taking credit for it herself. She was more likely to include the specialties of her mother or her aunts, among them the Broiled Mackerel from "Mother's Cook Book." One cannot know if the almost universal silence on her cooking reflected modesty, selflessness, or general Presbyterian denial of sensuality.

Actually, what would seem to be a prime requirement for cookbook authorship today may not have been so significant for her task. The elusive issue of Ella's culinary expertise suggests that cookbook compilers did not have to be gifted cooks; it was more essential that they have strong intra-community networks and be talented in administrative and social areas. In fact, the women who produced Suffolk County's cookbooks were pri-marily local leaders whose credentials were similar to Ella's, who may or may not have loved cooking, but who made wholehearted commitments to their cause.[15]

The Process: Sources, Methods, and Writing

Ella's methods, like those of other cookbook compilers, required recipe solicitation, sorting and editing, occasionally testing, and manuscript composing. Perhaps the most arduous job was recipe gathering. Ella had been collecting for at least twenty years before she began writing the manu-script, and she continued to receive recipes for at least another five years after that; it is likely that what started as a hobby later suggested the idea of the community book. Her early jottings in the first of several small note-books appear to be those of a housewife seeking to expand and modernize her repertoire. One recipe dated 1884, positioned about midway in this pad, suggests she had already been working for some time. Subsequent notebooks show a gradual evolution toward the charitable genre as she took more pains to write recipes completely and include donors' names. At the end of the century, her notebook recipes were still copied in her own hand, unsorted.

With the cookbook project in mind, Ella expanded her notebook collections with more active requests. A good many resulted from her flow of personal visits with local women (in person or by correspondence), following networking patterns common throughout Suffolk County. The sisters' diaries recorded the process with appropriate comments by Phebe: "T & Lizzie called with some receipts for Ellas book. . . . "[16] Likewise, Ella noted that she "went down to Mrs Rapier's after noon got rec-ipes . . . ,"[17] and "went down street after dinner—called at Mrs Hunttings she gave me a recipe for Molasses Crullers had a very pleasant call there—called at Miss Emily's she was most sick with a cold—Will send me her

Deviled Clams. ✗
Steam the clams. chop them
very fine, 4 soda cracker rolled
lumps of butter. 2 eggs.
little pepper, (cayenne sometimes
preferred) make as moist as
you can with the clam juice.
Fill the shells.
Put in the oven 15 minutes -

Cheese Scallop -
Soak a small teacup of bread
Crumbs in fresh milk, beat in
1 large egg - 1 tea spoonful of
melted butter - 3 oz grated cheese,
pepper and salt to taste.
Cover with dry bread crumbs
and bake a light brown.

Recipes for Deviled Clams and Cheese Scallop in Ella Smith's own hand from her cookbook manuscript. Courtesy Smithtown Historical Society.

recipe book soon— Called at Teas—she will send me recipes soon—."[18] Such social calls were integral to the weekly routine, so much so that Phebe identified the rare days without socializing as "alone" days.[19]

The Cookbook Community

The women who gave Ella recipes form an orderly social system consistent with the social visiting patterns described by social historians. Thus Ella's largest group of donors was comprised of family, the next group consisted of her local peers, and the third was formed of strangers who were the wives of her husband's or brother's business associates.[20] However, she also stretched the limitations of local visiting to include distant correspondents, celebrities, and published sources.

It is no surprise to find that the Smith family supplied the largest number of recipes. In a small village where nearly everyone was related, however distantly, it could hardly be otherwise. The multilevel social strata are easily visualized through Ella's family ties, and we can sense her obligation to keep relationships current regardless of economic or social position. Her daily dealings with mill-owning Blydenburghs, store-keeping Hunttings, and farmer Carlls were all kinship-related. With growing mobility, some of the family had relocated away from Long Island, and they often maintained social patterns through visits and correspondence. For example, Phebe spent December 1899 in Brooklyn, where she socialized with several relatives. Ella's collection reflected these relationships with such contributions as Belle's Invalid Recipes, sent on Presbyterian Hospital (New York City) stationery, and Caramels from Gertrude S. Strong in New Jersey.

The second-largest group was also local; these were usually fellow congregants who worked on Ella's committees. They also represented a range of local status, from prominent Mrs. Handley (Chicken Salad) to the modest school teacher, Miss Carrie Thompson (Boiled Bread Pudding). This group also included such acquaintances as Mrs. Theodore Roosevelt, who sent a hand-written Spice Cake recipe on White House stationery; Mrs. Roosevelt had entertained the Smiths at Summer White House cotillions in nearby Oyster Bay and involved herself in other Presbyterian charitable events in Smithtown. In contrast was Corn Cob Syrup, submitted by "a friend's mother who lives upstairs." Mrs. Drant, a wealthy newcomer to Smithtown, became acquainted with Ella through the church and the long-term friendship of their daughters; she offered Buttermilk Pudding.[21] When a friend moved, Ella maintained the relationship long-distance; for example, Mrs. W. E. Bowers, a local woman who relocated in Brownsville, Oregon, sent her "dear friend" a Gem Recipe.[22]

A third group, the wives of business associates, stood apart from the preponderance of Smithtowners in that they usually had no personal contact with Ella. For example, Theo's dealership in farm equipment required that he meet regularly with the distributor Mr. James B. Taylor of New York City, who probably returned Ella's hospitality by arranging for the large sheaf of candy recipes from his wife. Also in this category were numbers of recipes from Mrs. Matthew Reade and Mrs. Norton, Crescent City, Florida, apparent contacts of her brother, Coe Smith, who wintered there annually.

In addition to these classic network sources, Ella contacted relatively renowned outsiders with whom she had no personal relationship. This was a deviation from the standard patterns of Suffolk County community cookbooks, which concentrated instead on the specialties of local cooks. Thus Ella requested and included the recipe for Minnehaha Cake—"first premium" winner at the Nassau County Fair (1901)—sent by Florence Smith (unknown relationship); and Mrs. Titus's Sponge Cake, a prizewinner at the Rhode Island Fair.[23] Prominent restaurateurs also sent recipes; these included the many seafood dishes of Mrs. Frank Corwin's fashionable Long Island House, and the Cornbread and Sally Lunn from Mrs. Elizabeth M. Hudson's Griffin House, both in the county seat, Riverhead. Noted food writer and editor Maria Parloa sent recipes for Rice and Cornstarch Puddings on her *Ladies Home Journal* letterhead; her connection to Ella may have been initiated by Amy Kohlstad, a Smithtown stockholder on the *Journal* board. In the same mode, Ella borrowed from illustrious cooking schools and used recipes from Mrs. Haxtun's Cooking School, the New Haven Cooking School, the New York Cooking School, and the Sound Avenue Cooking Classes.

Published recipes were a fifth source of Ella's recipes and another departure from the common patterns of Suffolk County community cookbooks. She used a substantial number of these, without apparent request or permission. The recipes she copied were often simple variations on Smithtown cuisine and were not regionally distinctive. For example, recipes for plain and fruit fritters, from Delaware Water Gap, Pennsylvania, and Ellenville, New York, were copied into a section of locally obtained fritters of corn, parsnip, and apple. Since the manuscript was constructed by entering handwritten recipes first and the published ones afterward, the printed ones were apparently chosen to complement local donations and enlarge the chapters.

Many of Ella's published recipes originated in such works as *The Buckeye Cook Book* (1876) (originally a fund-raiser), the source of properly cited comments on breads for breakfast, tea, and supper; likewise, the East Winsted *Housekeeper's Friend* (1888) was credited for Fried Cakes.[24] Although it was not common practice for Suffolk County cookbooks to include published recipes, Ella found precedents in some books she consulted. *The Housekeeper's Friend* (1888) and *Tried and True* (Ellenville, New York, 1897) had tapped the most popular book authors of the day with Mrs. Rorer's Boiled Potatoes, Marion Harland's Potato Puff, and Miss Parloa's Lemonade, for instance.[25] Ella sought and borrowed local fund-raising cookbooks whenever she could, even when traveling: "3 April [1901, Brooklyn]: Woke up this morning found it raining hard. did not go out copied recipes some that Mrs. Lockwood gave me and some from a book she had—*Mites of Help.*"[26]

By 1905, when she began writing out her cookbook manuscript, Suffolk County towns had already printed ten charitable cookbooks, many of which were known to her—hence such recipes as Baked Omelet, from *The Practical Cook Book* (Northville, 1886, 1890).[27] Her correspondence with potential Suffolk County contributors included women from these communities, for example, Leona Downs of Northville or Mrs. Tuthill and Mrs. Latham of East Marion.[28] The efficiency with which recipes circulated through these women's networks, with no apparent thought of plagiarism, is nicely exemplified by the recipe for Six Months Cake, copied by Sarah H. Tuthill, East Marion, from *Our Favorites* (1900) and mailed to Ella without appropriate credit; Ella used it in her own manuscript over Mrs. Tuthill's name.[29]

Cuisine

From their names and their foods, we know that Ella's community was made up of established, native-born, white, Anglo-Saxon Presbyterians. Regardless of their sources, the recipes Ella collected, solicited, and copied fit their cultural patterns. Theirs was the dominant cuisine, late nineteenth-century English-American adaptations of coastal New England. It was simple cookery but rich in the products of a temperate climate, farm, and sea, and somewhat enlivened by Britain's imports from colonial Asia and India. The favored staples were wheat and corn, beef and pork (often as sausage, ham, and bacon), sea foods (clams and cod), winter root vegetables and pumpkins, summer salads and berries, orchard fruit (particularly apples), abundant dairy products, and eggs; New World corn and beans had replaced pease and broad beans; and cornbreads, cornmeal, pumpkin, and molasses had filtered into all elements of the meal. The typical English forms of pies, puddings, loaf cakes, roasts, simple sauces, and preserves still prevailed but were evolving in the late nineteenth century under the influences of developing technology (fuel, woodstoves, and canning), decreasing costs of white sugars and flours, and expanding urban leisure.[30]

Suffolk County cuisine was very much like that of its neighbors in coastal Connecticut, Rhode Island, and Massachusetts. Suffolk County residents had enjoyed a strong 350-year connection with southeastern New England's coastal towns; they crossed the waters of Long Island Sound frequently and easily to shop, conduct business, and socialize. It is no surprise to find that, with similar geographies and early ethnic histories, the food traditions of these neighboring regions were almost indistinguishable, as seen in the basic corn breads and various hominy corn dishes (called Samp Porridge in Suffolk County and Hulled Corn in Massachusetts), clam and oyster pies, lobscouse (thickened seafood stew), and chowders. Such New England regional dishes as Boston Baked Beans and Boiled Dinner had long since been assimilated into Long Island's eating patterns and appeared regularly in diaries.[31] Ella's manuscript included recipes she took from sources in Connecticut (Election Cake), Rhode Island (Sponge Cake), and Massachusetts (Delicate Cake) that were essentially identical to Smithtown recipes.

Although the daily standbys appeared regularly throughout the diaries of other Suffolk County women, in fund-raising cookbooks they were outnumbered by late nineteenth-century culinary innovations. These new dishes did not represent basic changes in the cuisine so much as they did extensions and elaborations on earlier upper-class cookery. This style-conscious component of evolving New England cuisine was clearly reflected in Ella's manuscript, in which the largest numbers of recipes were for new iced layer cakes, sweet desserts, candies, homemade preserves and pickles, sauced luncheon dishes, tea sandwiches, soups, and salads. Not to be confused with the hearty foods of daily eating, they were the dainty foods of hospitality, a rapidly spreading aspect of cuisine promoted by such influential institutions as the Boston Cooking School and *Ladies Home Journal.*

The sweets that predominated in charitable cookbooks were, in fact, the glue of village social interactions. The steady rounds of women's visits and calls that typified village afternoons were marked by the hospitality one offered and the gifts one brought. Although farm women were more likely to exchange seasonal surpluses (apples, hominy, asparagus, etc.), village women brought or served a piece of cake, a section of pie, or perhaps a glass of preserves or pickles. The need to have a ready supply of such gifts on hand was reflected in both weekday and Saturday work; the frequency of the diary entry "cooked and baked &c.," suggests the necessary precautions taken when unannounced company was common. The abundance of sweets and luxuries in Ella's manuscript were made only for special occasions—chicken salads and homemade candies for church suppers, soda pop for picnics, and lemon meringue pies or fresh coconut layer cakes for entertaining.[32] Like other local fund-raising cookbooks, Ella's attempted to reflect some aspects of local cuisine but was not intended as a manual for a balanced daily diet.

This statement of local culture through cuisine did not include minorities. Ella's was a period of strong anti-immigrant feeling, and this was reflected in the culinary world by the many established Americans who were more concerned with preserving native-born traditions than exploring new foods. Despite the publication of a handful of works on foreign cuisines, Ella's cookbook, like others from Suffolk County showed no interest in the ethnic foods of local Italians, Scandinavians, Irish, Poles, African Americans, or Eastern European Jews.[33] Of the two hundred and two recipes in Ella's large chapter on cakes, the few recipes named with foreign referents were not especially exotic. Her versions of Scotch Cakes (butter cookies, not shortbread), Denmark Cake (a spiced pound cake), Swedish Cake, Swiss Cake, and French Cake (standard baking powder cakes) were indistinguishable from common American preparations. Likewise, "Mrs. Rorer's Creamed Macaroni On Toast" was a simple variation on the English-American penchant for white sauce and snippets (toast triangles).

Editing and Writing

As recipes accumulated, they were subjected to a weeding-out process. The usual community cookbook involved a small committee of women who determined the selections with an eye to representing the membership and its cuisine, variety, and quality. Local cuisine was usually portrayed with a combination of pride in tradition and au courant sophistication, simply stated in the preface of one Suffolk County cookbook (ca. 1915): "The compilers have tried to collect the best recipes, old and new."[34]

Ella appears to have intended the same kind of balance; she made a point of identifying several old, local recipes, the backbone of local food culture. Among these were Mrs. David Carll's "Hard Molasses Ginger-bread (an old recipe)," Mrs. Strong's "New Year Cakes (old!)," and a sampling of dishes from "Mother" or Aunts Julia, Matilda, and Huldah. She also included a number of new and stylish recipes, among them Chicken Salad from prominent Mrs. Handley, and the "Lobster Bisque (Cooking Class Recipe) contributed by Mrs. A. B."

In addition to being representative, recipes had to be trustworthy, and thus a claim of reliability appeared in almost every Suffolk County work. Some of the cookbooks Ella borrowed declared their dependability with such titles as *Tried and True, Tried and Tested,* or *Reliable Recipes.* In Suffolk County, *The Practical Cook-Book* (Northville, 1886) proclaimed: "These recipes, given by members of the Society, have been tried and found to be reliable." Some thirty years later, reliability was still an important standard: *St. Ann's Cook Book* (Sayville, ca. 1915) swore by its donors "experience," that "all have been tried and proven."[35] In the days before test kitchens, basing such claims on local reputations did not imply a lazy committee. In a limited community, everyone's specialties were well known, having been tasted at church suppers and fairs or during the course of home entertaining or afternoon calls. It was important to the donors themselves to maintain standards, both out of self-interest and community benefit, and they undoubtedly submitted only those recipes good enough to be acknowledged publicly. It would have been unthinkable, in a small community, to risk one's reputation or status with untried or poor recipes. The strength of reputation is wonderfully illustrated by the childhood misadventure of an elderly Smithtown resident. She had been sent to a church food sale to buy a specific woman's cake, but she forgot the woman's name and chose the wrong one. To this day she remembers her mother's annoyed comment: "How could anyone buy anything she made!" followed by her family's teasing and the ignominy of eating that heavy and tasteless cake all week.[36]

Ella's concern with reliability was shown in occasional notations on testing. These recipes were not from her friends but always from published sources. To some degree this is strange, as it seems unlikely that Ella would have questioned the reliability of the established food writers she chose to cite. Perhaps the logic behind such testing grew from the impersonality of printed recipes and the community cookbook emphasis on personal testimony—the image of real women behind each dish. In this case the presence of a tester's name added personal involvement and responsibility. Thus we can understand Ella's comments, following a recipe for Chocolate Cookies: "This taken from Cleveland Baking Powder Book, tested by Mrs. Taylor of Otisville who says they are delicious."

In fact, the tested recipes were not alien to Suffolk County: Mrs. Rorer's Creamed Macaroni on Toast, "tested by M. A. T.," or Fish Pudding, taken from *Book of More Puddings*, "tested by Mrs. Millie Smith" were typical of New England variations in the use of common white sauce and pudding forms. It might also be noted that no personal recipes were tested; it would probably have seemed presumptuous and insulting to test a local woman's recipe, particularly when her reputation had preceded it.

Scrutinizing the recipes one by one, Ella marked them with blue or red pencil to signify acceptance or rejection. Although recipes would continue to arrive for at least another five years, by 1905 she had the selection well under way and she began to write. Early in January, with the conclusion of the Christmas holidays and Faith's return to Pennington Seminary, Ella turned to the manuscript: "Wed Jan 4 . . . *Began on my recipe book up in Faith's room. . . .*" In March, during three shut-in days of rain, snow, and mud, she "wrote recipes." Then all such references stopped.[37] At this point there is no evidence to say how long the writing process continued, who typed for her, or why she stopped.

Why Did It Fail?

Searching for a reason for the book's failure, we can eliminate the most obvious; there is no evidence that problems of ill health or family welfare interfered with her work. Ella lived and functioned well from 1905, when she began the manuscript, until her death some seventeen years later; Phebe died in 1915, Theo in 1918, and Faith lived a long and productive life.

A more likely explanation is the nature of the task facing her when she stopped. Presumably a basic conflict would have surfaced at that point, one that was fundamental enough to stop a woman as capable and determined as she was. Significantly, as she put her cookbook together, Ella would quickly have reached the stage where she should have been selling advertising, the controversial but essential labor that would have secured the funds to pay for publication. The required interplay of new work roles and religion may have been her book's undoing.

The Suffolk County women who produced fund-raising cookbooks raised production moneys with the support of the businessmen in town. In the nineteenth century this was no easy undertaking, as middle-class women had been forbidden such transgressions of the established male workplace. Their first steps away from the domestic sphere often engendered strong resistance and disapproval; their difficulties were described graphically in the introductory poem to Suffolk County's first cookbook (1886):

> Here come some Ladies with a roll
> But now I'm beggar-wise
> And if they're working for a fair
> I will not advertise
> He looked so cross and frowned so hard
> We did not dare to ask;
> so bought some pins
> And left the store,
> To find an easier task.

> Another man so gracious was,
> And looked so sweet and wise,
> When someone said "We've come to see
> If you would advertise";
> That we all thought "We'll get one here,"
> But no! for answered he,
> "If you don't till your papers
> Come back again at 3!"

He smiled us out and said "Goodbye"
Who nevermore we'd see
For if we ever called again,
He "not at home" would be.
One man looked so benevolent,
And took great interest
In what we told him of our work
And said it would be blessed.

He advertised right willingly,
And cheered us on our way
With kind regards and good advice
"How nice he was," said they.
"Yes, so he was," another sighed,
"But really, so polite,
He would have given twice the sum
If we had worked it right."

Oh! mercenary charity,
Benevolence and greed;
Oh! human nature students, please
Pass on and do not read.[38]

The poem highlights not only predictable male antagonisms to women's shifting roles but also women's problems in assuming a new image. Their self-effacing and wry commentary breathes discomfort at shifting from established, socially prescribed manners and passivity. Gradually, during the decades before 1920, Suffolk County cookbooks incorporated more advertisements; presumably women developed more effective attitudes and methods, and men welcomed the benefits of this advertising to both the community and their own enterprises. However, Ella may have been overcome by both her small, conservative town and her own deep rooting in nineteenth-century culture. The small, tradition-based village of Smithtown Branch did not welcome social change and offered the cookbook few financial resources. The village was growing at a relatively slow rate, eschewed the commercial developments of booming communities, and did little to welcome outsiders.[39] Significantly, all of Suffolk County's charitable cookbooks had been produced in successful entrepreneurial centers, where changing economics allowed more women's participation, rigid gender spheres were softening, and financial support for charitable cookbooks was forthcoming earlier.[40]

Ella's editorship also challenged her religious interpretation of food. Presbyterian value on plainness over sensuality was apparently not strong enough to prevent, stop, or redirect the manuscript, or Ella would neither have begun nor finished it. Yet, her own philosophy must have been reflected, to some degree, by the quotation she copied into her diary: "Be plain in dress and sober in your diet."[41] In general, the degree to which Protestant sects accepted this pronouncement varied according to denomination. For example, three churches in the Suffolk County village of Southold expressed remarkably different attitudes toward food. Of these, the Presbyterian women were the strictest. They voted to establish limitations on refreshments and to fine those who disobeyed: "It was decided by vote that supper shall be included in the meetings of the Society for the coming year—also that the supper shall be plain, consisting of either bread or biscuit, one kind of plain cake, one kind of fruit, and either cheese or meat [cold]."[42] They were also the least active in food fund-raising, producing only one charitable cookbook of the twenty-three published in Suffolk County (Southampton, 1907). It is likely that Ella's Presbyterian congregation shared at least some of this attitude, holding food secondary to their religious focus.[43] If so, her cookbook project may have met with a degree of disfavor.

Presbyterians stood in the shadow of the Methodist-Episcopalians, who published a larger percentage of books than their proportional number of churches. Their Southold publication, *Chop-Sticks* (1900), was a slim, twenty-page work, modish in both its layout and its cuisine, which emphasized cakes, puddings, pies, bread, salad, and luncheon entrees.

Even the stylish Methodist-Episcopalians of Southold could not hold a candle to the third group, the Universalist Ladies Liberal Sewing Society, whose reputation for good food and lively fun drew supporters from all churches. Their minutes were peppered with the pleasure of repeated experimentation in events and recipes and such good-humored expressions of delight as the following (1903): "The supper committee must be quite puffed up with pride, for what a supper they served—such delicious chicken salad, such scalloped potatoes and baked beans, such bread, such cake, such fruit—oh, such everything! . . . we are devotedly thankful for the great good cheer and merriment manifested by our members."[44]

It is no wonder Ella had problems. One cannot escape the paradox, perhaps most pressing for Presbyterians, in which so many churchwomen described their cookery as a religious act and saw benevolence as their duty, and were then required to enter the business world and raise funds in what was for many an unseemly, unreligious, and unwomanly act. As the poem above noted, religious and social ideals were compromised by cookbook compiling: "Mercenary charity, / Benevolence and greed."

Ella's strong ties to her conservative town and church kept her rooted in the nineteenth-century image of true womanhood. Her leadership within Smithtown culture was earned, in part, by her conformity to the prescribed image of women's roles—unswerving devotion to duty, and exertion of influence through private, passive example rather than active confrontation. One of her protégés wrote: "I would be a very disagreeable woman with so many living examples of Christianity about me to be gloomy or sad, & I will try more than ever to look up as the daisy does whether it rains or shines. . . . Your strong good sense and almost always unfailing good nature impress me or influence me in spite of what I say. . . ."[45] Ella did her good works quietly: "Only those closely associated with her have any idea of her many deeds of charity and they did not know one half."[46]

In addition to the book-related handicaps of town and social philosophy, Ella provided herself with still another stumbling block, her penchant for working alone. This was another departure from the model of successful cookbooks, which were generally assembled and printed by committees. The group offered great advantages in sharing the work, resources, and adjustments to new roles. Ella, by herself, had no allies in the work; her most logical supporter, Faith, had business experience and skills but visited home sporadically. In any case, Ella's preference for solitude grew with the years—her many, private hobbies, vacations alone, church leadership, even her social life showed an autonomous, detached quality. One can speculate on the forces that drove this capable woman inward; in any case, what began as an asset in cookbook compiling may later have become a trap.

Cookbook committees that typically gathered and edited recipes shared the responsibility of representing local people and their cuisine with accuracy and fairness. Committeewomen were often unidentified in print, perhaps to safeguard their reputations as editors, perhaps to shield them in the case of multiple entries, or perhaps as a method of maintaining the then socially correct image of women as private and passive.

Ella took a few steps out of the nineteenth-century domestic sphere, but she could not go the entire distance; although she had a reputation for "putting Smithtown on the map," the final steps fell to her daughter, Faith, the "first career woman in Smithtown."[47] It is ironic to think that the qualities that made Ella so exemplary in her world were also those that sabotaged her work.

A Tale of Three Cakes: On the Air and in the Books

Nelljean M. Rice

I

> What matters is that ordinary people understand and em-
> ploy the symbolic and cultural dimensions of food in their
> everyday affairs. Food is one of the most, if not the single
> most, visible badges of identity, pushed to the fore by people
> who believe their culture to be on the wane, their daughters
> drifting from their heritage. . . . [1]

It may seem strange to begin an essay on community cookbooks with the
question, "Who are we?" but the success of the genre answers this question.
"We are what we eat." This popular adage helps explain the interest shown
by anthropologists, sociologists, students of popular culture, historians,
and rhetoricians in the relationship of a people to what they eat. Workers
in these disciplines view the community cookbook as a representative
artifact of American cultural history. Its undiminished popularity speaks
to our continuing need to tie ourselves into various distinct but fluid
cultural units through the medium of food. If we believe that we are what
we eat, then the cooks and their recipes that feed us are our creators. We
venerate our creators in both daily and festival meals.

Mixing ingredients to create a dish and combining dishes to create a meal can be "read" as one of the primary rituals of American life. Because of this, our individually gathered stock of recipes serves as a cultural icon, providing a measure of continuity in a rapidly changing society. Susan J. Leonardi calls a recipe presented to community cookbook compilers "embedded discourse, and like other embedded discourses, it can have a variety of relationships with its frame or its bed."[2] The two or three sentence "stories" told by contributors place each recipe in a food tradition, illustrate something about the relationship between donor and recipe, and / or contain a testimonial from satisfied eaters. No other food publication captures the eating habits of a region in such a systematic (and sympathetic) manner. In fact, popular culture writers Jane and Michael Stern use the Walnut (Iowa) Centennial Cookbook as an important source of foodways and recipes in *Square Meals*. Choosing source material for *Square Meals*, the Sterns take their cues from the many cooks who rely on the locally compiled community cookbook (distributed by, say, the women of the First United Methodist Church) as one of the basics of their recipe collection.[3] Lynne Ireland sums up the relationship between community cookbooks and their readers when she says that the "compiled cookbook reflects what is eaten in the home. It is, in a sense, an autobiography" (108).[4] For its willing contributors, the community cookbook is then a way of eating the cake but sharing it, too.

In spite of the traditional community cookbook's popularity, the impact that media, especially radio and television, have had on our society has expanded the scope of the word "community" and expanded the formats available to the community cookbook. The written or orally delivered recipe, or the recipe demonstrated on a television cookery show serves to fill the gap created by the absence of an older relative in the home who can demonstrate the making of a particular favorite family dish to her apprentice, daughter, or granddaughter. The cook who does not belong to a church, PTA, or garden club group can still receive locally favorite recipes on regional radio or television shows, thereby participating in the foodways of her community in order to expand her repertoire of local favorites, without a particular group affiliation. Why are regional foodways so important to cooks?

A culture's desire for a continuous pattern of meals or specific foodstuffs has not been widely studied. Food events are a convergence of social and biological impulses that can turn even an ordinary meal into an event, or a special event into a meal. Because food is such a basic need and so much a part of ordinary life, its cultural importance tends to be overlooked or ignored. Yet as Charles Camp discusses in *American Foodways*, much of this culturally "transparent" activity is actually the very heart of our differences from others. A closer scrutiny of these differences can show us why they matter. Does a treasured family recipe have more value than great-grandmother's wedding gown? If it does, is it because all members of the family can eat the food made according to the recipe whereas the gown only can be admired? To understand the full impact of foodways on our culture we should follow anthropologist Mary Douglas's lead. Douglas believes that "food is a field of action. It is a medium in which other levels of categorization become manifest."[5] Anglo-Americans who traveled westward in the nineteenth century could take very little in the way of furniture, clothing, and utensils. But what they could, and did, take was a set of cultural assumptions. These givens often clustered around food choice, preparation, and presentation.

The westward expansion and the mobility of an immigrant population created the need for neighborly, yet professional, advice. Lonely women on isolated farms and ranches had few guides to "huswifery," unless they had carried with them one of the tomes of Eastern domestic ideology, such as Lydia Maria Child's *The American Frugal Housewife*, or unless a neighbor was close enough for daily consultation. These women missed the company of other women and had to rely on newspapers, infrequent community get-togethers, and what they could remember from home to help them triumph over the harsh conditions of rural life.

Even in the early twentieth century, a sense of isolation remained. When the crush of chores overwhelmed, when the driveway and the secondary road were blocked by mud or ice, the rural farm wife could join in the community of women by listening to the radio homemaker, of whom Evelyn Corrie Birkby of Sidney, Iowa, is among the best known. The midwestern radio homemakers, who have in the 1990s all but disappeared from the airwaves, served their listeners as a talking compendium of domestic advice; their most valued opinions came in the form of recipes. These women projected a community cookbook of the air. Mrs. Birkby chronicles the history of their success in *Neighboring on the Air: Cooking with the KMA Radio Homemakers.*[6]

Neighboring on the Air follows the community cookbook's standard format by grouping recipes under a particular category, such as "Meats," except the categories for Birkby have a more personal and historical interest and the recipes are presented as part of the stories of the individual radio homemakers. Most of the recipes are not merely "dropped in" but are rather tied to the women's histories by their names or the tales that the radio personalities told. In this way, Birkby is able to reveal indirectly much about the circumstances and personalities of her subjects. The astute recipe reader can thereby "read" the food story embedded in the radio homemaker history by contemplating recipe choice, the wording of directions for mixing and cooking, the choice of ingredients, and most importantly, the narratives that the homemakers themselves use to frame selected recipes.

II

That farmhouse seems elastic in its power of accommodating people.[7]

In the first half of this century, when Mrs. Birkby was growing up in the small rural towns of southwest Iowa as the daughter of a Methodist minister, she learned the lessons of a powerful domestic ideology that had its origins in the early Victorian conflation of heaven and the home. These lessons were taught through the examples set by mothers, sisters, grandmothers and aunts, themselves influenced by various popular domestic compendiums. For example, Mrs. Julia McNair Wright opens *The Complete Home* by stating: "Between the Home set up in Eden, and the Home before us in Eternity, stand the Homes of Earth in a long succession."[8] The early nineteenth century's *The American Frugal Housewife* by Lydia Maria Child, the most popular domestic manual, signified a trend toward works such as *Home* (1835) by Catherine Maria Sedgwick, and *A Treatise on Domestic Economy* (1841) by Catharine Beecher, which instructed American women on the proper organization of their households. Often in these works an older woman, such as Aunt Sophronia, "the Oracle of all" from *The Complete Home*, instructed newlyweds on the proper techniques of domestic science and visionary housekeeping, which always included significant detail on the gospel of good cooking.

The word "mission" resonates in the American psyche. After all, the

Puritans had a mission to create a new Eden in America. For the women proponents of domestic ideology, this sense of "mission" included their work within the American home. Writers such as Beecher, with a strong New England, Puritan background, were concerned that the waves of immigrant women were not sufficiently self-conscious (and Protestant) in their approach to making their homes domestic heavens. Out of a "profound veneration for the Divinely instituted Home," Mrs. Wright produced *The Complete Home* to serve as a "spring of strength and safety to the country at large."[9] The philosophy of the domestic compendium ties habits of food preparation to the creation of an ideal domestic environment. The value of preparing the "best" foods in the "healthiest" ways is consistently posited as one of the mainstays of the "Divinely instituted home." A desire for knowledge about the most effective recipes for invalids, or the ones most likely to nurture healthy children, led women such as Aunt Sophronia to keep a scrapbook. Just as these women saved scraps of material for quilts, they saved recipes for nourishing dishes and homeopathic cures, furniture polish and pesticides. Often, the idiosyncratic scrapbook took the place of the better organized (and more expensive) compendium, especially if it was supplemented by the compiled, or fundraising cookbook, which burgeoned in the years following the Civil War: "Well over two thousand titles were published by the end of the century, firmly establishing the place of the compiled cookbook in the hearts and kitchens of organized women everywhere."[10]

In *Perfection Salad*, a lively presentation of the history of domestic science, Laura Shapiro notes that as an outgrowth of and reaction to the combination of housekeeping and morality, late nineteenth-century "modern" women wished to "move through a day of chores and challenges like an invisible force for good, applying the laws of chemistry and biology to every mark of disarray."[11] Shapiro chronicles the success of this ideological movement through its codification in the Home Economics major at the college level. And although Shapiro does not state this explicitly, what she gives is the historical background, the "recipe," for a myriad of American communities whose women embraced the Protestant work ethic and the mission of "taming" the wilderness to make it fruitful. The Perfection Salad of Shapiro's title is like the summa cum laude degree for the American homemaker: the "link between home and heaven [was] forged by a perfect distribution of proteins, carbohydrates, and fats. . . ."[12] Nowhere

Evelyn Birkby (*center*) in the KMA studio with two unidentified guests.
Courtesy Evelyn Birkby.

is the quest for absolute apportionment more evident than in the community cookbook, the exemplar of neighborliness to which Evelyn Birkby has devoted her working career in a genre-bending way.

Mrs. Birkby first assayed community cookery writing as a young farm bride in southwest Iowa. In 1949 she was asked to write a weekly column for the local *Evening Sentinel* in Shenandoah, Iowa. "Up a Country Lane" has appeared continually ever since, even after the *Sentinel* was purchased by the *Shenandoah Valley News* early in 1994.[13] Mrs. Birkby also achieved regional celebrity as a radio homemaker with her "Down a Country Lane" program for Shenandoah's KMA radio. Recently, Mrs. Birkby has gained national recognition, appearing on syndicated television and National Public Radio, discussing and demonstrating her philosophy of neighboring. Birkby's ideas about community cookery so captivated Jane and Michael Stern that they contributed the foreword to Birkby's autobiography, *Up a Country Lane*, and styled her the "poet laureate" of radio homemaking.[14]

Up a Country Lane is a community cookbook, a community autobiography, and a personal autobiography. It combines chapters such as "Haying," "A Country Church," and "Saturday Night in Town" with recipes collected from Birkby's friends and neighbors in southwest Iowa. This book builds on Birkby's expansion of the compiled-cookbook genre begun with her earlier work, *Neighboring on the Air,* which re-creates the now all-but-lost world of radio homemakers.

The radio homemakers were successful because they provided camaraderie and helpful hints, using daily recipe sharing as the linchpin of their popularity. In effect, they became oracles in a community cookbook of the airwaves. The community cookbook is usually designed by a special interest group to earn money for a specific project. It has been employed often in rural areas to solidify ties among women joined by a specific church, school, or club society but scattered geographically. The selection of a well-beloved family recipe to donate to the community effort has provided many hard-working, unsung wives and mothers some measure of local fame in that their treasured recipe has, through the community cookbook, become a way of feeding a larger circle. This larger group comes to know the contributor as the "original author" of a current family favorite, perhaps even invoking her name each time the recipe is served. The radio homemakers tied into the community cookbook structure by enclosing their recipes (often provided by their listeners) in stories.

Mrs. Birkby's use of the community cookbook "convention," attaching the name of a recipe donor within her own history of radio homemaking and the story of her life, illustrates her ties to the form, even though her two books list her as "author." What she has provided is the kind of commentary on the background and circumstances attached to the recipes that the traditional users of the community cookbook already know from their social and civic connections to the contributors. For example, in *Neighboring on the Air,* Birkby tells the story of Jessie Young, who in 1926 became the first KMA radio homemaker to broadcast directly from her home. From an immigrant, impoverished background (Young's mother, Rosa Susanka, was, at the age of seven, washing dishes in a saloon to support herself), "Jessie did many jobs; among them she went from door to door to find customers to buy magazines, books, bluing, *and her mother's baked goods*" (emphasis added). Birkby follows this biographical detail with a recipe for one of the sort of cakes that Jessie Young would have offered door to door:

LAZY DAISY CAKE

Put 1 cup milk and 1 tablespoon butter on to heat in a saucepan. Beat 2 eggs till light and add 1 cup sugar, beating vigorously. Sift 1 cup flour, 1 teaspoon baking powder, and ½ teaspoon salt. Stir into the egg mixture and add vanilla. Add milk mixture, stirring carefully as added. Pour into 8 × 8 pan and bake 25 minutes in moderate oven. Frost with ⅔ cup brown sugar, ⅓ cup melted butter, 2 tablespoons thick cream, and ½ cup coconut. Spread on cake while warm and return to oven to caramelize.[15]

This simple recipe is a contribution to regional history in several ways. From Birkby's introduction, the reader can see that the cake was made to be sold. Possibly several were made each day. The caramelized frosting would not fall or run off, the 8 × 8 size and single layer made for easy transportation, and the touch of coconut in the frosting might have added exotic appeal for rural, small-town neighbors. The complex ideology and set of relationships needed to sustain the community is also implied by Birkby's placement of this recipe. Earlier, Birkby explains that Rosa Susanka's husband had deserted her and their four daughters, forcing Rosa to raise her girls using the homely skills of laundering, cleaning, sewing, and cooking for other people. Those of the community who could afford to pay the Susankas for their services earned kudos two ways. They demonstrated their own success at business or farming when they showed that they had enough money left over from the necessities to purchase a cake from Jessie, and they gained the respect of their friends because they were also helping a deserving family maintain its dignity and respect.

Even the title of the recipe may reveal its origin and purpose. Since nothing about the construction or the finished product looks like a drooping daisy, the reader might conclude that its name stems from Jessie's selling patter. Maybe she cajoled her customers by saying, "Just be *lazy* one of these *days*, and buy this cake for your family dessert." The luxury of *appearing* lazy, *and* by doing so also accomplishing a community good deed, must have been irresistible to those hard-working Iowa women schooled in the near impossible requirements of the "home equals heaven" metaphor propounded by the authors of the domestic ideology books. What freedom for the harried homemaker to say to herself: "I was such a lazy daisy today, buying one of Rosa's cakes." If the use of the word "lazy" proves problematic for some who know that no self-respecting Iowa wife would ever admit to even *thinking* that word in a positive context, those readers should understand the use of "lazy" here as a wry irony which maker, seller, purchaser and eater of the cake all would appreciate. Lazy daisy, indeed!

Who "named" the cake becomes immaterial when the power of the name enables Jessie and Rosa to sell more of them. It is no accident that Mrs. Birkby places this particular recipe at the beginning of Jessie Young's chapter in *Neighboring on the Air*, because Young's case is the perfect example of the commercialization of the community cookbook concept inherent in the radio homemaker programs.

III

> "Radio is the greatest factor in modern life today," Earl May stated shortly before he began broadcasting in September 1925 on his station, KMA, "The Cornbelt Station in the Heart of the Nation." Later, May declared the call letters an acronym for the slogan Keeps Millions Advised.[16]

With the advent of radio, the farmhouse, which metaphorically expanded to hold all those family, neighbors, and travelers who needed shelter and food, whirled into the air, so that any Kansas farmwife could say, with the flick of a switch, "I'm not in Kansas anymore." And if the housewife becomes Dorothy, then Earl May is the Wizard of Oz. During KMA's first year on the air, the Earl May Seed & Nursery Company "increased its business by 425 percent and added a million names to its mailing list."[17] May's radio homemakers not only endorsed products, they were also paid for their time on the air, so that while they expanded the community cookbook concept to its widest possible audience, they also commercialized what had been (up to their advent) a charitable tool. Still, each radio homemaker wished to stress the integrity of her endorsements, and Birkby confirms that desire in her account of Young's experience: "Jessie carefully thought through all her own commercials, but she did not work from a script. She would ad-lib twelve to thirteen commercials for her one-hour homemaker visit. Jessie recalled: 'I sold cosmetics, roses, fish, prunes, horse collars, harnesses, jackets, boots, jams, tires, blankets, and dress goods. I don't think you can mention anything that I didn't sell. But I never sold anything I didn't believe in. Listeners can tell right away if someone isn't being honest with them.' "[18] Commercials were couched in the form of advice; they were presented as a part of the *recipe* for happiness, just as were the actual recipes. As a result, the KMA homemakers, by sharing, and educating, helped give their employer an audience that thought of itself as an extended radio family. This sincere concern for their audience inspired the same type of loyalty that rural and small town folk have for the institutions most often associated with community cookbooks. Billy Oakley, the last radio homemaker on KMA, boosted the local sales of Bag Balm (a cream farmers use on their cows' udders) when she mentioned on her show "It's a Woman's World" that she used Bag Balm as a moisturizer.[19] Billie's recipe for soft hands was taken as gospel in the communities surrounding Shenandoah, Iowa. In the process, the manufacturers of the product benefited.

While Earl May founded KMA primarily as a vehicle to sell his Earl May Seed & Nursery Company products, he was quick to realize that the radio homemakers could sell anything as long as they could convince their listeners that the product would make their homes more "complete." The audience for the radio homemakers' oral texts was a ready-made one, holding certain expectations they had developed as devotees of a domestic ideology that emphasized cookery as an essential ingredient in making home a heaven on earth. Further, many of these listeners had participated in the process of the nonprofit community cookbook, either as donors of recipes or as readers. The leap into the air, so to speak, was easier to make when the radio programs included recipes shared woman to woman. "During her job interview [at the *Sentinel*] Birkby was told two things that stuck with her: 'Remember, there's [sic] many lonely people out there, especially the women. And always put in a recipe. Because if they don't use something else, they'll use the recipe.' "[20]

The glory days of radio homemaking began in the 1920s, escalated during the Depression years, and lasted until the proliferation of television in the 1960s. In the '30s and '40s, CBS broadcast Ida Bailey Allen's "National Radio Homemakers Club," which NBC countered with "Sisters of the Skillet." The government even offered an "Aunt Sammy" show built around recipes developed by the USDA Bureau of Home Economics.[21] However, the radio homemakers with the most devoted followings were the local women, like Jessie Young, Evelyn Birkby, and Billie Oakley, who projected a sense of connection with the community. The longest running show was "Kitchen-Klatter," which featured Mrs. Leanna Driftmier; it began in 1926 in Shenandoah, Iowa, at station KFNF, switched to KMA in 1939, and lasted until 1986. "Kitchen-Klatter" was syndicated throughout the Midwest from 1948 on, and its popularity helped create spin-offs—a business that produced food flavorings, cleaning products, and salad dressings, as well as *Kitchen Klatter Magazine,* which had a peak subscription list of ninety thousand. For twenty-eight years, Evelyn Birkby both wrote for the magazine and appeared as a "fill-in" homemaker on the radio show.[22]

Most of the recipes that the homemakers read to their listeners were, to use one of Birkby's favorite words, "special." They were not recipes that could be browsed in the latest issue of *Ladies Home Journal.* Each recipe, like the ones in community cookbooks, was connected to a story. Each story revealed the sense of community implicit in the recipe. The complex communication process inherent in the reading of a recipe over the air to a listener, who is writing it down in the midst of her morning chores, created another level of context or "story" for each recipe. Thus a recipe can be story, as well as food, in the serving of which the story of the copying might be told. Finally, the directions and their context become story again when the recipe is passed on.

This complex of exchanges works inside, yet helps to create, two "larger" stories. The first of these is the initial introduction to the recipe provided by the radio homemaker. These introductions most often tied the context of the recipe into some activity (such as threshing) familiar to the homemaker's listeners. Then, when a trusting atmosphere had been established, the homemaker could present the recipe knowing the directions were being copied down because the listeners wished to become, in some tangible way, a part of the radio homemaker's family. Serving a dish endorsed by this valued friend made the listener feel a part of an extended family. The second larger story concerns the serving of the recipe. As both the radio personalities and their listeners know, the farm community's practice of providing a meal as a "thank-you" for free labor is part of a social pattern in which quilting, harvesting, barnraising, and other seasonal farm jobs get done because folks pitch in and do them. A "payment" of food keeps the job / reward cycle informal and down home.

Billie Oakley's first recipe from Birkby's *Neighboring on the Air* illustrates the point perfectly.

INDIAN CAKE

2 cups sugar; ½ cup shortening (1 stick margarine); 2 eggs; ½ cup cocoa; ½ cup cold, strong coffee; 2 cups flour; 1 teaspoon soda; 1 teaspoon salt; 1 teaspoon vanilla; ½ teaspoon burnt sugar flavoring; 1 cup boiling hot water.

Mix in order given until smoothly blended except for the boiling hot water. Carefully blend in the hot water. Pour into greased and floured 9 X 13 baking pan. Bake in 350 degree oven for approximately 30 minutes. Cool, and top with the following frosting.

FROSTING

1 cup sugar, ⅓ cup water, ⅓ teaspoon cream of tartar, 2 egg whites.

Mix together in heavy pan the sugar, cream of tartar, and water. Bring to boil. Cook until syrup forms a hard ball in cold water. Stiffly beat the egg whites. Drizzle on boiling hot syrup while you continue to beat at a medium-high speed. Flavor with vanilla or your favorite flavoring. I prefer vanilla and almond. For a different flavor and a beautiful pink color, substitute maraschino cherry juice for water. Lovely.

Birkby comments:

> The Indian Cake has, in a way, become Billie's good-luck charm. The original recipe came from a 4-H girl to whom Billie had given a home permanent. The girl decided to bake her favorite cake and give it to Billie as a thank you gift. This became the cake Billie made through the years to take as a gift to welcome a new baby, to say her own thank you to a friend, to comfort a family that had had sorrow, or to take to a covered-dish dinner. "I have many memories tied up in that small cake," Billie says.[23]

Billie Oakley's Indian Cake, the first recipe she gave when her home-maker broadcasting began, shows community in action through the ritual use of food. The midwestern habit of neighborliness speaks to today's reader through the stories of the Indian and Lazy Daisy cakes. As with Jessie Young's cake, the ingredients are common and easily assembled, but the frosting is unusual. The maraschino cherry juice adds an exotic element. Like the Lazy Daisy cake, Oakley's cake has an unexplained, unusual name. Perhaps it recalls the Native American spirit of reciprocal gift giving. Or it may have been named because its color recalled the weathered Native American complexion. The use of margarine and commercial burnt sugar flavoring should also indicate to the careful reader that Oakley's recipe belongs to a time closer to our own.

Today's reader of Birkby's book can only speculate upon how many
Indian Cakes have been made by midwestern women, but the number may
bear out Earl May's radio call letter motto to "Keep Millions Advised."
When television began to feature homemaker shows in the early 1950s,
Billie Oakley was one of the few radio homemakers to also become a
television personality. By the late 1960s her "radio program was syndicated
over forty stations, including KMA. She also had a television cooking
show on KOLN-KGIN TV in Lincoln and Grand Island, Nebraska, in
Sioux Falls, South Dakota, and on Kansas and Iowa stations."[24] Oakley's
television performances reached people who perhaps were transplanted
from their home communities. Listening to her and watching her make
food gave these folks a chance to pretend they were back home in the
family kitchen.

Evelyn Birkby is determined that the legacy of goodwill created by
women such as Oakley, Jessie Young, and Birkby herself, a legacy evident in
individual recipe collections throughout the Midwest, will not be forgotten. She believes that the isolation felt by the early pioneers and farm
people can also be felt in today's cities. Even today, sharing a recipe is a way
to "reach out and touch someone," as one telephone company advertisement repeatedly urged us.

IV

> When radio stations came into existence in the 1920's, farm
> ers who owned both a radio and a telephone sometimes gave
> out a single long "general" ring which went to all the tele
> phones on their line. When they heard enough clicks to
> know the neighbors were listening, they would put the
> mouthpiece of the phone near the radio speaker and let the
> listeners hear the program.[25]

The old-fashioned "party line" phone, which several families shared,
should stand as a metaphor for the neighborliness that Evelyn Birkby
wishes to convey in her books. Not only did rural residents call the other
members of the party line so the whole line could listen to radio homemakers through the telephone, they also experienced each other's troubles
through the line. Often, as was the case in Birkby's community, there was a

person (usually self-designated) who served as the communications nexus of the neighborhood line. In a chapter titled "The Telephone," Birkby tells a story about Myrtle Brooks, the Mill Creek community's "unofficial communication center," that reaches to the powerful heart of community cookery. Myrtle was the most important source of information about local affairs. Today she might be labeled a busybody, but at that time Myrtle was the conduit through which all the local illness and tragedy flowed. If a farm wife heard from Myrtle, she immediately fired up her stove. In Myrtle's rural universe, food spoke words that could not be voiced in any other way.

Birkby, who at this time had already begun her career as a recipe communicator, coveted Myrtle Brooks's recipe for a banana cake. Each time Brooks brought the cake to a church social or pot-luck dinner, Birkby would ask for the recipe; and each time, Brooks would refuse, saying, " 'It's special. If I give you the recipe, you'll make it and get compliments, and it won't be mine any more!' "[26] At first this might seem like a rude response to a neighbor's request, but even today informal apprenticeship remains the norm in the American kitchen. Evidently, Birkby had to earn Brooks's trust. Evelyn Birkby was not a Mill Creek farmgirl by birth, so she had to prove her worth to the community by good deeds before she received the community wisdom in the form of its recipes. This impasse continued for two years until a different friend asked for Birkby's multi-grain bread recipe over the party line.

Immediately Myrtle Brooks cut into the conversation to implore Birkby to wait. It seems that Brooks had jumped out of the tub to listen in, and she needed to throw on her robe, turn on a light, and get a pencil, so she too could copy the bread recipe. The next morning Brooks called Birkby to thank her for waiting the night before. And, as Birkby continues: "Then, after a long pause and a deep breath, she concluded, 'By the way, I've decided to give you my banana cake recipe. I'll bring it to church Sunday.' "

MYRTLE'S FAMOUS BANANA CAKE

1¾ cups sugar; ½ cup butter; 2 eggs, beaten; ½ cup buttermilk; 1 teaspoon baking soda; 1 cup mashed bananas; 2 ¼ cups sifted cake flour; 1 teaspoon vanilla flavoring

Cream together the sugar and butter. (High grade margarine can be substituted for the butter, if you prefer, but that is something Myrtle would never do.) When mixture is light and fluffy, add the eggs and continue beating until smooth. Dissolve the baking soda in the buttermilk and stir into batter. Add bananas, cake flour, and flavoring. Mix well and pour into two greased and floured 8-inch pans or one 9-by-13 inch baking pan. Bake at 350 degrees for 30 to 45 minutes. Myrtle always frosted her cake with Brown Sugar Frosting: 3 tablespoons brown sugar, packed; 3 teaspoons butter; 3 tablespoons cream; 1½ cups powdered sugar; 1 teaspoon vanilla flavoring; dash of salt. Heat brown sugar, butter, and cream together over low heat, stirring, until well blended and sugar is dissolved. Remove from fire and stir in remaining ingredients, using enough powdered sugar to make spreading consistency. When smooth and creamy, frost the cake. Makes 20 servings.[27]

In the unspoken language of the Mill Creek community, this banana cake recipe conferred status because in Myrtle's mind this was not an everyday cake. If she shared her recipe, Myrtle Brooks would lose status every time someone else produced "her" cake at a community get-together. Yet Evelyn Birkby served her apprenticeship well and deserved to be rewarded. The most appropriate way to announce to Birkby that she had "arrived" in Mill Creek would be to arrange a recipe exchange, placing mistress and apprentice on equal footing. At the same time, the exchange must appear natural. The modern reader of Birkby's cookbook autobiography must wonder why Myrtle did not just keep her mouth shut and copy Birkby's recipe without divulging her own. But Myrtle Brooks could not let this opportunity pass. Using Mill Creek terms, "Myrtle's Famous Banana Cake" recipe, passed on to Evelyn Birkby, was Birkby's diploma, earning her a degree of sisterhood with the Mill Creek women. In *The Home Plot*, Ann Romines sums up the type of impulse that governed Myrtle's actions: "Immortality, for a woman, has often been a matter of attaching her name to a domestic artifact or process that will survive her, such as a recipe."[28]

The instinct that led Evelyn Birkby to write her autobiography as both an evocation of a vanishing rural lifestyle and as a cookbook reflects her heartfelt attachment both to the community in which she lived as a young wife, and to the form that symbolizes the attributes of a community most difficult to express. A whole social hierarchy is revealed parenthetically in the directions for making Myrtle's cake when Birkby says, "but that is something that Myrtle would never do."[29] By refusing to substitute margarine for butter in her recipe, Myrtle Brooks (and, by extension, Evelyn Birkby) has lined herself up with those who still believe that small, daily standards matter. The taste (in both senses of the word) of the community would be insulted by margarine.

Most of the recipes on which Birkby hangs her *Up a Country Lane* stories are not Evelyn Birkby originals. Rather, they are her version of the compiled, community cookbook. As a radio homemaker and food columnist, Birkby learned that food could be a way of releasing her imaginative powers. Through the use of gathered recipes, she could tell the stories of her friends and herself. Some things that could not be said could be implied in the strategic placement of a recipe in its narrative frame, or in a parenthetical aside buried in the recipe's directions. Although Birkby might not phrase it like this, she would agree with Mary Anne Schofield's comment that: "Food objectifies and then allows repetition of both the pleasure of the senses and the verifying of these senses. Food cooked, eaten, and thought about provides a metaphoric matrix, a language that allows us a way to get at the uncertainty, the ineffable qualities of life."[30] The success of Birkby's compiled cookbooks as foodways, community, and personal autobiography hinges on the small bit of advice that has remained at the center of all her endeavors: "Because . . . they'll use the recipe."

Juana Manuela Gorriti's
Cocina ecléctica: Recipes as
Feminine Discourse
Nina M. Scott

One of the books I brought home with me from my stint as a Senior
Fulbright Lecturer in Buenos Aires in 1987 was Argentine novelist Juana
Manuela Gorriti's *Cocina ecléctica* (The eclectic kitchen), a facsimile version
of the cookbook she compiled and edited shortly before her death in 1892;
it was republished in 1977.[1] It took me a long time to find the precise date
of its original publication, which turned out to be 1890. It seems appropriate to celebrate its centennial plus a few more, for it really is a remarkable
book.

I had bought Gorriti's book for several reasons. First, I am a passionate cook myself. Metaphors of the kitchen and culinary discourse thus
hold a particular attraction for me, as they did for a number of the Spanish American women authors I most admire: Sor Juana Inés de la Cruz,
the seventeenth-century Mexican nun and poet, and her countrywomen
Rosario Castellanos, who wrote the splendid short story entitled "Cook-

ing Lesson," and Laura Esquivel, creator of the popular novel and film *Like Water for Chocolate*. Puerto Rican novelist/poet Rosario Ferré observed in her theoretical essay "The Writer's Kitchen" something that also holds true for me: "For me writing and cooking often blend together."[2] Second, I am particularly interested in nineteenth-century women's literature, and in the ways in which the writers of that time designed strategies to give lip service to the woman as keeper of home and hearth while simultaneously breaking out of private into public discourse. Francine Masiello's excellent article on this topic points out how "the women of Argentina utilized the domestic sphere . . . to develop new codes of learning and enhanced their limited opportunities for public circulation by building intra-domestic networks of dialogue,"[3] a dialogue of which cookbooks formed an integral part. Third, I wanted to know more about Gorriti as a writer, especially given her status as Argentina's foremost woman of letters in the nineteenth century and her image as a flamboyant figure by anyone's standards.

Juana Manuela Gorriti (1818–1892) was the attractive, intelligent, and strong-willed daughter of a prominent landholding family in northern Argentina. Her father fought in both the war of independence from Spain and later on in the many civil wars that marked the early years of the Argentine republic; but as General Gorriti was on the losing side against the dictator Juan Manuel de Rosas, the family had to flee for their lives to Bolivia. There Juana Manuela fell in love with Manuel Isidoro Belzú, a young Bolivian officer, and married him when she was fourteen. He later was twice president of Bolivia. Belzú was ultimately assassinated. Theirs was a stormy relationship that resulted in permanent separation. Gorriti and her two daughters settled in Lima, where she supported herself by founding and running girls' schools, launching women's journals, and by publishing stories, essays, serialized novels, and travel literature. In spite of the fact that she had almost no formal education, Juana Manuela was an avid reader and a very cultured woman. She was an indomitable traveler, crossing and recrossing the Andes on horseback and, when possible, by railway; she also rounded the Horn by ship on a number of occasions in her frequent journeys between Lima, Buenos Aires, and La Paz. She was a prolific writer, much published and well received during her lifetime, and she is recognized today as one of the main precursors of the literature of the fantastic that is typical for the work of many of Argentina's most prominent writers: Jorge Luis Borges, Julio Cortázar, Silvina Ocampo, Luisa Valenzuela.

In spite of her literary successes, relatively little was written about Gorriti in her lifetime, and I felt that, given the communal nature of her particular cookbook, it might give me some clues as to the network of friends on which she, like so many nineteenth-century women writers, depended for support and survival. Experience has taught me that digging out actual texts written by early Spanish American women writers is often arduous enough, but reestablishing the social context out of which they wrote is even more difficult. The anecdotal nature of many of the recipes in *Cocina ecléctica* seemed to me to offer two ways of approaching Gorriti's text: I would see what information about her circle of friends I could glean directly from the cookbook, and I would then try to use this information as a springboard to other sources about Gorriti and her world.

A cursory glance at *Cocina ecléctica* shows it to have a surprisingly familiar format: a compendium of recipes sent in by a considerable number of women whose names appear at the end of their culinary contribution—just like innumerable contemporary fund-raising cookbooks put out by church groups, schools, museums, or symphony orchestras. I own a number of these, and what often makes them sell are recipes contributed by celebrities in the world of the arts: Luciano Pavarotti's meatballs or Yehudi Menuhin's Eggplant Casserole, for example. Gorriti's book, too, features recipes by celebrities, in her case well-known women writers such as the Peruvian novelists Clorinda Matto de Turner and Mercedes Cabello de Carbonera, and the Bolivian poet Adela Zamudio. There are a number of women who bear the names of illustrious South American families— Ascasubi, Irigoyen, Güemes, Palma, as well as Gorriti's two daughters— and many other acquaintances I could not identify.

I was intrigued by Gorriti's community cookbook format and wondered where on earth she got the idea. Were there other South American cookbooks organized along similar lines? When did this type of cookbook originate here in the United States? Was this format transmitted to Argentina via this country? Whereas it was impossible for me to research the history of Argentine cookbooks, I did ask a number of Argentinian friends if they could recall cookbooks with this particular format in their mothers' or grandmothers' collections. None of them could. I did have access to a Colombian work of this era, Aída Martínez Carreño's *Mesa y cocina en el siglo XIX* (Table and kitchen in the nineteenth century), which bore out the fact that Gorriti's type of cookbook was unknown in that country at least.[4] With respect to the United States, a letter to Barbara Haber, curator of printed books at the Arthur and Elizabeth Schlesinger Library on the History of Women in America, brought back some valuable information: the community cookbook originated around the time of the Civil War, "at Sanitary Fairs held to raise money for military casualties and their families. After the war was over, the ladies' aid societies formed during the war turned to local charities, and published their recipe collections to benefit hospitals, homes for the friendless, schools, and churches in every part of the country."[5]

But how did this idea reach Buenos Aires? Ricardo Rojas, the Argentine literary historian, provided what I conjecture to be a major clue. In his 1925 history of Argentine literature he includes a chapter on women writers and mentions the important role that U.S. schoolteachers, invited to Argentina by President Domingo Faustino Sarmiento in 1866, played in the formation of a whole generation of educated Argentine women: "The teachers brought down by him from the United States wasted no time in training outstanding Creole followers."[6] It seems entirely possible to me that Gorriti heard of the fund-raising cookbooks which were popular in the United States via one of these teachers, especially since she herself had founded schools in Lima and was in touch with women educators in both Peru and Argentina.[7]

No matter where Gorriti got the idea, the production of such a cookbook to earn money for herself made eminent economic sense. She was living on a pension paid to her by the Argentine government in recognition of her father's service to his country,[8] but she still depended on her pen for most of her livelihood and was by then seventy-one. Gorriti could draw on a wide spectrum of relatives and friends in the compilation of *Cocina ecléctica*, and from the comments of a number of her contributors it appears that her project met with great enthusiasm. After all, she was a very well known writer whose book was bound to sell, and the recipe exchange was a satisfactory arrangement for both parties: Gorriti appropriated their contributions for her own use but reciprocated by giving them the opportunity to appear as authors within her culinary text. Another impulse behind her book seems to have been a considerable degree of rivalry between herself and Countess Emilia Pardo Bazán, the famous Spanish novelist who was her contemporary and who was about to publish a work called *La cocina española antigua* (Old Spanish cooking).[9]

Having been fascinated for years by the subject of food and literature, yet still uptight about whether this was a "legitimate" scholarly concern (remember, this is 1987 we're talking about), I was amazed, reaffirmed, and delighted when I found Susan Leonardi's article, "Recipes for Reading," in—of all places—*PMLA*. Aside from her marvelous skills as a writer, Leonardi's article spoke to me because she took culinary discourse very seriously. In the act of recipe sharing she saw an "almost prototypical feminine activity" that functioned as a mark of women's relationships to each other: "The establishment of a lively narrator with a circle of enthusiastic and helpful friends reproduces the social context of recipe sharing—a loose community of women that crosses the social barriers of class, race and generation."[10] In the process of sharing their recipes, many of Gorriti's friends also told stories, embedding the former within personal anecdotes that reveal a great deal about themselves. *Cocina ecléctica* is thus a fabulous mirror of the community of women with which Gorriti interacted.

Her "Prologue" is very curious and yet, for her, also very typical. True to the philosophy of domesticity so popular in her time, Gorriti starts off by maintaining that "home is the domestic sanctuary; its altar is the hearth; its priestess and natural guardian, the woman." In the next breath, however, she distances herself from that traditional role: "Eager for other places, I threw myself into books and lived in Homer, in Plutarch, in Virgil and in all that group of Antiquity, and later in Corneille, in Racine; and still later in Chateaubriand, Hugo, Lamartine, without realizing that these men were renowned geniuses because . . . all of them had industrious and self-sacrificing women at their side who coddled them and fortified their minds with succulent tidbits, the fruit of a skill more suitable to a woman."[11] I have noticed the same tactic in Gorriti's creative writing: there is a very obvious discrepancy between the self-sacrificing domestic angels that people her fiction and Gorriti's own highly independent and unconventional self. She is not alone here: one notices a similar trend in other women writers of the nineteenth century, such as her friend Clorinda Matto de Turner, and the Cuban poet/novelist/playwright Gertrudis Gómez de Avellaneda. Gorriti not only separated from, but later divorced her husband, had a number of open affairs, and produced two further children out of wedlock; at times she dressed in masculine attire, and she became financially independent by dint of her writing and teaching.

In compiling her cookbook Gorriti arranged the recipes under the following headings: Soups, Sauces, Purées, Fish, Tamales, Fillings (both sweet and of fish or meat), Empanadas (similar to Cornish Pasties), Deep-fried Foods, Puddings, Poultry, Haute Cuisine, Rabbit, Vegetables, Barbecued Meats, and Desserts. With their mixture of European and indigenous dishes, the recipes reflect the hybrid culinary traditions familiar to many of Gorriti's friends. A dessert of raspberry cream, for example, is obviously European, while a recipe for tenderizing meat (wrap it in a clean napkin and bury it for three hours in a deep hole before barbecuing) clearly reflects the Argentine gaucho tradition.[12]

The broad range of contributors to *Cocina ecléctica* reveals a great deal about Gorriti's network of friends. The editor is effusive in her thanks to those who have made the book possible by their contributions but refrains from including herself in this group by not contributing even one recipe of her own.[13] One is immediately struck by the international scope of the participants. Besides Peru, Bolivia, and Argentina, the three countries in which she had lived most of her long and colorful life, Gorriti had contributions from Chile, Uruguay, Mexico, France, Belgium, Spain, Germany, and the United States. Sharing recipes for certain national dishes was often a source of considerable patriotic pride and tended to be couched in transports of lyrical prose, as in this description of *causa*, a Peruvian potato dish, and *chicha*, a beverage made of fermented corn: "Yes, causa is a joy to its numerous *dévotés* . . . a double cause of enjoyment for the pleasure of tasting it and for the obligatory glass of exquisite chicha which must follow it, and which in a transparent carafe can take its place among aristocratic wines, the recipe for which I will give here a little later."[14] Fellow Peruvian Clorinda Matto de Turner, the first Spanish American novelist to foreground the plight of the Indian, is quick to point out the indigenous roots of this drink, and to add a humanitarian observation: "This drink made of corn, the most nourishing of grains, is the sustenance of life and of strength for the Indian of the Bolivian and Peruvian mountains. With it he feeds himself, refreshes himself and also at times gets drunk, in order to forget his troubles."[15]

The ethnic diversity of South America is very evident in these recipes. A Bolivian contributor insists that nowhere is rabbit better prepared

"Tienda de chicha" (Chicha shop), cover illustration by J. Brown, after original by J. M. Groot, appearing on the front of *Mesa y Cocina en el Siglo XIX* (Table and kitchen in the nineteenth century) by Aída Martinez (1985). Courtesy Royal Geographical Society, London.

than in her country; her compatriot, the poet Adela Zamudio, concurs but makes a distinction in the condiments served with it: "You serve it to Creoles with a hot yellow pepper sauce and to foreigners with English mustard." Gorriti's daughter Edelmira contributed a recipe for *"humintas"* (a kind of tamal) which clearly underscored the contribution of the Indian in the preparation of these steamed packets of meat and corn wrapped in corn husks. Other recipes are purely European in origin, often obtained while members of these upper-class families were traveling abroad; often they are associated with famous persons such as Queen Victoria, Napoleon, Mme de Maintenon or the singer Adelina Patti. Some recipes are linked to South American history, such as *"Dorado San Martin"* (General José de San Martín was the hero of Argentine independence from Spain), or *"Balas del general"* (The general's bullets), a recipe that is narrated as pure dialogue between three lovely *criolla* ladies and an officer:

> "Mercy, General! Stay here one hour at least in order to eat a bite."
> "One hour, General! One hour and you will have forfeited nothing in your campaign."

"Oh, lovely ladies, it isn't bites I need but bullets."
"Well, you shall have them, General. Yes: one hour, one little hour
and you shall have bullets, I swear it."

True to her word, one of the three enterprising hostesses rapidly assembled
a platter of hard-boiled eggs stuffed with meat; when she served them to
the general, he pronounced them "Exquisite projectiles . . . they announce
my victory."[16]

In their excellent analysis of Gorriti's cookbook, Josefina Iriarte and
Claudia Torre confirm the historic framework of the recipes included in
this collection; in their opinion, these range from "heroic" or "epic" recipes
of the era of national independence, such as the "*Dorado San Martin,*" to
those of the subsequent "domesticated heroes," the bourgeois connoisseurs
of fine food who constituted the social élite of late nineteenth-century
Argentina.[17]

The social stratification of the contributors to *Cocina ecléctica* is very
obvious. They included married and single women, a few trained cooks, a
nun, and one man. Most of the women were upper-class, educated and, if
wealthy, usually also well traveled. Many expressed pleasure at being asked
to contribute and rejoiced at inserting their recipes into some amusing
anecdote, as we have seen above. On the other hand, the professional
cooks, probably because they belonged to a different social stratum, never
told stories. Among them, too, one gets an idea of demographic diversity.
One of the cooks is black—"*La negrita Encarnación*"; another, "Catalina
Pardini—Neapolitan cook," is probably part of the huge wave of Italian
immigration into nineteenth-century Argentina; and a third, from Lima,
records her feelings on knowing that Gorriti's book will allow her name to
appear there: "As though the exaltation of humble folk were to take place
through me, blind fate would have it that my poor and obscure name
should appear in this volume, where so many distinguished ones glitter."
At times it is clear that the mistresses appropriated their cooks' creations
without acknowledging the names of the latter: one Elvira Vela sent in a
recipe perfected by her cook and remarked, "How proud he would be if he
knew he was to appear in this learned book." However, she not only fails to
mention his name but signs her own to the recipe, modestly entitling the
pastry in question *Embozo a la Elvirita.*[18] Read with care, then, Gorriti's

recipes are a faithful cross-section of her upper middle-class society in the late nineteenth century.

As I mentioned in the introduction to this study, I was also interested in *Cocina ecléctica* as a springboard to reconstructing some of the network of women with whom Juana Manuela had contact, both in Lima and in Buenos Aires, and to finding out what the major concerns of these women were. Gorriti lived in Lima from 1850 to 1880. Besides supporting herself by teaching and writing, she also organized a famous literary salon where both women and men from Lima's intellectual circles met to perform music or to read poetry, fiction, or essays. Shortly before her death, Gorriti's son, Julio Sandoval, published the materials produced for his mother's *Veladas literarias* (literary evenings), and in an introductory letter to this work, the famous writer Ricardo Palma recalled with pleasure "those splendid evenings, of cordial, intimate moments of relaxation, enjoyed in the modest yet elegant salon of the illustrious Argentinian writer."[19] Gertrude Yeager's study of Gorriti's life documents a number of interesting observations about these gatherings: they lasted from about 8:30 in the evening to 3 in the morning, included famous writers as well as new talent, and also Gorriti's students. "From the beginning, what made the *veladas* unique was the inclusion of women, not only as observers but also as participants. . . . Each session included readings or performances by women of their compositions and a discussion of issues of interest to women. . . . The *veladas* were enormously successful, and as many as fifty or sixty people attended on a regular basis."[20]

The published *Veladas* document the salient preoccupations of Gorriti's circle of friends at that time: lectures on women's education and job training, historic and patriotic themes, literary studies, creative fiction and poetry. Uncovering biographical information about who these women were proved difficult, and I would have remained in the dark had not my graduate student Claudia van der Heuvel unearthed a two-volume study called *La mujer peruana a través de los siglos* (The Peruvian woman through the centuries), edited by one Elvira García y García in 1924 and 1925. These volumes contain a fascinating compendium of biographical information about Peruvian women, from pre-Columbian times to the time of the editor. Using *Cocina ecléctica* as a place to start, I made a list of all of the contributors from Peru (about half of the total number) and then checked these against the women mentioned in *La mujer peruana*. I was able to find eleven names, and when I compared their respective biographies, I found certain patterns emerging that proved very helpful for reconstructing Gorriti's network of women friends. Their stories were often much like hers, though somewhat less dramatic. Predictably, most women were from the upper class and most were, or had been, married. Several were widowed and in financial straits, having had reversals of fortune when their husbands died; like Gorriti, they turned to founding or teaching in girls' schools as well as to professional writing for newspapers and magazines to earn their livelihood. Most of these women had had a sketchy or even deficient early education, but all of them were devoted to literature and became well read by dint of great self-discipline.

Because of Gorriti's own precarious economic situation, and that of many of her peers, education for women was one of the group's most central concerns. Teresa González de Fanning, for example, a close friend as well as a contributor to the cookbook, was, like Gorriti, a creative writer, a journalist, and a founder of a *colegio* (high school) for girls; she contributed an eloquent essay about the necessity of job training for women. There is another interesting link here: Elvira García y García, the editor of *La mujer peruana*, is listed on the front page as a former director of the "Liceo Fanning." García frequently mentions the importance of Gorriti's salon for her and for other women of Lima—"those never-forgotten evenings," "those memorable evenings which up to now have not been revived." They were very obviously a major factor in the intellectual sustenance of these women.[21] As one of my other graduate students put it, "The *veladas* must have been their lifeline."

The reconstruction of Gorriti's context in Peru proved easier than in Argentina. Lily Sosa de Newton's extensive *Diccionario biográfico de mujeres argentinas* (Biographical dictionary of Argentine women) provided scant information on only two more women: a sculptor (María Aguirre de Vassilicós) and a writer from Santa Fe (Celestina Funes de Frutos); the latter appeared to be the only one of these women to have received a university degree.[22]

In the final analysis, then, *Cocina ecléctica* proved to be not only interesting reading in its own right but also a valuable tool, shedding light on Juana Manuela Gorriti and the women who formed her network of friends and soul sisters. Some of the fabric of these women's intertwined lives has come to light because of the gendered discourse of recipe sharing,[23] and so it seems only right to end on a culinary note. Did I find any recipes worth sharing with you? Two highly unusual ones come immediately to mind: *El huevo colosal* (The gigantic egg)[24] and *Helado de espuma* (Foam ice cream). The gigantic egg is made by separating a number of eggs into yolks and whites. Take two animal bladders, one smaller than the other, and place all the yolks in the smaller of the two. Tie it shut, place it in boiling water, and when the yolks are hard, remove the bladder. Place the outsize yolk in the center of the larger bladder, previously filled with the egg whites, tie it shut and boil until the whites are set. Peel off the bladder and serve "the gigantic egg, which makes a handsome impression at the table, when set upon a spicy sauce."[25]

The *Helado de espuma*[26] is also unusual in its preparation. Even though various contributors mention the use of freezers in the making of ice cream, according to this particular author Helado de espuma can be made without them, provided you live in the altiplano or other really high, cold regions. Rise at five in the morning, fill two zinc pails half full of milk, cover and proceed as follows:

> Wrap them in sheep skins well soaked in water strongly impregnated with saltpeter, or, lacking this, salt. Having placed them on the back of a horse, make him trot for three miles and bring him back at the same trot. The milk . . . , resting in its receptacle, roils like a stormy sea, and like the latter turns to a foam which rises, completely filling the empty space of the pail while the ice, simultaneously seizing control over the foam, ends up immobilizing it.[27]

This frozen mixture is then flavored with sugar and cinnamon and brought to the table immediately. Häagen Dazs, move over.

Recipes for *Patria:* Cuisine, Gender, and Nation in Nineteenth-Century Mexico

Jeffrey M. Pilcher

Laura Esquivel's best-selling novel *Like Water for Chocolate* dramatizes the importance of cuisine in Mexican culture. The heroine Tita is forbidden by custom to marry because as the youngest daughter she must care for her widowed mother. Worse still, her beloved, in order to be near Tita, agrees to marry her older sister. Unwilling to trade romance for respectability, Tita carries on an illicit affair through the medium of her cooking. Her dishes express her emotions: her sorrow brings people to tears, and her passion literally burns down the house. The novel even contains ex- cerpts from a handwritten cookbook in which she records her culinary se- crets, recipes that set her free from the restrictions of society.[1] Like Tita, nineteenth-century Mexican women wrote cookbooks in which they artic- ulated a vision of society different from the dominant view held by men.

As Esquivel's story suggests, women faced enormous pressure to conform to a rigid code of behavior. The restriction against the youngest daughter marrying so that she could care for her mother was only one of many demands placed on women. Mexican leaders expected them to serve the new nation but confined them to the domestic sphere, where they were supposed to raise patriotic sons and guard family morality. Intellectuals defined these values in an entire genre of instructional literature, including calendars and cookbooks that sought to teach women proper domestic behavior. This emphasis on building a moral family life increased under the dictatorship of Porfirio Díaz, who ruled from 1876 to 1911. During this time of modernization and industrial development, reformers encouraged women to work at home as a safeguard against vice on the streets.[2]

The Porfirian period was also the first time that significant numbers of Mexican women wrote their own cookbooks. These works included both manuscripts written by individuals and community collections of recipes published for charitable causes. This essay compares manuscript and community cookbooks with professionally written domestic manuals to explore the differences between male and female constructions of gender roles and national identity. Mexico's leaders dreamed of building a modern society based on European technology and ideology. But while women lived within the bounds of this patriarchal system, they did not always share its cultural foundations.

European Fashions, Creole Tastes

Challenges to the new Mexican nation seemed overwhelming in the first half century following independence. In 1821, after a decade-long civil war, the Spanish viceroy finally abandoned Mexico City, but patriot leadership soon splintered between liberal and conservative factions. Palace revolutions became the order of the day, allowing generals such as the flamboyant Antonio López de Santa Anna to play out personal ambition at the expense of both tranquility and the treasury. Internal strife reached its gravest point during the disastrous 1847 war against the United States, which cost the country half its territory. To counter this chronic instability, Mexican leaders sought to forge a sense of national identity, using secular education, religious icons, and patriotic festivals to instill a feeling of common purpose.[3] They invented a national cuisine as well, but class divisions frustrated their attempts to serve *la patria* (fatherland) at the dinner table.

The early republic extended privileges of citizenship to a narrow minority, and therein lay the origins of Mexico's instability. Creole elites monopolized the country's wealth and condemned the vast majority of Indians and mestizos to extreme poverty. Without hope for advancement, the destitute masses posed a constant danger of revolution against the rigid social structure. As a result, the conquistadors' heirs—and those wealthy enough to claim equal status—excluded the indigenous masses from political power and defined the new nation in European terms. But creole nationalists then faced the dilemma of asserting the uniqueness of a New World society built on Old World foundations. The nineteenth-century national cuisine becomes a symbol for their unsatisfying attempts to garnish sophisticated European culture with patriotic Mexican gestures.

Mariano Galván Rivera published Mexico's first cookbook in 1831, a decade after the nation gained independence. His work, which passed through a dozen editions and served as a model for cookbooks throughout the nineteenth century, possessed a sharp nationalist tone in both linguistic and culinary matters. The author denounced the Spanish Academy and insisted on using words of Mexican origin. He also praised spicy dishes as "truly national" and derided delicate European palates unaccustomed to chile peppers.[4] Although the most chauvinistic phrases disappeared from future versions, the insistence on a distinctive national taste continued to flavor the work. The 1868 edition, for example, included foreign dishes, but only after they had been "Mexicanized," that is, adapted to Mexican tastes.[5]

Defining this national cuisine remained a source of constant concern. A few years after Galván published his work, the *Nuevo y sencillo arte de cocina* (New and simple art of cooking) advertised recipes specifically "accommodated to the Mexican palate," which had no use for "European stimulants."[6] Nevertheless, in 1877 Narciso Bassols began his two-volume *La cocinera poblana* (The Puebla cook) with the pessimistic claim that cookbooks contained an abundance of useless foreign recipes.[7] Vicenta Torres de Rubio reiterated this attack on irrelevant cookbooks by observing that Mexicans neither season nor condiment their food according to European practices.[8] And in a community cookbook published in 1892, a group of women from Guadalajara declared that most authors copied recipes without concern either for quality or utility.[9] These assertions certainly contained an element of self-promotion by publishers trying to increase sales at the expense of French and Spanish competitors. But more importantly, they formed part of a campaign to unify the Mexican nation and subordinate social conflict.

The authors of this national cuisine came primarily from the liberal intelligentsia. Mariano Galván, the publisher of Mexico's first cookbook, also produced the Republic's first almanac as well as countless editions of women's calendars, travel guides, textbooks, and assorted other works.[10] Leading liberal newspaper editors also entered the cookbook trade, including Vicente García Torres and Ireneo Paz. One of the few female authors, Vicenta Torres, moved in liberal circles and even included in her work menus from political banquets.[11] Finally, Manuel Murguía dedicated a cooking manual to Mexican *señoritas* in 1856, two years after he printed the first edition of the Mexican national anthem.[12] These nationalist writers observed that Mexicans not only spoke the same language and shared the same history but also ate the same chiles and *frijoles* (beans).

The strategies used to create this national cuisine followed a few basic patterns, which have counterparts in the cuisine of post-colonial India analyzed by sociologist Arjun Appadurai.[13] The simplest method was to draw on local traditions by renaming regional recipes as national standards. An 1886 banquet attended by the Minister of Government and foreign dignitaries featured as the "national dish" *mole poblano*, a spicy stew from Puebla.[14] In a similar manner, people cooked everything from stuffed onions to barbecued meat *a la mexicana*, a conveniently ambiguous phrase often used in cookbooks to offset the preponderance of foreign recipes.[15] Cooks named dishes for national heroes: Moctezuma's dessert, insurgents' soup, Donato Guerra's cod, and *gorditas* from Guadalupe Hidalgo, the shrine of the national saint.[16]

Cookbook authors also took an inductive approach to the national cuisine by searching for culinary themes with national associations. They explored the Mexicans' common taste for "patriotic" frijoles and "truly national" chiles.[17] Menus provided a logical method of organizing these foods, thereby giving a coherent structure to the cuisine. Moreover, the uniform character of meals seemed to confirm the existence of a national cuisine. Well-to-do families took their main meal of the day in the early afternoon, following an invariable sequence of courses. The dinner began with a clear broth served with limes and chiles; next came a "dry soup" such as pasta or rice, followed by a main course of meat; the family then proceeded to frijoles before finally drifting off into a siesta.[18] Of course the popular classes could not afford such sumptuous feasts on a daily basis, which indicates the exclusive nature of this supposedly national cuisine.

Meat composed the central ingredient in elite meals from breakfast to supper. A quick glance at nineteenth-century cookbooks reveals an enormous variety of seasonings and dressings for meat.[19] Nor was this creativity limited to cookbooks; women prepared these diverse recipes on a daily basis. One foreign traveler observed that wealthy families ate the same meats prepared in different styles several times a week.[20] Fanny Calderón de la Barca, the wife of a Spanish envoy, described plates filled with meat, fish, and fowl served indiscriminately at every meal. She recorded that the wealthy ate meat for virtually every meal and in astonishing quantities, more than any other country in the world.[21]

Foreigners' accounts, with their ethnocentric biases, can also help identify the distinctive character of Mexican cuisine. Visitors from Europe and the United States almost invariably criticized these meat dishes as overcooked, and often blamed butchers for cutting meat in a "slovenly and injudicious manner."[22] But in fact, tradesmen carved beef to suit their customers' preference for well-done steaks. Mexicans abhorred the dripping, rare filets served in Europe and cut their meat in thin strips, pounding and marinating to tenderize them.[23] Such techniques often constituted the "Mexicanization" of European dishes: a recipe for *"bifstec" a la Chateaubriand* looks to foreigners like fajitas with French fries.[24]

Although Mexico's rich and famous preferred well-done meat, their carniverous diet nevertheless maintained a link with European traditions. Another part of Spain's culinary heritage was the preference for wheat bread. The conquistadors had subsisted on corn tortillas during the war against the Aztecs, but as soon as the fighting ended they demanded familiar European foods. Wheat continued to be a status symbol among the creole population, and by the eighteenth century bakeries flourished in all large cities.[25] One indication of the widespread wheat consumption comes from cookbooks' profuse recipes for bread soup as a way of utilizing leftover crumbs.[26] Unlike meat, Mexican bread earned the unanimous praise of foreign travelers, and William Bullock declared that "Europe cannot produce better."[27]

The elite preference for European foods such as meat and bread reflected their vision of the Mexican national identity. They hoped to build a modern, Western society on the foundations of Enlightenment philosophy and imported technology. Their blind adulation of foreign models had counterparts in the domestic sphere, where fashionable women hosted French dinners, wore French clothes, even affected French accents when speaking Spanish.[28] Vicenta Torres provided a culinary example of this appropriation of European culture. As one of the most beloved dishes of provincial Michoacán cookery she cited the *galatine*, a French dish prepared by boning poultry yet leaving the skin intact, then stuffing it with forcemeat and poaching it in broth.[29] For women unwilling to invest hours preparing such a dish and unable to pay a chef to do it for them, specialty shops sold gourmet foods such as pâté and pastry. Wine merchants also imported hams, cheese, olive oil, and salted fish in addition to barrels of Bordeaux and Jerez wines.[30] Banquet menus likewise demonstrate the infatuation with French haute cuisine. This quest for imported civility and taste reached its pinnacle in 1910 at the centennial of independence in a series of banquets honoring President Díaz, cabinet members, and foreign dignitaries. Not a single Mexican dish appeared at any of the score of dinners dedicated to this patriotic occasion. The French Sylvain Daumont Restaurant served most of the food, and G. H. Mumm provided all of the champagne. Even the Mexican colony in New York commemorated the centennial with French food.[31]

The Cuisine of the Streets

Just as French cuisine symbolized the modern nation aspired to by cosmopolitan Mexicans, Indian corn provided a metaphor for backward elements of society. Although urban elites had benefited from unprecedented economic growth, rural living conditions had changed little since the Spanish conquest. The vast majority of the people ate an essentially pre-Columbian diet of maize, beans, squash, and chiles, supplementing it with meat from European domestic animals only on rare festive occasions. The wealthy, with their carnivorous Western consumption habits, scorned this popular cuisine. Denying the nutritional and gastronomic merits of maize, they associated the grain with indolent villagers and immoral street people. Manuel Payno, a renowned author and gourmet, explained with remorse that etiquette forbade the consumption of corn tortillas and stuffed chiles because of their plebeian image and obliged fashionable Mexicans to eat English *rosbif*.[32]

Pre-Columbian civilizations developed a highly sophisticated cuisine, as the Spanish conquistadores discovered when they reached the New World. Fernando Cortés and his men wrote with awe of Moctezuma's lavish banquets, which included scores of different fish and game served in elaborately spiced dishes.[33] While commoners could not afford such extravagant meals, they nevertheless ate a balanced diet of maize, beans, squash, and chiles, which supplied carbohydrates, protein, minerals, and vitamins respectively. Indeed, pre-Columbian agriculture was productive enough to support a population of 25 million people.[34] The cornerstone of Mesoamerican cuisine was the tortilla, a flat maize griddlecake that could be folded around vegetables, chiles, or beans to form a taco. On festive occasions cooks molded their maize dough into elaborate confections such as tamales. These cakes wrapped in corn husks illustrate the common people's approach to culinary art. Instead of using expensive ingredients such as duck or deer, women created exquisite dishes by twisting and pleating the corn dough into delicate forms and spicing them with a variety of herbs and chiles.[35]

Pre-Columbian cuisine survived into the nineteenth century not only in isolated villages but also in Mexcio City. Immigrants had flooded from the countryside to the capital in the decades before independence and thousands of people, unable to find adequate housing, slept and ate in the streets.[36] The frugal peasant kitchen adapted easily to this precarious urban existence, since cooking required only a few simple utensils: a grinding stone to prepare the corn dough, a small griddle to cook the tortillas, and a ceramic pot for the beans. Women could set up small braziers on street corners and sell enchiladas and stews to passing pedestrians.[37] These curb-side kitchens became ubiquitous, prompting one official to complain that virtually every street and plaza in Mexico City had a resident cook.[38]

Foreign travelers remarked about the enormous variety of food available from vendors in the capital. Women wandered the streets with baskets of corn confections such as tamales, *quesadillas,* and *gorditas,* while men carried improvised ovens with pastries and *barbacoa* (barbecued meat). Fiestas provided the primary focus for Mexico's popular cuisine, as they had since the days of Moctezuma. In the week before Christmas, people exchanged food and drinks in *posadas,* festive reenactments of the holy family's search for shelter in Bethlehem.[39] All Souls Day or the Day of the Dead was another popular holiday on which adults offered ritual foods to departed relatives while children devoured candy skeletons.[40] The most spectacular celebration of the year came during Holy Week, when great crowds converged on the capital from distant villages and ranches. Throngs of people danced through the streets, guzzling fruit drinks and devouring ice cream in a movable feast of popular cuisine.[41]

Although the wealthy often objected to the spectacle of dirty, half-naked people congregating around curb-side cooking pots, in many central nineteenth-century Mexico City locales, such as the Street of San Juan and the Plaza of San Pablo, improvised restaurants were renowned for their superb dishes.[42] Politicians and intellectuals such as Mariano Otero and Guillermo Prieto also visited taverns to buy quesadillas and *carnitas* from vendors whose cooking fires filled the unventilated buildings with smoke. These saloons often owed their reputations more to the tasty food than to the quality of their drinks. Discriminating diners favored the enchiladas served at the bars of "Uncle Juan Aguirre" and "The Granny." Plebeian foods also invaded many of the wealthiest homes of the capital as respectable women sent their maids out to buy barbacoa and tamales off the streets.[43]

Mexicans of all classes consumed Indian foods, but the process of modernization brought increasing attempts to restrict this popular cuisine. Authorities launched ongoing campaigns against the traffic hazard of street vendors.[44] Sanitary regulations also restricted the sale of vegetables and mushrooms by small-time merchants, but these proclamations were invariably repealed because of the popular outcry.[45] Meanwhile, an alternative to lower-class cuisine appeared in the form of restaurants catering to the elite's taste for French food. The Tivoli and Sylvain Daumont gained reputations as the most snobbish of the capital's establishments, although a more relaxed atmosphere prevailed in The Archbishop, managed by the redoubtable "Don Frijoles" (Mr. Beans).[46]

Published cookbooks reinforced elite disdain for lower-class foods. One book, supposedly "accommodated to the Mexican palate," contained not a single recipe for tamales, enchiladas, or quesadillas.[47] Another manual written in 1868 for a French audience explained that tortillas appeared on even the most affluent tables, but only in provincial cities. The recipes assured Parisian readers that sophisticated continental cuisine prevailed, at least in Mexico City.[48] A lack of written recipes does not prove that elites never ate popular foods. The Indian servants who did the cooking hardly needed instructions for making enchiladas, and virtually all were illiterate anyway. Nevertheless, cookbooks often contained positive condemnations of serving Indian foods. The most severe censure came from the *Diccionario de cocina* (Dictionary of cooking), published in 1845, which pointedly questioned the morals of any family that ate tamales—the food of "the lower orders."[49]

Many wealthy Mexicans wished to create the image that they ate exclusively French food, but a more accurate picture of class distinctions can be obtained by examining the context of meals. The 1831 *Cocinero mexicano* placed popular dishes such as enchiladas and tamales in the category of light brunches, eaten in the morning when there was no chance that strangers might come visiting.[50] Picnics in the country offered another suitable occasion for eating tamales.[51] A later edition of Galván's cookbook explicitly distinguished between the situations for elite and common foods. Among family members and intimate friends, it explained, one could safely eat stuffed chiles, mole poblano, or even enchiladas and tamales. But for formal brunches, and always at dinner, one should adhere to European customs.[52] These rules did not appear only in stuffy etiquette manuals. Guillermo Prieto, no stranger to lower-class enchilada-makers, described mole as excellent for intimate family gatherings but preferred the complex Spanish stew, *olla podrida,* for banquets.[53]

The superior social status of European foods became most obvious at year-end holidays. Christmas Eve supper, perhaps the most formal celebration of the year, followed a rigid tradition. The menu contained virtually nothing of domestic origin, from the appetizers of dried fruits and nuts to the Spanish wines and sherry. In a land blessed with superb fresh seafood, on this most important night Mexicans served *bacalao a la vizcaína* (dried cod Biscay style). The dish was attractive primarily as a demonstration of wealth; after spending outrageous amounts on the imported Norwegian fish, housewives also had to buy imported olives, capers, and olive oil for the traditional recipe.[54]

By 1900 Porfirian elites had come to view popular cuisine not only as unfashionable but also as a positive menace to society. Using the language of the newly developed nutritional science, Engineer Francisco Bulnes attributed Indian backwardness to the supposed inadequacy of maize-based diets.[55] Psychologist Julio Guerrero went further, stating that criminal behavior resulted from the "abominable" foods eaten by the lower classes.[56] Reform efforts therefore emphasized public cooking classes as a means of weaning the lower classes from corn. Not coincidentally, police inspectors led the recruiting campaign, an indication of the perceived importance of diet in maintaining social order. These classes, which were used to attract students to vocational schools, emphasized European models, such as modest French family cooking. Teachers inveighed against the "disgraceful habit" of eating spicy foods and advised their students to give up Mexican dishes in favor of English cooking—a drastic measure indeed.[57] Ultimately, these educational campaigns not only failed to transform the popular diet, they may actually have helped to undermine the domestic ideal they sought to uphold.

Cookbooks and the Creation of National Communities

Benedict Anderson has persuasively argued that modern nations were forged not through the development of tribal customs in the distant past but in the eighteenth century as a product of the Enlightenment. The standardization of vernacular languages through the spread of print and literature allowed people from different ethnic groups to imagine "national" communities that had not previously existed. Nineteenth-century Mexican elites certainly used instructional literature to attempt to mold a patriarchal nation based on Western European models. Cooking manuals contributed to this identity by assigning women to a domestic role within the nation and spelling out acceptable cultural (eating) practices. But standards of domestic morality and national identity created by male authors did not necessarily reach a complaisant female audience. Indeed, community cookbooks produced in Porfirian Mexico imagined an alternate vision of the nation and of the female place within it.[58]

Nineteenth-century Mexican standards of domesticity established an inherently unequal relationship, placing a woman under the authority of her husband. She could legitimately leave him only if he beat her *excessively,* and the law defined adultery as a crime for females but not for males. The culinary arts provided a natural medium for inculcating these gender roles because the kitchen was a primary focus of domesticity. Even women with servants spent a large part of each day making sure their family was well fed.[59] Professional cookbook authors explicitly supported the subservient role of women within the domestic world. In the introduction to one family manual, María Antonia Gutiérrez cautioned that a woman must "maintain a pleasant and agreeable home so that her husband would not abandon her."[60] Jacinto Anduiza elaborated this theme in an 1893 cookbook that attributed many of the worst domestic calamities to failures in the kitchen. He warned that men dissatisfied with their wives' cooking would seek their pleasures in taverns and bordellos.[61] Many upper- and middle-class women accepted—at least in public forums such as newspaper letter columns—the image of matrimony as a burden requiring constant work and self-abnegation on their part to assure their family's happiness and honor. Nevertheless, manuscript works and community cookbooks contained other possible constructions of the domestic sphere.

Even to begin expressing themselves, Porfirian women had to break a long-standing male monopoly on the cultural capital of literacy. Jean Franco has shown that during the colonial period clergymen exercised editorial control over female authors such as the poet Sor Juana Inés de la Cruz, and after independence liberal intellectuals took over the task of instructing women in their duties of citizenship.[62] By the end of the nineteenth century, however, works by female authors had begun to expand through Porfirian educational campaigns. One measure of this literacy came from the growing popularity of manuscript cookbooks, which had impressed foreign visitors as early as 1880. Fanny Gooch observed that affluent Mexican ladies took great pride in their handwritten volumes, although she noted that a hired cook often followed her own recipes and ignored her mistress's instructions.[63] Simone Beck, the famous French cooking teacher, recalled that her mother had likewise filled notebooks full of recipes even though a hired cook did the actual work.[64] In the 1890s, these manuscripts developed into community cookbooks as women came together to publish their recipes. Indeed, cookbooks may actually have helped spread writing skills by providing women with a medium for expressing themselves, a poetry familiar from their hours in the kitchen.

These nonprofessional books testify first to the sociability of Mexican women, for housewives carried on a brisk market in recipes as well as gossip. María Luisa Soto de Cossio, a rancher's wife in Hidalgo, included in her personal cookbook dishes from her grandmother, Aunt Gabriela, and a neighbor named Virginia. She also copied out recipes from the published *Recetas prácticas,* a volume she may have borrowed from a friend.[65] Manuscript cookbooks even served as albums recording family traditions, with dishes handed down from mothers and grandmothers. The fact that the older women were often illiterate added further to the value of their daughters' books. The exchange of cooking tips also reached beyond the extended family to become the focus for Catholic charities, which were one of the few legitimate female activities outside the home. A group of matrons in Guadalajara prepared a recipe manual to support the local orphanage, and several community cookbooks from Mexico City were dedicated to works such as cathedrals for Saint Rafael and Saint Vincent DePaul.[66]

In 1896, Vicenta Torres extended this community of cooks throughout the republic in her *Cocina michoacana,* a serialized guide to the cuisine of Michoacán. Printed in the provincial town of Zamora and sold by subscription, it began with local recipes submitted by women within the state. Nevertheless, she soon expanded her audience to reach cooks from all over the country. A woman from Celaya sent her recipe for Heroic Nopales (cactus lobes); from Guadalajara came a green chile lamb stew; a Mexico City matron offered her favorite meat glaze; and a reader in the border town of Nuevo Laredo even sent her Hens from the Gastronomic Frontier. By printing recipes from throughout Mexico, Torres provided the first genuine forum for a national cuisine. Contributors exchanged recipes with middle-class counterparts they had never met and began to experiment with regional dishes, combining them in new ways that transcended local traditions. Thus, women began to imagine their own national community in the familiar terms of the kitchen, rather than as an alien political entity formulated by men and served up to them in didactic literature.[67]

Torres and her collaborators conceived of their work as a community cookbook, first for the state of Michoacán and later for the entire nation, in which they shared in the common oral culture of the kitchen despite the distances separating them. Confident that readers were familiar with the basic techniques of cooking, they provided correspondingly vague instructions. One woman wrote simply to fry pork chops in "sufficient quantities of pork fat" until well done and to serve with "hot sauce to taste." A contributor to another community cookbook listed among the ingredients for mole poblano: "of all spices, a little bit." A recipe for stuffed chiles read: "Having roasted and cleaned [chiles], fill with cooked zucchini squash, onion, oregano, etc." It went without saying that cooks would adjust their seasonings to taste, for recipes served merely as written keys to a much fuller language of the kitchen.[68]

Certainly cooks adapted the recipes they found in cookbooks to fit their personal tastes. María Luisa did not simply copy verbatim the dishes presented in the *Recetas prácticas*; she simplified procedures, removed extraneous ingredients, and on one occasion found it necessary to change "stirring frequently" to "stirring continuously," a lesson perhaps learned at the expense of a ruined dinner.[69] Moreover, women read selectively, passing over impractical dishes such as Manuel Murguaia's absurd recipe for stuffed frijoles, which involved cooking beans—"but not too soft"— slicing them in half, inserting a bit of cheese, dipping them in egg batter, and frying them in oil.[70] Male chefs, for whom cooking provided a degree of status, may have delighted in such outlandish preparations, but housewives tended to view cooking as an everyday chore and therefore stressed practicality.

Women also used cuisine as a means of defining a uniquely religious version of the national identity. Torres and her correspondents, while not afraid to experiment with the techniques of foreign haute cuisine, emphasized national dishes that often held religious significance. Most prominent were the colonial moles, "those essentially American dishes," which they considered indispensable for festivals such as the Day of the Dead. Another culinary tradition with patriotic affiliations developed around the Virgin of Guadalupe. Having first appeared to an Indian in 1531, the saint gained a universal appeal in Mexico that was even recognized by anticlerical liberals such as Ignacio M. Altamirano. The Porfirian regime acknowledged the Virgin's power as a national symbol in 1895 by formally crowning her the patron saint of Mexico. Vicenta Torres paid homage a year later by inserting in her cookbook a recipe for *gorditas* (small corn griddlecakes) from the Villa de Guadalupe Hidalgo, the location of the Virgin's shrine.[71]

The Virgin's incorporation into the national cuisine illustrated not only the religious character of female patriotism but also the peculiar selection process that transformed local dishes into national symbols. Residents of Guadalupe Hidalgo made a living by selling the plump, sweet, silver-dollar-sized corn griddlecakes to visiting pilgrims. But among their own families they celebrated December 12, the Virgin's day, by eating barbecued goat with *salsa borracha* (drunken sauce). Nevertheless, the plaza gorditas ultimately gained recognition as the food of the Virgin, so that by 1926 a newspaper ran a cartoon showing a man refusing to accompany his plump wife (in Spanish, also a *gordita*) on a trip to the Virgin's shrine with the excuse: "Why take a *gordita* to *la villa?*"[72]

As in the case of gorditas, this exchange of recipes even began to cross established class and ethnic lines, perhaps because women worried less than men about the social stigma attached to Indian dishes. Unlike the usual practice of segregating enchiladas into a ghetto labeled "light brunches," the *Recetas prácticas* integrated these foods among other recipes for meats and vegetables. Another cookbook prepared by a charitable women's organization in Mexico City gave more recipes for enchiladas than for any other type of food.[73] Vicenta Torres made a virtue of including recipes of explicitly Indian origin, assuring readers that these "secrets of the indigenous classes" would be appropriate at any party. Along with tamales, she included *gordita* cordials, *pozole de Quiroga* (a hominy stew), and *carnero al pastor* (shepherd's mutton), but out of deference to her Porfirian audience, she carefully set them apart with the label "*indigenista.*"[74]

But care must be taken in interpreting this acceptance of native food as an indication that ties of gender were breaking down lines of class. Even middle-class women, after all, could generally count on a household servant to do the difficult work of grinding corn and chiles. Moreover, these same women shared with elites an admiration for French haute cuisine. Yet they also embraced a genuinely Mexican national cuisine based on colonial moles and even pre-Columbian tamales that were rejected by Eurocentric male elites. Being excluded from power themselves, perhaps women simply had less motivation to maintain the distinctiveness of creole culture. After all, they based their image of the nation on the Virgin of Guadalupe, a symbol shared with the Indian masses, rather than on the trappings of Western industrial society idealized by elite men.

A Mestizo Cuisine

Cuisine has fulfilled an important task in defining gender roles and national identity. Mexican leaders of the nineteenth century hoped to build a modern, patriarchal nation based on Western European models. Cookbooks provided a valuable means of indoctrinating women into this new order by emphasizing European dishes and disparaging Indian foods. In this way, intellectuals hoped to cleanse Mexico of the vestiges of its pre-Columbian past. Corn became a symbol for disorderly and unsanitary elements of society such as street people and backward villagers. Women were considered especially vulnerable to the immoral influences of the streets, hence the need to keep them locked away in the kitchen. Reformers focused particularly on lower class women in an attempt to improve family diets and morality and thereby transform the proletariat into imitations of the bourgeoisie.

The Porfirian order and its ideal of imported progress collapsed with the Revolution of 1910. From this social upheaval emerged a new group of leaders who sought to reformulate the sense of national identity and create an ideology with broad appeal to the Indian and mestizo masses. The revolutionaries launched a cultural campaign to legitimize themselves as representatives of the mestizo "cosmic race." They glorified the pre-Columbian past in murals, museums, and movies, and decried the deposed dictator as a toady to foreigners. The culinary expression of this new ideology was stated succinctly by a leading nutritionist, Rafael Ramos Espinosa. He formulated the simple equation that people who ate only corn were Indians, those who ate only wheat were Spaniards, while Mexicans were those people fortunate enough to eat both grains.[75]

Mestizo cuisine was not identified as a national standard until the 1940s, but the roots of its recognition lay in the Porfirian period. Cookbooks written after World War II, which offered Indian foods as a symbol of the Mexican nation, grew out of the community works produced at the turn of the century. The social gatherings of women sharing family recipes developed into organized cooking classes, and successful teachers in turn provided recipes for women's magazines and published cookbooks of their own. Their ties to oral culture nevertheless remained close, as can be seen from the hospitable author who invited readers to her Mexico City home for further instruction.[76] The most prominent teacher, Josefina Velázquez de León, traveled throughout the republic, holding cooking classes and collecting regional recipes. She published more than 150 cookbooks exalting tamales and enchiladas as culinary manifestations of Mexican nationalism. Her audience came from the rapidly growing middle class, the wives of businessmen and professionals who shared a vision of the mestizo nation. Although stark inequalities remained between rural and urban diets, maize had finally regained its place at the Mexican banquet table.[77]

Laura Esquivel's novel once more provides an apt metaphor for the transformation of Mexican cuisine and society. After the death of her mother, Tita turns down a respectable marriage to an American doctor in order to carry on an illicit affair with her Mexican lover. In the same way, Mexicans have begun to give up the slavish imitation of foreign models and show pride in their Indian heritage. Foreign influences certainly persist, with American fast food displacing French haute cuisine as a modern status symbol. Nevertheless, the Indian dishes scorned by nineteenth-century elites have been enshrined as the national cuisine. Pozole, formerly a "secret of the indigenous classes," now serves as the symbol of Guadalajara's cooking. And tamales, once the food of the "lower orders," have become the heart of the country's haute cuisine. Tita learned "the secrets of love and life as revealed by the kitchen"; modern Mexican women followed that same path to define their national identity.

Cooking, Community, Culture:
A Reading of
Like Water for Chocolate
Cecelia Lawless

Laura Esquivel has written an unclassifiable work that simultaneously breaks and brings together boundaries of genre so as to concoct something new in Mexican literature. *Like Water for Chocolate: A Novel in Monthly Installments with Recipes, Romances, and Home Remedies,* or in the original Spanish, *Como agua para chocolate: Novela de entregas mensuales con recetas, amores y remedios caseros*[1] is a mixture of community recipe book, how-to household book, socio-political and historical documentation of the Mexican Revolution, psychological study of male/female as well as mother/daughter relations, gothic narrative, and ultimately, an extremely readable novel.

In the following pages I would like to explore the culinary aspects of this popular Mexican novel. In linking the act of narration and the act of cooking, this novel doubles as a community cookbook. The novel intrigues me because it equates cooking and eating with both a sense of self and a sense of community. Like community cookbooks, which so often cross and collapse formal borders and share some characteristics of auto-

biography, history, etiquette, and folklore texts, this novel crosses boundaries as well. It collapses borders—those between fiction and instructive
cookbook; reading about food and wanting to eat food; woman as pro-
vider of sustenance and woman as object of consumption. Indeed, rewriting and rethinking borders is a primary focus of this text. *Like Water for
Chocolate* takes place along the Mexican American border, so that the setting underscores the novel's exploration of the limitations of the woman's
role in the kitchen, and its movement between the forms of novel and
community cookbook.

My interest in *Like Water for Chocolate* lies in the very basic beginnings
of questioning and uncovering—"cooking-up"—the layers of possibility
that this expansion of cookbook into novel presents. In essence, every
analysis of literary work acts as a recipe that has its roots in the Latin
recipere, which implies an exchange, a giver and a receiver. Lisa Heldke points
out that "foodmaking . . . tends to invite us to see itself as a 'mentally
manual' activity, a 'theoretical practical activity'—a 'thoughtful practice.'"[2]
Heldke's choice of words demonstrates a collapsing of boundaries between
theory and practice where cooking can act as a potential site for this kind
of reconstructive thought process. As literary critics we wish to stimulate
the mental palates of our readers so as to share our thoughts and create a
dialogue for the exchange of intellectual nourishment. In the work at hand,
I will experiment with various theoretical ingredients and ground this
essay in the pivotal question: How does this cookbook/novel participate
in the act of creating community among its readers?

Food exerts a powerful force in defining a cultural milieu; it commands societal attention, both utilitarian and artistic.[3] The hunting, gathering, and preparation of food is often a shared endeavor in a community.
In particular, cooking, with all its creative potential, can become a revela-
tion of not only the cook's identity but can point beyond to his or her
community. In her studies of culinary autobiographies, Anne Goldman
asserts that the "very domestic and commonplace quality of cooking
makes it an attractive metonym for culture . . . presenting a family recipe
and figuring its circulation within a community of readers provides a metaphor nonthreatening in its apparent avoidance of overt political discourse
and yet culturally resonant in its evocation of the relation between the
labor of the individual and her conscious effort to reproduce familial
traditions and values."[4]

Food and its preparation is often a mere excuse for bringing a community together. As George Booth points out, "a meal in Mexico seems to be primarily social, with alimentation taking a back seat."[5] Certainly this association between food and sociability is a strong factor in *Like Water for Chocolate*, where constant slippage occurs between the narrative and cookbook discourses of the text. This novel demonstrates a particular Latin quality that encodes dining as a rite of eating, speaking, *and* narrating about food. As you eat, you tell stories of other great gastronomic moments. Eating and storytelling become intertwined. In such a way, food operates on various levels and rarely ceases to act as a mode of communication, a base for community. To share a meal with someone is always more pleasant than to eat alone, and in *Like Water for Chocolate* the cooks prepare delicacies for family and social gatherings, and ultimately for the readers.

The tradition of sharing recipes in Mexico has been predominantly oral. Perhaps because of that oral tradition, Mexican cooking has welcomed experimentation and incorporated hybrid methods and ingredients, combining the European with the indigenous in a culinary outcry of freedom against the limitation of written rules. Although recipe books do not have a long tradition in Mexico, Bernardino de Sahagún, *Historia general de las cosas de Nueva España*, and Bernal Díaz del Castillo, *Historia verdadera de la conquista de la Nueva España*, are indispensable sixteenth-century records of the rituals and intricacies of the cooking and eating habits of the pre-Hispanic Aztecs in Mexico.[6] These texts demonstrate that food preparation has a long and generous history in Mexico. In the nineteenth century, community cookbooks became a fashionable expression of culinary artistry and an endeavor to link Mexican nationalism with European elitism. But these cookbooks were aimed at a very specific literate audience. Only in the past two decades, however, have popular cookbooks really appeared on the Mexican market. Today such diverse titles as *Así es la comida* (literally, Thus is food), *Técnicas culinarias* (Culinary techniques), and *Breviario del mole poblano* (Study of mole poblano [a national dish]) can easily be found in bookstores.[7] This history contrasts with Europe where cookbooks were among the earliest printed books,[8] and with the United States, where cookbooks were considered part of the reading repertoire necessary for colonial and pioneer women. *Like Water for Chocolate* also serves to personalize and individualize the vast repertoire of Mexican culinary dishes, as it mixes modern gustatory pleasures with a sense of specifically indigenous Mexican ingredients.

For upwardly mobile North Americans, food preparation and consumption are often viewed as leisurely activities rather than as diligent work or a mere means of survival. In fact, during the past decade among a certain class of people, food preparation has taken on a quality of sophisticated trendiness, demanding money, time, and superficial knowledge of exotic recipes from Thailand, Ethiopia, the Tex-Mex region, and so on. As in past centuries, culinary boundaries begin to collapse to create a more globalized culinary community. In sharing recipes across the borders of literature and academia, Susan Leonardi claims that she and other cooks participate in a practice uniting women across social barriers.[9] But the art of cooking is produced within a certain social context and so encodes a political problematic that needs to be discussed. Cooking, viewed as manual and everyday labor, automatically becomes associated with and assigned to those people marginalized by class, gender, and race. Although dictated by place, class, or economics, food can become a common language for all through need and hunger.

Like Water for Chocolate tells the story of three sisters, the youngest of whom, Tita, is destined by family tradition to cook for and look after her mother. Because of her enforced celibate destiny, Tita's one and only love, Pedro, cannot marry her. Instead, Mamá Elena suggests that he marry the oldest sister, Rosaura. He accepts this proposal as a way to live under the same roof as Tita. Right up to the last chapter, the plotline follows with unnerving accuracy the recipe for a gothic novel. Here is Eve Sedgwick's summary of the European gothic; note how she manipulates the same "you" address and implicit command mode that a typical recipe would use: "You know the important features of its mise en scene: an oppressive ruin, a wild landscape, a Catholic or feudal society. You know about the trembling sensibility of the heroine and the impetuosity of the lover. You know about the tyrannical older man [woman] with the piercing glance who is going to imprison . . . them. You know something about the novel's form: it is likely to be discontinuous and involuted, perhaps incorporating tales within tales, changes of narrators, and such framing devices as found manuscripts or interpolated histories."[10] The introduction of food in *Like Water for Chocolate* serves to subvert or at least parody these very conventions. In spite of many troubles—a brush with insanity, the jealousy of her sister, repression by her mother—Tita manages, through her cooking, to develop her own language and sense of self, combining erotics with independence.

Thus the novel challenges a conventional kind of classification, such as the gothic, and the traditional emplotment of Mexican women's lives in order to highlight an already existing community of hardworking and creative female cooks who rely on the indigenous recipes of Mexico for self-expression.

While reproducing and simultaneously subverting a traditional and easily accessible plotline, and while foregrounding Mexican nationalism through indigenous ingredients, Esquivel creates an experimental novel with historical echos, exemplified in her use of monthly installments—*folletines*. Each chapter begins with a title page that includes the author's name. The next page outlines the recipe of the month's ingredients and, on the following page, the narrative begins with a "preparation" (Manera de hacerse) and proceeds with the traditional third person impersonal voice of a cookbook. "Place five egg yolks, four whole eggs, and the sugar in a large bowl"[11] (En una cacerola se ponen 5 yemas de huevo, 4 huevos enteros y el azúcar).[12] This signifier "se," the impersonal "one," shifts from one writer or reader to a projected community of cooks and diners. The recipe continues with intermittent dashes and sprinkles of Tita's story. Each chapter ends with the promise of another recipe. This is a popular strategy for enticing the reader, often used in Mexican *fotonovelas* (photonovels) and the avidly consumed *libros semanales* (weekly books).[13] The narrative of Tita is embedded in that of the food. These detailed recipes, which sometimes start in ways unusual for Western readers, such as how to rear and prepare a turkey for *mole de guajolote*, combine with the tantalizing story of Tita. Cooking and life intermingle and become so closely blended that just reading the title of each recipe evokes the flavor of Tita's story.

The narrative of *Like Water for Chocolate* itself becomes a kind of recipe—a how-to-book on surviving a mother's tyranny, finding love in the midst of familial and social struggle, returning to a paradisaical home, or building a community. Is this a cookbook or a novel? In Mexican bookstores, *Like Water for Chocolate* appears on the shelves with best-sellers *and* in the area designated for cookbooks.[14] Once more the text plays with the supposed importance of established boundaries. Esquivel superimposes a romantic narration upon the enlarged semiotic field of the cookbook to blur literary lines. Combining the familiar motifs of recipes and the romance she defamiliarizes cultural territory to create ambiguity. Such ambiguity of traditional feminine territory acts as a point of entry for readers—

a place to construct a sense of self and simultaneously a place that offers a potential "recipe" for community.

Read as a cookbook/novel (with the stress on cookbook), *Like Water for Chocolate* provides a cultural poetics that is defined by an interplay of voices combined with taste and aroma. In effect, the text overthrows a visual paradigm for a sensual one. Western thought has relied heavily on the visual to create distance between the subject and the object,[15] so that to interject other senses such as taste, touch, and smell, all vital to the cooking process, radically revises traditional ways of "seeing" and thinking. In this way *Like Water for Chocolate* becomes a performative culinary memoir that encourages its use as novel *and* cookbook. At both of these narrative levels the reader can almost enter the text at will. Particularly when assembling the recipes, the reader/cook/bricoleur[16] can follow the exact measurements and directions to reproduce an invariant, unchanging product, or working within dimensions of previously learned structures, produce something new. The use of the impersonal *se*, one, potentially refers to Tita the protagonist and to the reader simultaneously. Implicitly, then, the inclusiveness of the subject "se" reaches out to others in the cooking community.

This community includes both Mexicans and non-Mexicans (we should not forget the extraordinary popularity of this text both inside and outside of Mexico). This community cookbook, like its nineteenth-century predecessors, emphasizes the labor involved in producing various recipes; but unlike earlier cookbooks, *Like Water for Chocolate* stresses the reproduction of the specifically Mexican cultural cooking practice. However sentimentalized and romantic the surrounding storyline may be, this combined cookbook/novel insists on a historically grounded sense of cultural specificity. This emphasis on ethnicity provides Tita with the authority to speak against the potential politics of assimilation by America. Thus, in its doubling as community cookbook and novel, *Like Water for Chocolate* empowers the main protagonist, Tita, against any invasive forces. I think that this aspect unconsciously contributes to the popularity of the text (and film) because it metamorphoses an everyday, supposedly non-threatening, activity such as cooking. Cooking in *Like Water for Chocolate*, and eating, and documenting the cooking and the eating give an individual and a whole community a powerful sense of identity.

In teaching both the novel and the film in undergraduate courses I have witnessed firsthand the effect that the text has on its audience and its potential to provide a base for community building. Students want to share their recipes, tell their own stories of grandmothers' and aunts' recipes and love lives. This enthusiasm for the genre has led students to make testimonial videos of their families' histories as well as compile their own cookbooks, create poems, and so on. Even though few of these students come from Mexico, as a result of working with Esquivel's text, they have developed a new sense of their own national identities and a new level of self-assertion, inspired by Tita and her story. In this way, the reading of *Like Water for Chocolate* has instilled in students a form of solidarity and a sense of community. Cooking foregrounds Tita's Mexican ethnicity. In his ethnographic studies Michael Fischer points out that ethnicity "is not something that is simply passed on from generation to generation, taught and learned . . . [rather the] process of assuming an ethnic identity is an insistence on a pluralistic, multidimensional, or multifaceted concept of self: one can be many different things."[17]

As Tita's sense of self and her creative development as a cook grow through the action of the novel, so too do the novelistic and cookbook narratives reach out toward a sense of community that will nurture her. This community, in part formed through the sympathetic audience reading and cooking her recipes, in part composed by the other female cooks in the novel, is achieved, like an autoethnographic record, through a "complex series of linguistic maneuvers required to locate the self with respect to a sense of community and ethnic traditions."[18] In *Like Water for Chocolate* these linguistic strategies issue from the recipes themselves, for recipes can serve as the "conscious and careful work necessary to maintain and reproduce such cultural practices as a means of authorizing the subject."[19] The cookbook/novel can produce the means to more than material nourishment, it may reproduce as well those cultural practices and values that provide a community with a means of self-definition and survival. Recipes, then, articulate or voice Tita *and* they embody her: they create a communal subject as well as an individual authority. These recipes also participate in the formation of her identity as a young Mexican woman, from a particular class, and with a particular stigma—as the youngest daughter she is destined by family tradition to serve as cook and caretaker for her mother until death. Tita thus stands out as different from her two sisters, cut off from a sense of community with them. She is trapped, unable to completely identify with mother, sisters, or the Indian cooks around her. The question remains whether through these same identifying recipes she can break free from an assigned self to form her own sense of self. To achieve this she must find and have the support of a strong community. Until Tita acknowledges this need for community she can fall into the trap of recipe-sharing that does not include a dialectical give and take. Debra Castillo points out this aspect of recipes and cooking in the preface of her book on Latin American women writers: "The recipe serves as an index of female creative power; it also describes a giving of self to appease another's hunger, leaving the cook weakened, starved."[20]

While confined to the kitchen, Tita has drawn strength there from the community of Indian women in her life who have taught her to see ghosts and read recipes that others have trouble deciphering. At one point, her sister Gertrudis, now a revolutionary general, tries to complete one of Tita's desserts, *torrejas de nata*. Gertrudis knows the vocabulary of military maneuvers, but the language of the recipe is completely foreign to her: "Gertrudis read this recipe as if she were reading hieroglyphics. She didn't know how much sugar was meant by five pounds, or what a pint of water was, much less what this ball business was"[21] (Gertrudis leía la receta como si leyera jeroglíficos. No entendía a cuánta azúcar se refería al decir cinco libras, ni qué era un cuartillo de agua y mucho menos cuál era el punto de bola).[22] For the first and only time in the text a man, Gertrudis's faithful bodyguard, Treviño, enters the kitchen to help with the cooking. Like Gertrudis, he knows nothing about food preparation, but with the aid of a gastronomic dictionary they are able to figure out the process, and the dessert is a success. Gertrudis cannot understand her sister's recipe because she participates at a different level of discourse—fighting in the revolution, taking part in the larger stage of Mexican history. Rather than marry or stay in the home she has expanded her gender identity to become a revolutionary soldier; in doing so she is no longer at ease in the kitchen and has lost touch with women's voices, as embodied in Tita's recipe. The legacy from Mexico's strict nineteenth-century society cannot provide her with the space in which to cook *and* fight; the traditionally private (female) and public (male) realms have not come together for Gertrudis. Ironically in this instance, the revolutionary woman who has left home, commanded troops, and killed people still remains dependent on a man and on man's words for help in the kitchen. In contrast, Tita has no need of dictionaries, icons of the patriarchal written word, because she has been raised by Nacha, the Indian cook of the house, and thus comes from a different community, one based on oral knowledge.

Nacha, who is in her eighties, dies near the beginning of the novel but in times of crisis appears to Tita to help her and functions as a good mother substitute in contrast to the bad biological mother, Mamá Elena.[23] Although marginalized as Indian women, Nacha, Chenca, and Luz del Amanecer, play vital roles in Tita's life: they act as a formative community for her. These are the women who aid, teach, and encourage Tita's cooking skills, and they accomplish this through their presence, not through a logocentric position. This physical and spiritual presence falls into the traditional Mexican cooking apprenticeships described by Jose Luis Loredo:

> In our country culinary technique is still studied through a hands-on apprenticeship rather than a systematic and intellectual teaching. The most common form of learning is to attach oneself to people with more experience and to try to capture their 'secrets' instead of receiving knowledge from a more formal source. Recipe books generally are collections of recipes whose memorization could not awaken or stimulate the interest of either student or teacher.[24]
>
> [En nuestro país, la técnica culinaria se estudia todavía más a través de un aprendizaje empírico y manual que mediante una enseñanza sistemática e intelectual. La forma más común es colocarse al lado de una persona con mayor experiencia y tratar de captar sus 'secretos', en vez de recibir los conocimientos en forma ordenada. Los libros de cocina son en general colecciones de recetas, cuya memorización no podría despertar o estimular el interés ni del alumno, ni del profesor.][25]

In *Like Water for Chocolate* the culinary "secrets" are made public. And while *Like Water for Chocolate* enforces an idea of culinary apprenticeship that favors human contact over textbook learning, it simultaneously functions as a text that disproves its own premise by stimulating an interest and joy in cooking for its audience, as witnessed by the popularity of both the novel and the film in Mexico and abroad.

Like Water for Chocolate as film and text has been avidly consumed by its audiences. I would like to suggest that there exists a direct connection between reader reception and the concept of community-building. As noted by the *New York Times* in August 1994, the film version has been the most popularly received of any Latin American film in the history of the United States.[26] This film, directed by Alfonso Arau, Laura Esquivel's former husband, appeared after the book publication and at a particularly uneasy moment in U.S.-Mexico relations. The visual impact of seeing a tightly produced, "comfortably" magic realist story from Mexico was very propitious for American politicians dealing with the possibly negative effects of the recently passed North American Free Trade Agreement (NAFTA). In a sense, the film and the book helped to allay the fears of ordinary Americans who viewed Mexicans as gobbling up displaced American jobs. Instead, they saw attractive Mexican characters merely consuming large amounts of food. Relations with the United States, especially as evoked in the film, are cordial and nonconflictive. The language barrier appears as an almost nonexistent issue since most of the major Mexican characters in the film are bilingual. And although Gertrudis's biological father is a mulatto, the issue of race is visually ignored by the film since Gertrudis is played by a vividly blond actress. What we see instead is the implicit bridging of communities through the subtle "Hollywoodization" of a strongly Mexican story.

Although the second best-selling novel in Mexico in 1989, *Like Water for Chocolate* was not always well received by critics there. For example, Antonio Marquet, writing in *Plural,* is quite disparaging:

> The defects of the novel are very evident (actually it brings together all the typical elements of 'popular literature'): it is simplistic, Manichean; moreover, the novel appeals to an infantile sense of logic, it is plagued by banal conventionalisms, devoid of any definite stylistic intention, and has no other aspiration than that of being trendy.[27]
> [Los defectos de la novela son muy evidentes (en realidad reúne todos los elementos típicos de la 'literatura popular'): es simplista, maniquea; en ella hay, además, una lógica que pretende ser infantil, está plagada de convencionalismos banales, despojada de una intención estilística definida y no tiene otra aspiración que ser novedosa.][28]

Even though some of these points may be well taken, Marquet describes in exaggerated detail the negative aspects of the novel. Nevertheless, *Like Water for Chocolate* is "novedosa," and it attracts an unusually large reading public, particularly female readers. For traditional critics though, this appeal to and popularity with the female audience in Mexico only emphasizes the "low" cultural quality of the novel. However, popular response to *Like Water for Chocolate* demonstrates that there exists a female community of readers that could potentially be rather powerful in their numbers and buying power, and this community inspires fear in many sectors of Mexican society.

Like Water for Chocolate as film and text has been consumed by a large public in and outside of Mexico. In the act of experiencing an expansion of their cultural horizons—either historical, geographical, or culinary—a "community" of viewers / readers has been created. For some time in the United States and in Mexico, and I am sure in other places as well, talk about *Like Water for Chocolate* flourished. Although a form of American cultural imperialism may be at work (particularly in the film), the discussions the film and text have generated, in which people recognize the romanticizing of Tita and Mexico in a golden primitive past, may actually discourage a form of critical imperialism. In contrast to the film, for example, the cookbook / novel can be approached as more "writerly": because of the actual recipes included in the text, the reader becomes a producer rather than mere consumer of film / text.[29] Indeed, I would argue that both film and novel place "on the table" expanded forms of communication for potential present and future communities through the visual and written displays of culinary virtuosity. Communities can come about through talking about food and sharing gastronomic pleasures as well as through the communal eating of food.

Tita communicates with Nacha, Luz del Amanecer and Chenca through the recipes that she learns or shares with them. All of these women are superlative cooks. Part of their talent lies in their openness to experimentation with innovative ingredients. Experimentation carries through at the level of narrative and cookbook as well, for *Like Water for Chocolate* functions without a sense of closure. This lack of ending, a continual call for openness, invites the creation of an inclusive community. As Susan Leonardi points out, "the social context of recipe sharing results in a loose community of women that crosses the social barriers of class, race, and generation."[30] This adage can apply to fictional characters as well as to critics. *Like Water for Chocolate* seduces us into trying the recipes and following the storyline. This invitation to reproduce the recipes and continue the story lays a foundation for community-building. It also calls attention to the boundaries inherent in sharing culture. The bringing together of novelistic and cookbook narratives leads readers to question the conflations and distinctions between the community constructed within the text itself and the community of readers created outside it. In this sense *Like Water for Chocolate* also serves as a point of departure for a theoretical model regarding women and their place in Latin American culture; that is, within the literary object one can find the pleasures of fiction as well as strategies for theory.[31]

In *Like Water for Chocolate* the kitchen, for example, metamorphoses into a productive site for the discourse of the triply marginalized—the Indian, the servant, the woman. The cultural production of a recipe takes place within the zone of a kitchen where the woman appears as producer instead of merely reproducer. As we have seen, the kitchen is a site of production of self, even though traditionally it is seen as an enclosing prison. Through a discourse of commands, the women in *Like Water for Chocolate* break out of the ideological constraints of the kitchen as "women's space." Rather than a constraint, the kitchen here serves to open into other sites or becomes converted from a colonized space into one of possibility. Josefina Ludmer writes:

> It is always possible to have a space from which you can practise that which is prohibited in other spaces; it is always possible to annex other areas and to set up other territories. And this practice of transfer and transformation reorganizes the given sociocultural structure.[32]
> [Siempre es posible tomar un espacio desde donde se puede practicar lo vedado en otros; siempre es posible anexar otros campos e instaurar otras territorialidades. Y esa práctica de traslado y transformación reorganiza la estructura dada, social y cultural.][33]

The apparent limitation of the kitchen becomes transformed into knowledge that is enriched by cooking, as so eloquently expressed by Sor Juana, a historical mouthpiece for Tita: "What could I not tell you, my Lady, of the secrets of nature I have discovered while cooking! That an egg holds together and fries in fat or oil, and that, on the contrary, it disintegrates in syrup. That to keep sugar liquid, it suffices to add the tiniest bit of water in which a quince or some other fruit has soaked. But, Madam, what is there for us women to know, if not bits of kitchen philosophy? . . . And I always say, when I see these details: If Aristotle had been a cook, he would have written much more.[34]

Sara Castro-Klarén also speaks of Latin American women's need for a site of articulation: "The search, therefore, is not for identity but rather for a space from which we can speak"[35] (La busqueda, por tanto, no es identidad sino de un espacio desde el cual podemos hablar).[36] That space, as the title of the volume in which Castro-Klarén's article appears tells us, is in the kitchen, with "la sartén por el mango" (literally, the frying pan by its handle), "ready to start cooking." The kitchen can powerfully embody this space of articulation when there exists a community to support, maintain, and continue the innovation or renewal of tradition.

Tita's kitchen, therefore, becomes a zone of transformation where the woman rebels against the colonizing aspects of the traditional kitchen. And here I use the word "colonize" under the guidance of Chandra Mohanty, who argues that "however sophisticated or problematic its use as an explanatory construct, colonization almost invariably implies a relation of structural domination, and a suppression—often violent—of the heterogeneity of the subject in question."[37] In other words, although Tita finds herself in the traditional site of the kitchen, where women have been domestically relegated, she sets up her own territoriality. Some argue that herein lies the power of women who do "reign" from their kitchens. I would contend though that to be shunted somewhere by a patriarchal force and then claim it as a source of power is not enough. Instead, Tita, from her traditional position as cook and spinster, uses the kitchen *and* the recipe to expand the confines of the site and to set up her own discursive territoriality from which to voice herself as subject. She makes the private become a realm for the public by sharing her recipes with those in the house and outside of it, as well as with the readers of her story. Through the reusing of space—the kitchen—and language—the recipe—Tita builds community.

The community of cooks in *Like Water for Chocolate* stands in contrast to the shifting foundations of home and family evoked in the cookbook/novel. Esquivel presents the story as narrated by a cook to show the longevity of the recipe and its power to tell a story. But in Esquivel's process of deterritorializing a traditional feminine space,[38] the nondisputed concepts of home and family lose their stability. For example, the De la Garza ranch house, feudal in all its trappings, appears to act as a region of refuge for this family of women. Traditional moral rights and spiritual bonds to the particular territory of the home appear to be acknowledged even during the violent times of the Revolution. A detailed account is given of how Mamá Elena defends her house from voracious revolutionary soldiers through her forceful rhetoric and her steely gaze, which subdues even the captain of the troops. In a later episode, however, when Mamá Elena is attacked and left a paraplegic and a female servant is raped, the text dismisses the scene quickly in a brief paragraph.[39] The sacred space of home has been violated, women and food have been consumed, but the story must go on for there remain more recipes to disclose. In thus displacing the traditional importance of the home site with the privileging of reading recipes, the text explicitly opens the doors of this closed concept of home, acknowledging that its appeal—safety, stability, and community—ineluctably slides into an appeal for totality, closure, and exclusion. Thus, the traditional concept of home as a positive female site that ignores the home's more sinister, prisonlike qualities, has been replaced in *Like Water for Chocolate* by a more open concept of a tenuous place disruptible by armies, jealousies, and destructive passions. The comforting idea of home linked to nostalgia for an integrated organic wholeness, so often present in romantic novels, is replaced by the literally organic food matter that is prepared by Tita for her family, friends, and other people like her.

Throughout the novel there exists a close relation between food and the body. While the looks and touches of amorous fire between Pedro and Tita come directly from a handbook of gothic tropes, the textual language infuses these tropes with a startling culinary force. Gestures of love—Tita and Pedro must invent a language of signs due to the constant vigilance of Mamá Elena—are communicated, consumed, and consummated through food. For example, when Pedro gives Tita her first rose, she thinks that the best way to preserve it would be to convert it into a special dish, *codornices en pétalos de rosas* (quail in rose petals). She makes this delicacy with such love, tenderness, and attention that the piquant dish animates everyone with generous, passionate feeling. This feeling, inspired by the meal, changes the life of Tita's sister, Gertrudis, who is overcome by physical rapture and runs naked through the countryside to be embraced by a soldier whom she soon exhausts with her desires. Radically, Tita herself has become incarnate in the food:

> A strange alchemical process had dissolved her entire being in the rose petal sauce, in the tender flesh of the quails, in the wine, in every one of the meal's aromas. That was the way she entered Pedro's body, hot, voluptuous, perfumed, totally sensuous.[40]
> [Su ser se había disuelto en la salsa de las rosas, en el cuerpo de las codornices, en el vino y en cada uno de los olores de la comida. De esta manera penetraba en el cuerpo de Pedro, voluptuosa, aromática, calurosa, completamente sensual.][41]

In this lavish description, food transforms Tita's body into the site of desire to be consumed; simultaneously, food articulates her desires. A new intermediary space has been created for the subject, Tita: "With that meal it seemed that they had discovered a new system of communication, in which Tita was the transmitter, Pedro the receiver, and poor Gertrudis the medium, the conducting body through which the singular sexual message was passed."[42] (Parecía que habían descubierto un código nuevo de comunicación en que Tita era la emisora, Pedro el receptor y Gertrudis la afortunada en que se sintetizaba esta singular relación sexual, a través de la comida.)[43] Ironically, it is the third party, Gertrudis, who benefits from this culinary/revolutionary language. Yet this incident also demonstrates that community is created by more than just two people; that is to say, for Tita to have the fullest possible effect on her beloved Pedro, the presence of a third party, Gertrudis, is needed. Food can be shared between two people, but when there are more present, particularly in a censored environment such as this one, additional people can create community, communication, and solidarity.

Like many gothic romances and/or event-oriented cookbooks, *Like Water for Chocolate* concludes with a wedding. And just as the recipes in the other chapters merge with the narrative in an almost seamless fashion, so here the reader is seduced into believing that we will witness the wedding of John Brown and Tita: "This wedding . . . had a special significance for her. For John too. He was so happy."[44] (Esta boda . . . tenía un significado muy especial para ella. También para John. Él estaba tan feliz.)[45] In fact, however, we find Tita once more in the kitchen, this time preparing an elaborate wedding feast for Esperanza, the daughter of Pedro and Rosaura, and Alex, the son of John Brown. During the wedding dance, when we are explicitly told that Tita is now thirty-six years old, Pedro (now a widower) finally proposes marriage. For a woman in her late thirties still to be unmarried in Mexico highlights that she is an old maid, rejected, or worse, a woman of ill repute. Yet, after so many years, it looks as if true love will conquer all. Then, because of the sensuous effect of Tita's food, all the guests quickly leave the ranch for love-making activities. Tita and Pedro find themselves alone together for the first time in their lives as a "legitimate" couple. Finally, Tita is no longer the *virgen/solterona* nor "the other woman."

They fall into each other's arms and Pedro dies consumed by happiness. His death occurs because, as John once explained to Tita, each person has a box of matches inside the body that can be lit one by one or that may disastrously all burn together: "If a powerful emotion should ignite them all at once they would produce a splendor so dazzling that it would illuminate far beyond what we can normally see . . . summoning us to regain the divine origin we had lost"[46] (si por una emoción muy fuerte se llegan a encender todos de un solo golpe producen un resplandor tan fuerte que ilumina más allá de lo que podemos ver normalmente . . . y nos llama a reencontrar nuestro perdido origen divino).[47] These loaded words— "nuestro perdido origen divino"—imply an ideal, original home, what Fredric Jameson has called a "utopian impulse" that represents a longing for a transformed world where men and women would live together harmoniously, a world based on the traditional female values of love, family, and community.[48] To join Pedro in death, to not be alone, Tita consumes many actual matches while thinking of passionate, explosive scenes with him. She bursts into flames that ignite one of the few things that she made for herself, a knitted quilt, and so the fire devours her and the whole ranch. Read traditionally, Pedro and Tita meet in the tunnel of light, reminiscent of the birth canal, to enter heaven, a final refuge—a final home.

This "happy" ending of the novel becomes quite problematic for a reader desiring some depiction of enlightened community-building. Tita turns her back on the world and on community in choosing to pursue a "home" with her beloved. This is one of the most seductive, dangerous, and commonly accepted criteria of the concept of home—lack of growth or change. We often forget that the home serves as a site that implies journey *and* arrival—a dynamic tension between leaving and returning.[49] Tita, however, falls into the clichéd trap of reaching for an idealized, utopian, static concept of home.

Until the last chapter / installment it appears that Esquivel wishes to subvert the Western, patriarchal view of the home as the interior / inferior space for women. With its complex depictions of the kitchen, recipes, and cooking as potential sites for building a discursive community of women capable of confronting systems of power and domination, *Like Water for Chocolate* appears to participate in a "homing" motion of entering the kitchen, through the cookbook discourse, and leaving the kitchen, through the narrative discourse. Instead, Tita sets the ranch and what it represents on fire by literally cooking herself—the ultimate female sacrifice of self. This is a consumption of the idea of home, not a consummation.[50] Ultimately, *Like Water for Chocolate* subverts the idea of home as interior / inferior space for women by actually devouring both the home as house and as woman.

The only thing that remains of Tita after the fire is a cookbook from which her great-niece reconstructs and narrates Tita's story. As in *One Hundred Years of Solitude*, the written word resists destruction. This time, though, the words of the cookbook represent a strong strain of *women's* writing. The secrets of cooking are passed on to the great-niece and to the reader—representing an act of trust in recipe-sharing. In this manner, although the ending of *Like Water for Chocolate* may seem like a betrayal, the survival of the text shows that in writing these recipes and in her romance Tita brings her private acts into the shared public domain of the reader.

Tita does follow her man even into death, but her story and her recipes supplement the traditional role of the romantic heroine. Her text confers a higher status and power to the traditionally devalued personal sphere of the kitchen. Through her recipes Tita provides us not only with a means to enter into Mexican life, she also invites us into the gourmet delights of her kitchen, her own territory. After the death of Mamá Elena, Tita converts this traditionally restrictive and oppressed site for women into a liberating, creative space so that we readers wish to try her recipes in our own kitchens. Just as Jean Franco demonstrates how certain words such as "mother" have been reconstructed through the activities of *las madres de la Plaza de Mayo*,[51] so Tita participates in a reconstruction of the kitchen and its tools as a positive site for change. A new domain appears in

Like Water for Chocolate, not a room of one's own, not a merely public or private self, not a domestic realm—it is a space in the imagination that accommodates the inside, the outside, and the liminal elements of in between—a site of community for those who read recipes and those who use them.

In *Like Water for Chocolate* the theory of recipes becomes actualized in the aftereffects produced by eating Tita's food: to merely read or dream up a recipe has little impact until the cook uses that recipe to transform food into flavorful dishes for the eater. The syntax of the recipe, its structure and its ultimate message, is founded on a series of commands. The (usually) impersonal addresser directs the addressee from a site of assumed knowledge where one of the cooking lessons, namely creativity, is ignored. The reader of *Like Water for Chocolate* will follow the given recipe, not necessarily improvise with the recipe.[52] Perhaps this explains the creativity and variety so well savored in Mexican cooking: precisely because there is a lack of tradition of cookbooks and written recipes, inventiveness has become part of the structure of sharing recipes through oral tradition within families. Tita, Nacha, Luz del Amanecer, Chenca, even Gertrudis participate in cooking as a starting point for inventiveness. For example, Gertrudis resorts to a dictionary and Luz del Amanecer mixes her indigenous knowledge with Spanish ingredients. These women create a dialogue with the recipe, they inject outside sources into a realm normally marked by closure to establish an interdisciplinary discourse.

Tita maintains the home through her cooking and household activities, so that she manages to fold the lives of family members into one another, in a very different manner from the chain of domesticity her mother had constructed. Tita's power, unlike Mamá Elena's, does not come from her "territoriality" or her attachment to the land and thus to nature. Rather, although Tita's realm has been reduced to the kitchen, her power over the domain of pots and pans and their secret ingredients affects almost all of those who eat from them. The accepted distinction of a passive feminine nature and male enterprise has been disturbed here. Within the bounds of the text, Pedro, the only man in charge on the ranch, hardly appears to work: we never see him in action. And except for an occasional medical visit, John Brown, the American, does not exhaust himself with work either. Instead, *Like Water for Chocolate* describes women's work and their thriftiness and inventiveness with the materials they have around them in confecting food, soap, diapers, and relationships, even in the midst of scarcities caused by the Revolution.

Cookbooks can be read as historical records of culture. It should not be forgotten that this novel does take place in a particular historical time with the Mexican Revolution in the background, during a period of bloodshed and violence. Yet, *Like Water for Chocolate* appears as a direct eulogy of Mexico and its culinary, familial traditions. The sense of history's pain and difficulty is erased by the keen nostalgia the text evokes and by the film's depiction of lush colors and glorification of appetizing food and love. Even though the mother directly feels the effect of the historical time when she is attacked, this family still represents a feudal landowning group whose suffering is minor in comparison to that of others. The very title of the text and the formatting of the book in *folletines* (installments) emphasizes the text's attempt at authenticity. Thus, *Like Water for Chocolate* represents food and its preparation as metonyms for the reaffirmation and maintenance of tradition. In light of the NAFTA treaty and relations between Mexico and the United States, it is politically useful and poignant that this text/film suggest that Mexico is quaint, old, and above all, not advanced, unthreatening.

Tita becomes such a good cook precisely because she puts herself, literally and figuratively, into what she prepares. I would argue that this merging of praxis and theory is an important aspect of community cookbooks. For example, when Tita is in the United States, far from her culture and her country, she loses the ability to speak. Only the flavor of a certain soup brings back memories of Tita's childhood and the soothing presence of Nacha. Tita is once more able to "rememorar" a recipe and with it, language again becomes possible. Such signs in *Like Water for Chocolate* as "woman," "kitchen," and "community," are in a process of shift in their presentation and in their reception. Luisa Valenzuela would point out that in this re-evaluation of a woman's space, language too is affected: "What we women will do, and are now doing, is to effect a radical change in the electrical charge of words. We are inverting their poles, making them positive or negative depending on our own needs and not following the rules of inherited, phallocratic language."[53] In *Like Water for Chocolate*, terms such as "cookbook," "gothic," "feminine," "home" are also redefined and re-molded in Esquivel's (post)modern attempt to create a place, a community from which her character Tita can speak.

At the same time, food and its language of recipes are traditionally considered a gendered discourse—the woman's domain, hence marginalized—and therefore not a discourse of empowerment. In her *PMLA* article of 1989, Leonardi voices the preoccupation of the female critic who wonders if her academic colleagues will question her intellectual abilities since she appears to have so much "extra" time to spend thinking, researching, and writing about food (let alone the time it takes to prepare): "Would the tensions that academic women face between the domestic and the professional make it more or less difficult for them to extend credibility toward a writer who begins with a recipe? . . . Do I erode my credibility with male academics by this feminine interest in cooking, cookbooks, and recipes?"[54] We need to explore this tension between gendered theory and practice, to dare to let go of our theoretical homes, systems of meaning, and political identities to realize a community of possibilities out of the *experience of displacement* where women often read, write, and work in the interstices of male culture. Esquivel's text experiments with precisely this problem.

Notes

Bound Together: Recipes, Lives, Stories, and Readings

1. *Our Sisters' Recipes,* ed. Nettie Kaufman (Pittsburgh, 1909).
2. Carolyn G. Heilbrun, *Writing a Woman's Life* (New York: Ballantine, 1988), 11.
3. Patrocinio P. Schweickart, "Reading Ourselves: Toward a Feminist Theory of Reading," in *Gender and Reading: Essays on Readers, Texts, and Contexts,* ed. Elizabeth A. Flynn and Patrocinio P. Schweickart (Baltimore: Johns Hopkins University Press, 1986), 56.
4. Elaine Showalter, "Common Threads," in *Sister's Choice: Tradition and Change in American Women's Writing* (Oxford: Oxford University Press–Clarendon Press, 1991), 147.
5. Ibid., 175.
6. As an example of this continuing process, see Patricia P. Buckler and C. Kay Leeper, "An Antebellum Woman's Scrapbook as Autobiographical Compo-

sition," *Journal of American Culture* 14 (1991): 1–8. My colleague Lisa Klein has presented papers on Renaissance women's samplers and other needlework as self-representation: "The Pious Needlewoman of the Renaissance" and " 'This so fayre example': Biblical Family Dramas in Seventeenth-Century English Needlework," delivered respectively at the 1992 SUNY-Binghamton conference, "Roles of Women in the Middle Ages," and at the 1994 Shakespeare Association of America seminar, "Material Girls: Women's Texts in the Seventeenth Century."

7. Susan S. Arpad, " 'Pretty Much to Suit Ourselves': Midwestern Women Naming Experience through Domestic Arts," in *Making the American Home: Middle Class Women and Domestic Material Culture 1840–1940*, ed. Marilyn Ferris Motz and Pat Browne (Bowling Green: Bowling Green State University Press, 1988), 13.

8. Sally L. Kitch, *This Strange Society of Women: Reading the Letters and Lives of the Woman's Commonwealth* (Columbus: Ohio State University Press, 1993), 242, 278.

9. Lillian Schlissel, *Women's Diaries of the Westward Journey*, 2nd ed. (New York: Schocken, 1992), 10.

10. While social mores of the past certainly dictated against women participating in public debate and publication, women were by no means locked out of America's literary business, even in the early and mid-nineteenth centuries. As Susan Coultrap-McQuin shows in *Doing Literary Business: American Women Writers in the Nineteenth Century* (Chapel Hill: University of North Carolina Press, 1990), "by the 1850s women were authors of almost half of the popular literary works," and "by 1872 women wrote nearly three-quarters of all of the novels published" (2). However, the same society that permitted their publications also denigrated these women authors for going beyond the bounds of "true womanhood" and gentility, and simultaneously, criticized their work for dwelling on domestic issues! (Ibid., 7–17.)

11. Karen J. Blair, *The Clubwoman as Feminist: True Womanhood Redefined, 1868–1914* (New York: Holmes & Meier, 1980), 3; Anne Firor Scott, *Natural Allies: Women's Associations in American History* (Urbana: University of Illinois Press, 1991), 2.

12. Robert Scholes, *Textual Power: Literary Theory and the Teaching of English* (New Haven: Yale University Press, 1985), xi.

13. Deane W. Curtin, introduction to *Cooking, Eating, Thinking: Transformative Philosophies of Food*, ed. Deane W. Curtin and Lisa M. Heldke (Bloomington: Indiana University Press, 1992), xiii.

14. Ibid.

15. Angela Little, "An Academic Ferment," *Journal of Gastronomy* 2 (1986): 24–25.

16. Curtin, introduction to *Cooking, Eating, Thinking*, xiv.

17. Lisa M. Heldke, "Foodmaking as a Thoughtful Practice," in *Cooking, Eating, Thinking,* ed. Curtin and Heldke, 203.

18. By "invention" I mean those choices that improvise or stylistically alter a given pattern or genre. To repeat exactly a pattern invented by another is certainly a choice, and it could be a choice laden with ideological positioning, but I wouldn't call it artistic invention.

19. Ann Romines, *The Home Plot: Women, Writing and Domestic Ritual* (Amherst: University of Massachusetts Press, 1992), 296.

20. Interdisciplinary studies have contributed to this legitimacy, I think. The growth of American Studies, Women's Studies, Cultural Studies, and Popular Culture have all allowed greater investigation of women's texts and activities previously isolated from serious study, along with greater acceptance of readings of all cultural products.

21. Margaret Cook, *America's Charitable Cooks: A Bibliography of Fund-raising Cook Books Published in the United States (1861–1915)* (Kent, OH: [privately printed], 1971).

22. Mary Douglas, *Food in the Social Order: Studies of Food and Festivities in Three American Communities* (New York: Russell Sage Foundation, 1984), 30.

23. Lynne Ireland, "The Compiled Cookbook as Foodways Autobiography," *Western Folklore* 40 (1981): 108, 109.

24. Ibid., 110–11.

25. Laura Shapiro, *Perfection Salad: Women and Cooking at the Turn of the Century* (New York: Farrar, Straus and Giroux, 1986), 14–15; 5.

26. Barbara Kirshenblatt-Gimblett, "Recipes for Creating Community: The Jewish Charity Cookbook in America," *Jewish Folklore and Ethnology* 9 (1987): 8–11.

27. Susan J. Leonardi, "Recipes for Reading: Pasta Salad, Lobster à la Riseholme, and Key Lime Pie," *PMLA* 104 (1989): 340–47.

28. Ilene Alexander, Suzanne Bunkers, and Cherry Muhanji, "A Conversation on Studying and Writing about Women's Lives Using Nontraditional Methodologies," *Women's Studies Quarterly* 3–4 (1989): 99–100.

29. I borrow this phrase from Ann Romines, whose *Home Plot* best helped me to place community cookbooks within a literary context.

"Tried Receipts": An Overview of America's Charitable Cookbooks

1. Gertrude Frelove Brebner, *The All-American Cook Book* (Chicago: Judy, 1922). This quotation is from the dedication. The title page further illuminates the Cause: "The proceeds from the sale of this book are to be devoted to the relief of disabled, needy and unemployed ex-service men and their dependent families. As far as is practicable, all work of preparing and selling the book is being done through the employment of ex-servicemen."

2. *Lord Fairfax's Kitchen. A Collection of Tried Recipes from Winchester Housekeepers* (n.p., n.d.). Margaret Cook, *America's Charitable Cooks: A Bibliography of Fund-raising Cook Books Published in the United States (1861–1915)* (Kent, OH: [privately printed], 1971) estimates that this was published in Winchester, Virginia, in 1892.

3. L. L. McLaren, *High Living* (San Francisco: Paul Elder and Company, 1904). This quote is from the preface by Edward H. Hamilton. A second edition of *High Living* appeared in 1906 immediately after the great San Francisco earthquake. The funds were then contributed to provide relief for earthquake victims.

4. *The Landmarks Club Cook Book* (Los Angeles: Out West Company, 1903). This quote is from the introduction by Charles F. Lummis.

5. *Massachusetts Woman's Temperance Union Cuisine* (Boston: E. B. Stillings & Co., 1878). This book was "published by the Ladies of the M.W.C.T.U., in Aid of the Fair, in Horticultural Hall, April 22, 1878."

6. See, e.g., Karen J. Blair, *The Clubwoman as Feminist: True Womanhood Redefined, 1868–1914* (New York: Holmes & Meier Publishers, 1980); Karen J. Blair, *The History of Women's Voluntary Organizations, 1810–1960* (Boston: G. K. Hall & Co., 1989) (a guide to sources, published as part of the G. K. Hall Women's Studies Publications); Sophonsiba Preston Breckenridge, *Women in the Twentieth Century: A Study of Their Political, Social, and Economic Activities* (New York: McGraw-Hill, 1933, rep. New York: Arno Press, 1972); Jane Cunningham Croly [Jennie June, pseud.], *The History of the Woman's Club Movement In America* (New York: Henry G. Allen and Co., 1898); Mary L. Ely and Eve Chappell, *Women in Two Worlds* (New York: American Association for Adult Education, 1938; Lori D. Ginzberg, *Women and the Work of Benevolence* (New Haven: Yale University Press, 1990); Janet Gordon and Diana Reische, *The Volunteer Powerhouse: The Junior League* (New York: Rutledge Press, 1982); Nancy A. Hewitt, *Women's Activism and Social Change, Rochester, New York, 1822–1872* (Ithaca, NY: Cornell University Press, 1984); Faith Rogow, *Gone to Another Meeting: The National Council of Jewish Women, 1893–1993* (Tuscaloosa: University of Alabama Press, 1993); Amos G. Warner, *American Charities. A Study in Philanthropy and Economics* (New Brunswick: Transaction, 1989) (a new edition with a new introduction by Mary Jo Deegan; originally published by Thomas Y. Crowell and Co. in 1894); Frank Dekker Watson, *The Charity Organization Movement in the United States* (New York: Macmillan, 1922); Mary I. Wood, *The History of the General Federation of Women's Clubs* (New York: History Department, General Federation of Women's Clubs, 1912).

7. Janice B. Longone and Daniel T. Longone, *American Cookbooks and Wine Books, 1797–1950* (Ann Arbor: Clements Library and the Wine and Food Library, 1984).

8. Sara M. Evans, *Born for Liberty: A History of Women in America* (New York: Free Press, 1989).

9. Madeline Lee, "Women Did What They Could," review of Evans, *Born for Liberty, New York Times,* August 20, 1989.

10. Margaret Cook, *America's Charitable Cooks: A Bibliography of Fund-raising Cook Books Published in the United States (1861–1915)* (Kent, OH: [privately printed] 1971).

11. The following is a sample of such fair-related cookbooks: *Helps for Young Housekeepers* (Fair Given by the Bethany Band of Merry Workers, San Francisco, 1875); *A Friend in Need* (St. Aloysius Church Fair, Washington, D.C., 1887); *The Ladies' Handbook* (Universalist Church Fair, Gardiner, Maine, 1886); *Grand Rapids Receipt Book* (Ladies' Fair, Congregational Church, Grand Rapids, Michigan, 1873); *Favorite Recipes* (Ladies of Art Booth, First Congregational Church Fair, Kansas City, Missouri, 1903); *Tested Recipes* (Fair in Aid of the Daughters of the Republic of Warner, New Hampshire, 1894); *Culinary Cullings* (Ladies Fair in Aid of Building Fund of YMCA, Newburgh, New York, 1883); and *Souvenir Cook Book* (Carnival and Fair of Harry Howard Hook & Ladder Co. and Reliance Engine & Hose Co., held in the New Firehouse, Port Chester, New York, 1907). And in Massachusetts: *Nantucket Receipts* (Fair for the New England Hospital for Women and Children, Boston, 1870); *Dedham Receipts* (Fair in Aid of Homeopathic Hospital, Boston, 1871, and also Fair in Aid of the Dedham Public Library, Dedham, 1871); *Massachusetts Women's Christian Temperance Union Cuisine* (Fair in Horticultural Hall, Boston, 1878); *Housekeeper's Assistant* (Coral Street Methodist Episcopal Church Christmas Fair, Worcester, 1878); *The Tried and True Cook Book* (Ladies Fair, Universalist Church, Worcester, 1881); *The Housekeeper's Friend* (Annual Fair and Festival, Methodist Episcopal Church, Dorchester, 1882); *The Household Friend* (Methodist Episcopal Church Loan Exhibit and Bazaar, Chelsea, 1883); *The Woman Suffrage Cook Book* (Festival and Bazaar, Boston, 1886); *The Ladies Delight* (G.A.R. Fair, Dorchester, 1886); *Crumbs of Comfort* (Ladies of the Housekeepers' Table, at a Fair held in honor of the First Universalist Church, Charlestown, 1888).

12. Mrs. Leslie R. Andrews, and Mrs. J. Reaney Kelly, *Maryland's Way. The Hammond-Harwood House Cook Book* (Annapolis, MD: Hammond-Harwood House, 1963).

13. *City Mission Cook Book* (Lawrence, MA: Women of Greater Lawrence, n.d.).

14. *Choice Recipes of the Mother's Club. Recipes by Twentieth Century Cooks* (Buffalo, NY: Mothers Club, 1913).

15. Linda Deziah Jennings, comp., *Washington Women's Cook Book* (Seattle: Washington Equal Suffrage Association, 1909).

16. Following is a sample of the diverse groups sponsoring fund-raising cookbooks: the Theo-broma Club (Montevallo, Alabama, 1901); the Bethany Band of Merry Workers (San Francisco, 1879); Helping Hand Club (New Almaden, California, 1890); Ladies' Sewing Circle (Arcata, California, 1902);

the Ten Minute Circle (Auburn, California, 1902); Ergatikan Circle (Fresno, California, 1905); Women's Work Society (Los Angeles, 1907); Young People's Society of Christian Endeavor (Oakland, California, 1907); Semper Fidelis Circle (Stockton, California, 1907); Sunshine Society (Santa Monica, California, 1910); Floral League (San Francisco, 1911); Twentieth Century Club (Berkeley, 1914); Philalethean Club (Montrose, Colorado, 1911); Whatsoever Circle (Torrington, Connecticut, 1889); the Flower Committee (Torrington, Connecticut, 1907); United Workers (Greenwich, Connecticut, 1910); Comfortable Society (Branford, Connecticut, 1914); New Century Club (Milford, Delaware, 1904); Standard Bearer's Society (Wilmington, Delaware, 1915); Fresh Air Fund (Washington, D.C., 1912); Progressive Culture Club (Titusville, Florida, 1910); Women's Committee for Industrial Work (Atlanta, Georgia, 1915); Monday Club (Quincy, Illinois, 1890); Shakespeare Club (Jerseyville, Illinois, 1895); Halcyon Society (Belleville, Illinois, 1900); Helpers Circle (Rock Island, Illinois, 1904); Mothers' Round Table (Woodlawn, Illinois, 1910); Associated College Women Workers (Chicago, 1912); Week End Club (De Kalb, Illinois, 1912); Star Society (Pekin, Illinois, 1914); Every Wednesday Club (Hampshire, Illinois, 1915); Cosmos Society (Greenfield, Indiana, 1906); the Mite Society (Bristol, Indiana, 1907); Working Girls' Association (Evansville, Indiana, 1910); Progressive Class (Fountain City, Indiana, 1914); Proteus Club (Des Moines, 1900); Pella's Dutch and American Housekeepers (Pella, Iowa, 1901); the You and I Club (Lawrence, Kansas, 1879); the Domestic Science Club (Hutchinson, Kansas, 1907); Willing Workers (Morrowville, Kansas, 1915); Free French Movement (New Orleans, 1900); Thursday Afternoon Whist Club (Portland, Maine, 1914); Clionaian Social and Dramatic Club (Baltimore, 1915); the Cooking Class of the Young Ladies' Saturday Morning Club (Boston, 1875); Women's Educational and Industrial Union (Boston, 1887); Knights and Ladies of Honor (Worcester, Massachusetts, 1887); Ladies of the Housekeepers' Table (Charlestown, Massachusetts, 1888); Pickle and Preserve Table Committee (Somerville, Massachusetts, 1888); Lend-a-hand Club (Barre, Massachusetts, 1894); the Thought and Work Club (Salem, Massachusetts, 1897); Association of Women Workers (West Roxbury, Massachusetts, 1910); the Loyal Workers' Society (Springfield, Massachusetts, 1914; Tuesday Ten (Grand Rapids, Michigan, 1898); Ramblers Club (Minneapolis, 1911); the Sojourner's Club (Kirksville, Missouri, 1915); "Home Workers" Society (Lewiston, Montana, 1902); Tabitha Society (Axtell, Nebraska, 1915); Ladies' Circle of Industry (Peterboro, New Hampshire, 1905); the Cake Committee (Orange, New Jersey, 1905); Financial Aid Society (Stanhope, New Jersey, 1906); Free Dispensary and Relief Association (Sing Sing, New York, 1887); the Reading-room Association (Pleasantville, New York, 1894); the Palm Strewers' Circle (New York, 1899); Baraca Society (Hornell, New York, 1907); Women's Poultry Club (Saratoga Springs, New York, 1909); Artistic Needle

Workers (Marshfield, Oregon, 1905); Busy Bees (Willoughby, Ohio, 1915); Croquet Club (Norristown, Pennsylvania, 1898); Belgian Relief Committee (Reading, Pennsylvania, 1915); Silver Thimble Society (Jackson, Tennessee, 1906); Woman's Literary Club (Barton, Vermont, 1902); Buds of Promise Class (Montpelier, Vermont, 1904); and the Tuesday Night Workers (Appleton, Wisconsin, 1887).

17. The author has served as a judge for these awards since their inception and as collection development consultant for the Tabasco library.

18. From the Statement of Purpose, Tabasco Annual Community Cookbook Awards entry form.

Cooking Up Stories: Narrative Elements in Community Cookbooks

1. Robert Scholes expands the notion of codes usefully in his *Textual Power: Literary Theory and the Teaching of English* (New Haven: Yale University Press, 1985): "The writer, the reader, and the text—all are coded: by language, the most comprehensive code, and by other social and institutional systems that can be described and understood in terms of the notion of code" (47). Inventions are those variations in a genre that produce style, novelty, uniqueness, "art."

2. Jay Clayton, *The Pleasures of Babel: Contemporary American Literature and Theory* (New York: Oxford University Press, 1993), 10.

3. Wallace Martin, *Recent Theories of Narrative* (Ithaca, NY: Cornell University Press, 1986), 82.

4. Susan S. Arpad, "'Pretty Much to Suit Ourselves': Midwestern Women Naming Experience through Domestic Arts," in *Making the American Home: Middle Class Women and Domestic Material Culture 1840–1940*, ed. Marilyn Ferris Motz and Pat Browne (Bowling Green: Bowling Green State University Press, 1988), 11–26.

5. Wolfgang Iser, "The Reading Process: A Phenomenological Approach," in *Reader-Response Criticism: From Formalism to Postmodernism*, ed. Jane P. Tompkins (Baltimore: Johns Hopkins University Press, 1980), 50.

6. Domna C. Stanton, preface, *The Female Autograph: Theory and Practice of Autobiography from the Tenth to the Twentieth Century* (Chicago: University of Chicago Press, 1984), vii.

7. Martin, *Recent Theories*, 75.

8. Estelle C. Jelinek, *The Tradition of Women's Autobiography: From Antiquity to the Present* (Boston: Twayne, 1986), xiii.

9. Ibid., 186–87.

10. Lynne Ireland, analyzing 1970s "compiled" cookbooks from the midwestern United States, decided that generally these books "serve as a fairly accurate

guide to the food habits of the group which produced them." See "The Compiled Cookbook as Foodways Autobiography," *Western Folklore* 40 (1981): 112. This bears investigation, however. I think about the numbers of people who often use prepared foods yet buy cookbooks that contain elaborate recipes and may even contribute a recipe to a church- or school-supporting charitable cookbook.

11. Jelinek, *Tradition of Women's Autobiography*, xiii.

12. Hayden White, "The Value of Narrativity in the Representation of Reality," in *On Narrative*, ed. W. J. T. Mitchell (Chicago: University of Chicago Press, 1981), 5. White's association of "history proper" with a stronger narrative structure and sense of closure (lacking in annals and chronicles), and with "moral meaning, a demand that sequences of real events be assessed as to their significance as elements of a *moral* drama" (20), makes me wonder if certain community cookbooks might not be read as histories. That strong sense of moral significance is certainly present in many of the cookbooks, and the neat orderliness of the cookbook, the oft-present legitimizing statements of local community authorities or of the book's compiler, seem to participate in what White says occurs in the creation of history: "The representation of real events arises out of a desire to have real events display the coherence, integrity, fullness, and closure of an image of life that is and can only be imaginary" (23).

13. Radcliffe College's Schlesinger Library contains an excellent collection of fund-raising cookbooks from the 1870s to the present, with strong representation of New England texts; the Library of Congress holds a number of early texts; Johnson and Wales University also maintains quite an extensive collection, as does the University of Iowa. Bibliographies specifically covering community cookbooks are spotty, the basic text here is Cook's *America's Charitable Cooks*, covering books published in the United States between 1861 and 1915. Later texts are indexed within general cookbook bibliographies only.

14. *Who Says We Can't Cook!* Women's National Press Club (Washington, DC, 1955).

15. *Black Family Dinner Quilt Cookbook*, National Council of Negro Women (Washington, DC, 1993).

16. *Louisiana Legacy*, Thibodaux Service League (Thibodaux, LA, 1982).

17. *Pirates Pantry: Treasured Recipes of Southwest Louisiana*, Junior League of Lake Charles (Lake Charles, LA, 1976).

18. *What's Cooking at Columbia: A Recipe Book*, Columbia University Committee for United War Relief (New York, 1942).

19. *Nos Meilleures Recettes*, Le Club Féminin de Liaison Franco-Americaine (Washington, DC, 1947), 23, 26.

20. *A New Daily Food*, ed. Lydia Shillaber, Ladies of St. Paul's Church (Morrisania, NY: Bedell & Bros., 1885).

21. Ibid., 13.

22. *Florence Cook Book*, Ladies of the Mission Circle in Florence (Northampton, MA, 1897).

23. *Needlework Guild Cook Book*, Needlework Guild of the First Presbyterian Church (Jamestown, NY, 1907).

24. Ibid., 148, 149.

25. *Who Says We Can't Cook!* 38.

26. *The Greek Palette: A Cookbook*, Greek Ladies Philoptochos Society "Myroforoi," Saints Constantine and Helen Greek Orthodox Church (Lawrence, MA, 1987).

27. Ibid., 15.

28. *Cook Along with Us*, Sisterhood of Temple Beth Sholom (Peabody, MA, 1964); *The Best Little Cookbook in Texas*, Junior League of Abiline (Abiline, TX, 1981).

29. Peter Brooks, *Reading for the Plot: Design and Intention in Narrative* (New York: Knopf, 1984), 37.

30. Ibid., 9.

31. *Out of Our Kitchen Closets: San Francisco Gay Jewish Cooking*, Congregation Sha'ar Zahav (San Francisco, 1987). Tzvetan Todorov finds that the "minimal complete plot can be seen as the shift from one equilibrium to another"; see his "Structural Analysis of Narrative" (1969), reprinted in *Contemporary Literary Criticism: Modernism through Poststructuralism*, ed. Robert Con Davis (New York: Longman, 1986), 328. The shifts in fund-raising recipe books may have occurred before the text's productions, as with the Jewish congregants who came out of the closet; yet that shift repeats itself in the text, as recipe donors and editors present themselves and their foods for our acceptance—ask us to break bread with them.

32. Ann Romines, *The Home Plot: Women, Writing and Domestic Ritual* (Amherst: University of Massachusetts Press, 1992), 17.

33. *A New Daily Food*, ed. Shillaber, 13, 14.

34. *Our Sisters' Recipes*, ed. Nettie Kaufman (Pittsburgh, 1909).

35. *Cook Book*, Atlanta Woman's Club (Atlanta, GA, 1921).

36. Ibid., 3.

37. *Simply Simpático: A Taste of New Mexico*, Junior League of Albuquerque (Albuquerque, 1981); *Bay Leaves*, Junior League of Panama City, Florida (Panama City, 1955).

38. *Bay Leaves*, 10, 102.

39. *Mariechen's Saxon Cook Book*, ed. Elva J. Crooks, Central Verband der Siebenbuerger Sachsen of the United States (Cleveland, 1955).

40. Ibid., 26. Occasional bilingual cookbooks or cookbooks incorporating bilingual elements did appear earlier, as in the case of *St. Paul's Bazaar Kochbuch und Geschaeftsfuehrer* (Chicago, 1882).

41. Ibid., 40.

42. *The Sephardic Cooks,* Congregation Or VeShalom Sisterhood (Atlanta, 1977).

43. *The Center Table,* rev. ed., Sisterhood Temple Mishkan Tefila (Boston, 1929).

44. Charles Camp, *American Foodways: What, When, Why and How We Eat in America* (Little Rock, AR: August House, 1989), 29.

45. *Angel Food,* St. Barnabas Episcopal Church (Lafayette, LA, 1979).

46. Ibid., 68, 69.

47. *The Historical Cookbook of the American Negro,* National Council of Negro Women (Washington, DC, 1958).

48. *Pots and Politics: An Historical Cookbook,* Washington State Women's Political Caucus (Seattle, 1976).

49. *Canyon Cookery: A Gathering of Recipes and Recollections from Montana's Scenic Bridger Canyon,* Bridger Canyon Women's Club (Bozeman, MT, 1978).

50. Ibid., 14, 15.

51. Martin, *Recent Theories,* 127.

52. Deborah Cameron, introduction to *The Feminist Critique of Language: A Reader* (London: Routledge, 1990), 4.

53. *A New Daily Food,* ed. Shillaber, 15.

54. *Legendary Cookbook,* Llano Fine Arts Guild (Llano, TX, 1985).

55. *Stirring Tales Spun by the Fire,* Ladies Aid Society of Grace M. E. Church (Albany, NY, 1902).

56. *The Dandy Cook Book,* Ladies Aid of Candia Village Church (Candia, NH, 1941).

57. Susan Sniader Lanser, *Fictions of Authority: Women Writers and Narrative Voice* (Ithaca, NY: Cornell University Press, 1992), 6.

58. Romines, *Home Plot,* 296.

59. Florence Howe, introduction to "T. S. Eliot, Virginia Woolf, and the Future of 'Tradition,'" in *Tradition and the Talents of Women* (Urbana: University of Illinois Press, 1991), 17.

Claiming a Piece of the Pie:
How the Language of Recipes Defines Community

Earlier versions of this chapter appeared in *Cultural Performances: Proceedings of the Third Berkeley Women and Language Conference,* Mary Buchultz et al. (Berkeley, CA: Berkeley Women and Language Group, 1994), 133–43; and as a talk at the American Anthropological Association annual meeting (1993).

1. This analogy is often used by avid cookbook readers. A telling example makes it into print on a jacket blurb on *The Minnesota Ethnic Food Book* (1993), quoting Minneapolis restaurateur and cookbook author Giovanna D'Agostini (aka Mama D): "I read cookbooks like novels, and it's great to read a book as good as this one." Mama D goes on to endorse the book for its role in sustaining cultural continuity, saying that the book "will help us to preserve the traditional dishes of our mothers and grandmothers so that our children and grandchildren will enjoy the dishes we enjoyed."

2. See Barbara Kirshenblatt-Gimblett, "Recipes for Creating Community: The Jewish Charity Cookbook in America," *Jewish Folklore and Ethnology* 9 (1987): 8–12; and David Remnick, "News in a Dying Language," *New Yorker* 64 (1994): 40–47, for parallels in their respective discussions of Jewish charity cookbooks and Yiddish newspapers.

3. Michael Owen Jones et al., "Foodways and Eating Habits: Directions for Research," *Western Folklore* 40 (1981): 12.

4. Deborah Schiffrin, *Approaches to Discourse* (London: Basil Blackwell, 1994).

5. Marcia Adams, *Cooking from Quilt Country* (New York: Clarkson N. Potter, 1989).

6. *A Garden of Eatin'*, Ladies of St. Therese Catholic Church (Appleton, WI: 1971).

7. Laurel Robertson et al., *Laurel's Kitchen: A Handbook for Vegetarian Cookery and Nutrition*, 7th printing (Berkeley: Nilgiri Press, 1980).

8. Irma S. Rombauer and Marion Rombauer Becker, *Joy of Cooking*, 30th printing (Indianapolis: Bobbs-Merrill, 1983).

9. Jane Brody, *Jane Brody's Good Food Book: Living the High-Carbohydrate Way* (New York: Norton, 1985).

10. William Labov, *Language in the Inner City: Studies in the Black English Vernacular* (Philadelphia: University of Pennsylvania Press, 1972).

11. Donald Polkinghorne, *Narrative Knowing and the Human Sciences* (Albany: State University of New York Press, 1988), 15.

12. Esther B. Aresty, *The Delectable Past* (New York: Simon and Schuster, 1964), 222..

13. M. F. K. Fisher, "The Anatomy of a Recipe," in *With Bold Knife and Fork* (New York: Paragon Books, 1968).

14. Aresty, *Delectable Past*, 47, 52.

15. Fisher, "Anatomy of a Recipe," 23.

16. Labov, *Language*, 363.

17. Brody, *Jane Brody's*, 632.

18. *Betty Crocker's Cookbook* (New York: Golden Press, 1979), 289.

19. Labov, *Language*, 365.

20. H. Paul Grice, "Logic and Conversation," in *Syntax and Semantics 3: Speech Acts,* ed. Peter Cole and Jerry L. Morgan (New York: Academic Press, 1975), 41–58. It could be argued that a violation of any of Grice's conversational maxims, such as Quantity, Relevance, or Manner, is what causes the difficulty when a Recipe is perceived as hard to follow. The "speaker" has made erroneous assumptions about the "hearer's" ability to receive the message, about shared background.

21. Amy Shuman, "The Rhetoric of Portions," *Western Folklore* 40.1 (1981): 72–80, discusses the social consequences of food apportionment, illuminating its importance in social behaviors. This may be a conditioning factor in where and how portion amount is positioned in recipes.

22. Labov, *Language,* 365.

23. Ellen Buchman Ewald, *Recipes for a Small Planet* (New York: Ballantine, 1973).

24. *Pies from Amish and Mennonite Kitchens,* collected and ed. Phyllis Pellman Good and Rachel Thomas Pellman (Lancaster, PA: Good Books, 1982).

25. Charles Goodwin, "Audience Diversity, Participation and Interpretation," *Text* 6 (1986): 283–316.

26. *The California Heritage Cookbook,* Junior League of Pasadena (Garden City, NY: Doubleday, 1976).

27. *A Synod of Cooks,* Chichester Diocesan Association for Family Social Work (Hove, Eng.: n.d. [early 1990s]), 28.

28. Alessandro Duranti, "The Audience as Co-author: An Introduction," *Text* 6 (1986): 244.

29. We may not realize it today with the mass production of food, but even earlier in this century, egg sizes were not standardized, nor was flour uniform in terms of gluten and moisture content, and baking soda was preferred as a leavening agent over baking powder (see Aresty, *Delectable Past*). What is implied by something as apparently straightforward as a recipe ingredient may not be what it seems. To evoke Gertrude Stein, an egg is an egg may not be an egg.

30. For a discussion of the community cookbook as a social autobiography, see Lynne Ireland, "The Compiled Cookbook as Foodways Autobiography," *Western Folklore* 40 (1981): 107–14.

31. Allison Kyle Leopold, *Victorian Sweets* (New York: Clarkson N. Potter, 1992), 12.

32. As in Ireland, "Compiled Cookbook"; Kirshenblatt-Gimblett, "Recipes"; and Anne L. Bower, unpublished "*Our Sisters' Recipes:* Cooking Up a Community."

Growing Up with the Methodist Cookbooks

1. I could not have written this essay without the help of my parents, Ruth Rogers Romines and Elmer Romines, who spent many hours patiently an-

swering my questions about the Methodist cookbooks and the history of Houston, Missouri. My sister, Marilyn F. Romines, generously helped me to recover and extend my cookbook memories. My cousin, Gayla Kay Romines Bratton, shared her mother's copy of the 1907 Methodist cookbook, and my friend Freeda Baker Stewart found and shared her (Baptist) mother's well-worn copy of the 1907 cookbook. I'm grateful for the long memories and vast expertise of my friends Edna Johnson Duff, Wave Campbell Akins, and Vera Kirkman Douglas, all longtime members of the Houston cooking community, who enthusiastically discussed this project with me. And I am especially thankful for the example and practice of my two grandmothers, Mayme Munson Rogers and Bess Mitchell Romines: good cooks and good writers, both.

2. *Cook Book*, Women's Missionary Society, M. E. Church (South Houston, MO, 1934), subsequently, CB'34.

3. *Cook Book*, First Methodist Church of Houston, Missouri (1941), subsequently referred to as CB'41; *Cook Book*, Ladies' Aid of M. E. Church (South Houston, MO, 1907), subsequently referred to as CB'07; and *Methodist Church Cook Book* (Houston, MO, 1967), subsequently referred to as CB'67.

4. CB'67, 98.

5. Ibid., 28.

6. CB'34, 29.

7. Ibid., 102.

8. CB'67, 90.

9. CB'34, 84.

10. CB'07, 24.

11. CB'41, 6.

12. Ibid., 36, 32.

13. Ibid., 30.

14. CB'07, 6.

15. CB'34, 9, 36.

Speaking Sisters: Relief Society Cookbooks and Mormon Culture

1. Providence Second Ward Relief Society, *Joyful Cooking* (Providence, UT: Watkin's Printing, 1963); Millville Second Ward Relief Society, *Millville Favorites* (Olathe, KS: Cookbook Publishers, 1987); Lakeside Relief Society, *Country Thyme Flavors* (Olathe, KS: Cookbook Publishers, 1986).

2. Ezra Taft Benson, "To the Mothers in Zion," Address at Fireside for Parents. Salt Lake City, February 22, 1987, 2–3.

3. *Country Thyme Flavors*, 1.

4. Leonard J. Arrington and Davis Bitton, *The Mormon Experience: A History of the Latter-day Saints* (Urbana: University of Illinois Press, 1992), 299.

5. *Millville Favorites*, 61, 56.

6. Ibid., 73.

7. *Joyful Cooking*, 72.

8. *Millville Favorites*, 30, 75, 8, 10.

9. *Country Thyme Favorites*, 99.

10. *Joyful Cooking*, vii.

11. Susan J. Leonardi, "Recipes for Reading: Pasta Salad, Lobster à la Rise-holme, and Key Lime Pie," *PMLA* 104 (1989): 340–47.

12. Mary Field Belenky, Blythe McVicker Clinchy, Nancy Rule Goldberger, and Jill Mattuck Tarule, *Women's Ways of Knowing: The Development of Self, Voice and Mind* (New York: Basic Books, 1986).

13. *Millville Favorites*, 68.

14. *Country Thyme Favorites*, 31, 77.

15. Ibid., 91, 28.

16. Ibid., 57, 91.

17. *Joyful Cooking*, 42.

18. Lyn Mikel Brown and Carol Gilligan, *Meeting at the Crossroads: Women's Psychology and Girls' Development* (Cambridge: Harvard University Press, 1992).

19. *Joyful Cooking*, 116; *Millville Favorites*, 35, 47; *Country Thyme Favorites*, 124.

20. *Country Thyme Favorites*, 57, 50, 34.

21. Janet L. Surrey, "Eating Patterns as a Reflection of Women's Development," *Women's Growth in Connection: Writings from the Stone Center*, eds. Judith V. Jordan, Alexandra G. Kaplan, Jean Baker Miller, Irene P. Stiver, and Janet L. Surrey (New York: Guilford Press, 1991), 244.

22. Luce Irigaray, "The Bodily Encounter with the Mother," *The Irigaray Reader*, ed. Margaret Whitford (Cambridge, MA: Basil Blackwell, 1991), 43.

23. *Country Thyme Favorites*, 46; *Millville Favorites*, 135.

24. Irigaray, "Bodily Encounter," 44.

25. *Millville Favorites*, 100.

26. *Joyful Cooking*, 151.

27. Irigaray, "Bodily Encounter," 43.

Voice, Stories, and Recipes in Selected Canadian Community Cookbooks

1. Grey Granite Curling Club (Owen Sound, Ontario), *Granite Goodies: 40th Anniversary Cookbook of the Grey Granite Club* (Winnipeg, Manitoba: L. Rasmussen, 1991), 116.

2. Roland Barthes, "The Death of the Author," in *Modern Criticism and Theory: A Reader*, ed. David Lodge (New York: Longman, 1988), 157 (First published in *Image-Music-Text*, ed. and trans. Stephen Heath [n.p.: Fontana, 1979]).

3. Grey Granite Curling Club, *Granite Goodies*, viii.

4. *The New Shorter Oxford English Dictionary on Historical Principles: Thumb Index Edition*, vols. 1 and 2 (Oxford: Clarendon Press, 1993), 1461. "Baste" appeared in the late fifteenth century, "braise" in the middle of the eighteenth century. Over time, "julienne" has changed its meaning: in the early eighteenth century, it referred to a soup of vegetables, with carrots as the prime ingredient; in the late nineteenth century, it took on its present meaning of a specific method of cutting vegetables.

5. Mikhail Bakhtin, "From the Prehistory of Novelistic Discourse," in *Modern Criticism and Theory*, ed. Lodge, 150 (first published in *The Dialogic Imagination: Four Essays by M. M. Bakhtin*, ed. Michael Holquist, trans. Caryl Emerson and Michael Holquist [Austin: University of Texas Press, 1981].)

6. Bakhtin, "From the Prehistory of Novelistic Discourse," 150; 130.

7. Ibid., 131.

8. Chatsworth United Church Sunday School (Chatsworth, Ontario), *Chatsworth United Church Sunday School Cookbook* (Winnipeg, Manitoba: Gateway Publishing: n.d.), 49; Grey Granite Curling Club, *Granite Goodies*, 80.

9. Georgian Bay Gourmets (Georgian Bay, Ontario), *Georgian Bay Gourmet: Summer Entertaining* (Weston, Ontario: Southam Murray Printing, 1983), 3.

10. *Live: Regis and Kathie Lee* (Buena Vista Television, ABC TV, date unknown).

11. Bakhtin, "From the Prehistory of Novelistic Discourse," 131.

12. Barthes, "Death of the Author," 163.

13. Wolfgang Iser, "The Reading Process: A Phenomenological Approach," *New Literary History* 3 (1972): 220–21.

14. See Grey Granite Curling Club, *Granite Goodies*, 188; 75; 107; 73; 95; 92; Georgian Bay Gourmets, *Georgian Bay Gourmet*, 14; 18; 12.

15. Stanley Fish, "Interpreting the *Variorum*," in *Modern Criticism and Theory*, ed. Lodge, 320.

16. Iser, "The Reading Process," 227.

17. Bakhtin, "From the Prehistory of Novelistic Discourse," 140–41.

18. Michel Foucault, "What Is an Author?" trans. Joseph V. Harari, in *Modern Criticism and Theory*, ed. Lodge, 198 (first published in *Textual Strategies: Perspectives in Post-Structuralist Criticism*, ed. J. V. Harari [Ithaca, NY: Cornell University Press, 1977].)

19. Bakhtin, "From the Prehistory of Novelistic Discourse," 143.

20. YMCA, *Y Cookbook* (n.p., 1969), 29; 26; 32; 26; 31; 28; 80.

21. Iser, "The Reading Process," 214.

22. St. Andrew's Presbyterian Church (Chatsworth, Ontario), *St. Andrew's Cookbook*, illustrated by Betty MacKinnon; type-setting by Cynthia Cameron (n.p., n.d.), 15.

23. Grey Granite Curling Club, *Granite Goodies*, 108.

24. Chatsworth United Church Sunday School, *Cookbook*, 16.

25. Grey Granite Curling Club, *Granite Goodies*, 23; Temple Hill United Church, *Temple Hill United Church 1887–1987: 100th Anniversary Cookbook* (n.p., 1987), 97.

26. Iser, "The Reading Process," 223.

27. Susan Winnett, "Coming Unstrung: Women, Men, Narrative and Principles of Pleasure," *PMLA* 105 (1990): 514–15.

28. Grey Granite Curling Club, *Granite Goodies*, 8; 23; 113; 111.

29. Foucault, "What Is an Author?" 203; Winnett, "Coming Unstrung," 515.

Empathy, Energy, and Eating:
Politics and Power in *The Black Family Dinner Quilt Cookbook*

1. Irma S. Rombauer and Marion Rombauer Becker, *Joy of Cooking*, vol. 1 (New York: Signet, 1964), 587–88.

2. Margaret Atwood, "Introducing *The CanLit Foodbook*," in *Literary Gastronomy*, ed. David Bevan (Amsterdam: Rodope, 1988), 51.

3. Dorothy I. Height and the National Council of Negro Women, Inc., *The Black Family Dinner Quilt Cookbook: Health Conscious Recipes and Food Memories* (Memphis: Wimmer Companies, 1993).

4. National Council of Negro Women, Inc., *Black Family Reunion Cookbook* (Memphis: Wimmer Companies, 1991).

5. *Black Family Dinner Quilt Cookbook*, 5.

6. Ibid., 5–6.

7. Ibid., 12, 40, 114.

8. Ibid., 22, 198.

9. Ibid., 18–19.

10. Ibid., 42–43.

11. Ibid., 157.

12. Ibid., 158–59.

13. Ibid., 192–93.

14. Susan J. Leonardi, "Recipes for Reading: Pasta Salad, Lobster à la Riseholme, and Key Lime Pie," in *Cooking by the Book: Food in Literature and Culture*, ed. Mary Anne Schofield, (Bowling Green: Bowling Green State University Popular Press, 1989), 129.

15. Leonardi, "Recipes for Reading," 131.

16. Laura Esquivel, *Like Water for Chocolate: A Novel in Monthly Installments with Recipes, Romances, and Home Remedies,* trans. Carol Christensen and Thomas Christensen (New York: Doubleday, 1992), 7.

17. Charles Camp, *American Foodways: When, Why, and How We Eat in America* (Little Rock, AR: August House, 1989), 24, 29, 51; Jack Goody, *Cooking, Cuisine, and Class: A Study in Comparative Sociology* (Cambridge: Cambridge University Press, 1982), 13.

18. Linda Keller Brown and Kay Mussell, eds. *Ethnic and Regional Foodways in the United States: The Performance of Group Identity* (Knoxville: University of Tennessee Press, 1984), 4.

19. Reay Tannahill, *Food in History,* new, fully rev. and updated ed. (New York: Crown Publishers, 1988), 68.

20. Ibid., 69.

21. Maude Southwell Wahlman, "African Symbolism in Afro-American Quilts," *African Arts* 20 (1986): 70, 76.

22. William Ferris, ed., *Afro-American Folk Art and Crafts* (Boston: G. K. Hall & Co., 1983), 65.

23. *Black Family Dinner Quilt Cookbook,* 5–6.

24. Ibid., 200.

25. Ibid.

26. Ruth L. Gaskins, *Every Good Negro Cook Starts with Two Basic Ingredients: A Good Heart and a Light Hand* (New York: Simon and Schuster, 1968).

27. *Black Family Dinner Quilt Cookbook,* 213.

28. Gaskins, *Every Good Negro Cook,* vii, 2.

29. *Black Family Dinner Quilt Cookbook,* 9.

30. Anne Romines, *The Home Plot: Women, Writing and Domestic Ritual* (Amherst: University of Massachusetts Press, 1992), 294.

31. Patricia Yaeger, *Honey-mad Women: Emancipation Strategies in Women's Writing* (New York: Columbia University Press, 1988), 3.

32. Andrea Nye, *Feminist Theory and the Philosophies of Man* (New York: Routledge, 1988), 148.

33. Hélène Cixous, "The Laugh of the Medusa," in *Women's Voices: Visions and Perspectives,* ed. Pat C. Hoy II, Esther H. Schor, and Robert Di Yanni (New York: McGraw-Hill, 1990), 487.

34. Mary Anne Schofield, ed., *Cooking by the Book: Food in Literature and Culture* (Bowling Green: Bowling Green State University Popular Press, 1989), 1.

35. Leonardi, "Recipes for Reading," 134.

The Moral Sublime:
The Temple Emanuel Fair and Its Cookbook, Denver, 1888

1. The fair was described in considerable detail in the local press and is mentioned in Marjorie Horbein, *Temple Emanuel of Denver: A Centennial History* (Denver: Temple Emanuel, 1974). I also consulted the Temple Emanuel Archives and the local press for the week of the fair. This essay was written at the invitation of Dr. Jeanne Abrams, Director of the Ira M. Beck Memorial Archives of Rocky Mountain Jewish History at the Center for Judaic Studies, University of Denver (Colorado). The Beck Archives were recently dedicated and are part of the special collections at Penrose Library, University of Denver. This essay was the basis for a public lecture on March 10, 1994, sponsored by the Rocky Mountain Jewish Historical Society, at the Beth Medresh Hagadol Synagogue. My warm thanks to Dr. Abrams for bringing the cookbook to my attention and to Professor John Livingston for his helpful suggestions.

2. On the Jewishness of cold fish, see Barbara Kirshenblatt-Gimblett, "Kitchen Judaism," *Getting Comfortable in New York: The American Jewish Home, 1880–1950*, ed. Susan Braunstein and Jenna Joselit (New York: Jewish Museum, 1990).

3. These issues are discussed in greater detail in Kirshenblatt-Gimblett, "Kitchen Judaism."

4. Allen duPont Beck, *The Centennial History of the Jews of Colorado, 1859–1959* (Denver: University of Denver, 1960), 65.

5. "The Hebrew Fair," *Rocky Mountain News*, October 23, 1888, p. 10.

6. "The Jewish Fair," *Rocky Mountain News*, October 23, 1888, p. 2.

7. See "The First Charity Fair," in *Frank Leslie's Illustrated Newspaper*, April 30, 1864.

8. Beverly Gordon, "Playing at Being Powerless: New England Ladies Fairs, 1830–1930," *Massachusetts Review* 27.1 (Spring 1986), 144–60. See also, Mary Bosworth Treudley, "The 'Benevolent Fair': A Study of Charitable Organization among American Women in the First Third of the Nineteenth Century," *Social Service Review* 14 (1940): 509–22; and Rodris Roth, "The New England, or 'Old Tyme,' Kitchen Exhibit at Nineteenth-Century Fairs," in *The Colonial Revival in America*, ed. Alan Axelrod (New York: Norton, 1985), 159–83.

9. Bertram W. Korn, *American Jewry and the Civil War* (Philadelphia: Jewish Publication Society of America, 1951), 103.

10. Korn, *American Jewry*, 105.

11. On Jewish participation in world's fairs, see Barbara Kirshenblatt-Gimblett, "Exhibiting Jews," *Destination Culture* (Berkeley: University of California Press, 1998 [in press]).

12. Korn, *American Jewry*, 99.

13. April 20, 1864.

14. Korn, *American Jewry*, 3. For a discussion of Jewish voluntary associations during this period, also see Hasia R. Diner, *A Time for Gathering: The Second Migration, 1820–1880* (Baltimore: Johns Hopkins University Press, 1992).

15. Korn, *American Jewry*, 12.

16. November 11, 1870; December 2, 1870.

17. December 9, 1870.

18. Korn, *American Jewry*, 100–101.

19. Ibid., 104.

20. The Purim balls were masked balls. Referring to house visits, the *Jewish Messenger* (April 1, 1870) even claims that "the mask, in this country, seems to be affected solely by us Israelites."

21. Mary P. Ryan, *Women in Public: Between Banners and Ballots, 1825–1880* (Baltimore: Johns Hopkins University Press, 1989).

22. *Frank Leslie's Illustrated Newspaper*, April 16, 1864.

23. Gordon, "Playing at Being Powerless," 154.

24. *Frank Leslie's Illustrated Newspaper*, April 30, 1864.

25. "Insanity Fair," *Frank Leslie's Illustrated Newspaper*, April 23, 1864; "Town Gossip."

26. Gordon, "Playing at Being Powerless," 153.

27. See Ann Firor Scott, *Natural Allies: Women's Associations in American History* (Urbana: University of Illinois Press, 1991), who traces the history of women's efforts from charity to reform and from volunteerism to professional careers, from the 1790s to World War I.

28. See Barbara Kirshenblatt-Gimblett, "Recipes for Creating Community: The Jewish Charity Cookbook in America," and "Jewish Charity Cookbooks in the United States and Canada: A Bibliography of 201 Recent Publications," *Jewish Folklore and Ethnology Review* 9.1 (1987): 8–12, 13–18. The discussion that follows is drawn from these articles.

29. This cookbook was produced by the St. Laurent (Quebec) B'nai Brith and edited by a team headed up by Norene Gilletz, who has since gone on to write her own highly successful kosher cookbook, *The Pleasure of Your Food Processor.*

Ella Smith's Unfinished Community Cookbook:
A Social History of Women and Work in Smithtown, New York, 1884–1922

1. Ella Smith Recipe Collection, Smith Family Papers, Smithtown Historical Society Archives, Smithtown, New York.

2. Of the twenty-three pre-1920, Suffolk County fund-raising cookbooks used in this study, only four identified the women who had compiled them. The remaining cookbooks were skimmed for prominent names; in all cases the most active women were descended from old, distinguished families, married

to prominent businessmen, and involved in a broad range of philanthropic activities.

3. Frederick Kinsman Smith, *The Family of Richard Smith of Smithtown, Long Island: Ten Generations* (Smithtown: Smithtown Historical Society, 1967), 3, 24, 338–39, 464; Charlotte Adams Ganz, ed., *Colonel Rockwell's Scrap-book, Short Histories, Dwellings, Mills, Churches, Taverns, 1665–1845, Township of Smithtown, Suffolk County, Long Island, N.Y.* (Smithtown: Smithtown Historical Society, 1968), 127.

4. Catherine Beecher and Harriet Beecher Stowe, *The American Woman's Home or, Principles of Domestic Science; Being a Guide to the Formation and Maintenance of Economical, Healthful, Beautiful, and Christian Homes* (New York: J. B. Ford & Co., 1869); Ganz, *Colonel Rockwell's Scrap-Book,* 164. For use of Beecher works on Long Island, see Eunice Telfer Juckett Meeker, "Ladies Village Improvement Society Cookbooks" (unpub. research paper for the L. V. I. S. [East Hampton, 1992], 20).

5. Minutes of the Ladies' Aid Society and the Women's Missionary Society, 1880–1922, First Presbyterian Church of Smithtown Archives, Smithtown, New York.

6. Ella Smith, diaries; a sampling of her activities include a church sale, December 17, 1900; help with church supper, February 1, 1904; cleaned, May 17, 1904; taught Sunday School, May 20, 1904; papered walls, September 7, 1905; decorated church, February 5, 1916; picked berries, June 22, 1920.

7. Phebe Smith, diaries. "Keeping house" seems to have included various aspects of Ella's activities, among them cooking and covering Theo's business.

8. Phebe Smith, diaries, November 22, 1900: "Ladies Aid . . . Treasurer resigned, . . . gave me 9 votes declined . . ."; February 11, 1909: "Mrs Abbey called AM to get me to be chairman on some committee. Nix . . ." (Ella Smith Recipe Collection).

9. Phebe Smith, diaries, February 4, 1903; February 3, 1906; November 14, 1907; September 30, 1908; November 6, 1908.

10. Ella Smith Scrap Books and Recipe Collection, Smith Family Papers, Smithtown Historical Society Archives; for subscriptions, see Ella Smith, diaries, August 15, 1901, end pages 1904, January 5, 1921.

11. Ella Smith, scrapbooks; diaries, August 1904; January 6, 1905; August 1907; June 1917; August 1918; July 1921; Theo Smith, Smithtown, to Ella Smith, April 17, 1891; July 24, 1892; September 7, 1894; July 22, 1897; August 23, 1899; October 24, 1909 (collection of the author).

12. Mary E. Sturtevant, New Bedford, Massachusetts, to Ella Smith, September 12, 1904; packets of recipes copied from cookbooks included those from Mrs. Irvin of Ellenville, New York (*Tried and True*); Mrs. Curran of Scranton, Young Ladies' Society, comp., *A Cook Book of Tried and Approved Recipes* (Scran-

ton, PA: First Presbyterian Church of Scranton, 1897); Mrs. Lockwood of Brooklyn, New York, *Mites of Help.*

13. Ella Smith, diaries, September 16, 1895; February 7, 1898; February 10, 1900; February 1, 1904; April 9, 1904; February 2, 1918; February 8, 1918; November 13, 1918. Mrs. Call, Sadie Darling, Mrs. Hallock, Mrs. Strong were all listed in Ladies' Aid records.

14. Phebe Smith, Long Island City, to Faith Smith, St. Johnland, April 12, 1892; these and other letters cited throughout the paper are from the author's collection; Phebe Smith, diaries, January 29, 1909.

15. Meeker, "Ladies Village Improvement Society Cookbooks," 7; although only five of Suffolk County's fund-raising cookbooks identified the committees, genealogical studies on their names and those appearing frequently in the others represented old, prominent families.

16. Phebe Smith, diaries, April 13, 1901.

17. Ella Smith, diaries, July 29, 1904.

18. Ella Smith, diaries, March 8, 1901.

19. Phebe Smith, diaries, February 4, 1904; October 4, 1904; January 29, 1905.

20. Nancy Tomes, "The Quaker Connection: Visiting Patterns among Women in the Philadelphia Society of Friends, 1750–1800," in *Friends and Neighbors, Group Life in Ameirca's First Plural Society,* ed. Michael Zucherman (Philadelphia: Temple University Press, 1982).

21. Norman "Bud" O'Berry, Smithtown Historian, interview with author, St. James, New York, October 24, 1984.

22. Mrs. W. E. Bowers, Brownsville, Oregon, to Mrs. Theo Smith, Smithtown Branch, December 10, 1910.

23. Ella Smith Recipe Collection; Ella Smith, diaries, November 17, 1904.

24. The Women, comp., *Centennial Buckeye Cook Book* (Marysville, OH: First Congregational Church, 1876), later reprinted commercially as *The Buckeye Cook Book* (from 1884 to 1905); Cook, *America's Charitable Cooks,* 207; Ladies' Aid Society, *Housekeeper's Friend* (West Winsted, CT: M. E. Church, 1888).

25. Ladies' Aid Society, *"Tried and True," A Cook Book of Domestic Receipts and Housekeeper's Manual* (Ellenville, NY: Methodist Episcopal Church, 1897), 45, 93.

26. *Buckeye Cookery and Practical Housekeeping. Tried and Approved, Original Recipes* (Minneapolis: Buckeye, 1876), copied in Ladies' Aid Society, *The Housekeeper's Friend* (West Winsted, CT: M. E. Church, 1888); *Mites of Help,* discussed in Ella Smith, diaries, April 3, 1901; Ladies' Aid Society, *"Tried and True,"* 45, 93; Mrs. Marsh, Delaware Water Gap, to Ella Smith, Smithtown, November 4, 1890; Mrs. Spurge, Smithtown, to Ella Smith, Delaware Water Gap, October 4, 1900.

27. It is not clear from Ella's notes if she used the first, handwritten edition, Young Ladies B.W. Society, *The Practical Cook Book* (Northville: Congre-

gational Church, 1886), or its subsequent, printed revision: Ladies of the Mutual Benefit Society, *The Practical Cook Book* (Northville: Congregational Church, 1890).

28. Ella Smith to Fan Latham, November 17, 1901, Ella Smith Letters collection of author; Ella Smith diaries, January 24, 1904; Ella Smith recipe collection.

29. Loren A. Rowley, ed., *Our Favorites. A Collection of Cooking Recipes Approved and Recommended by Ladies of East Marion* (East Marion: [privately printed] 1900).

30. For a detailed description of the cuisine, see Sandra L. Oliver, *Saltwater Foodways: New Englanders and Their Food, at Sea and Ashore, in the Nineteenth Century* (Mystic, CT: Mystic Seaport Museum, 1995).

31. For Baked Beans, see Mrs. Hubbard, diary, July 1881; Phebe Smith, diaries, April 19, 1901; for boiled dinner, see Mary Handley, diary, February 6, 1868; Carrie H. Davis, diary, May 1882; Phebe Smith, diaries, April 3, 1906.

32. Laura Downs, interview with author, Northville, October 17, 1994; Phebe Smith, diaries, June 13, 1903; April 25, 1906.

33. Helen Campbell, *In Foreign Kitchens: With Choice Recipes from England, France, Germany, Italy, and The North* (Boston: Roberts Brothers, 1893); Berthe Julienne Low, *French Home Cooking Adapted to the Use of American Households* (New York: McClure, Phillips & Co., 1904).

34. [Title page missing], *St. Ann's Cook Book* (Sayville: St. Ann's Episcopal Church, ca. 1915), 1.

35. Ibid.; *Practical Cook Book* (Northville, 1886), 3.

36. Helen Thompson Jones (1913–   ), interview by the author, Smithtown, January 23, 1995.

37. Ella Smith, diaries, January 4, 1904; January 12, 1905; February 10, 1905; March 10, 1905.

38. *Practical Cook Book* (Northville, 1890), 2. The poem is not directly attributed to a particular writer, although the word "selected" follows the last line, perhaps indicating extraction from another text.

39. Norman "Bud" O'Berry, Smithtown Historian, interview with the author, St. James, October 24, 1984.

40. *Brooklyn & Long Island Business Directory*, 1890–91 and 1897 (Brooklyn: Lain & Healy); *Montauk Business Directory of Long Island (Nassau and Suffolk Counties, N.Y.* (Jamaica: Montauk Directory Company, 1911).

41. For Protestant attitudes toward food, see Colleen McDannell, *The Christian Home in Victorian America, 1840–1900* (Bloomington: Indiana University Press, 1986), 45–51; Philip Greven, *The Protestant Temperament, Patterns of Child-Rearing, Religious Experience, and the Self in Early America* (New York: Alfred A. Knopf, 1977), 206–17, 296, 300–305; Ella Smith diaries, end pages, 1905.

42. Ladies Sewing Society, Minutes of the Annual Meeting, June 19, 1884, Presbyterian Church Archives, Southold, New York.

43. Ladies' Aid Society, comp., *The Southampton Cook Book* (Southampton, NY: Presbyterian Church, 1907).

44. Joella Vreeland, *The Southold Sisterhood, Sociables and Serious Business: The Story of the Ladies Liberal Sewing Society* (Southold: First Universalist Church, 1985), 46 and passim; personal interview, October 16, 1994.

45. Mrs. Annie M. Spurge, Smithtown, to Ella Smith, Smithtown Branch, October 4, 1900.

46. Obituary notice in the Minutes, Women's Missionary Society of Smithtown, undated [1922].

47. Clifford E. Crafts, Jr., of Crafts, Smith, Nowick and Goodwin Insurance Agency (Faith's partner), personal interview, Smithtown, November 19, 1984; Faith Smith, obituary, *Smithtown Messenger*, December 23, 1976; Ganz, *Colonel Rockwell's Scrap-book*, 127.

A Tale of Three Cakes: On the Air and In the Books

1. Charles Camp, *American Foodways: What, When, Why and How We Eat in America* (Little Rock, AR: August House, 1989).

2. Susan J. Leonardi, "Recipes for Reading: Pasta Salad, Lobster à la Rise-holme, and Key Lime Pie," in *Cooking by the Book: Food in Literature and Culture*, ed. Mary Anne Schofield (Bowling Green: Bowling Green State University Popular Press, 1989), 127.

3. Jane Stern and Michael Stern, *Square Meals* (New York: Knopf, 1984).

4. "The Compiled Cookbook as Foodways Autobiography," *Western Folklore* 40 (1981): 107–14.

5. Camp, *American Foodways*, 56; "Standard Social Uses of Food: Introduction," *Food in the Social Order: Studies of Food and Festivities in Three American Communities*, ed. Mary Douglas (New York: Russell Sage Foundation, 1984), 30.

6. Iowa City: University of Iowa Press, 1991. Quotations from this text will henceforth be cited as *Neighboring on the Air*. In a November 6, 1994, phone conversation, Mrs. Birkby informed this author of Melinda Lee and Jackie Olden, two Los Angeles radio homemakers who are currently broadcasting; she also referred me to the following article about them: Kathie Jenkins, "Queens of Call-In Cooking," *Los Angeles Times*, September 1, 1994, sec. H, 10, 11, 20.

7. Julia McNair Wright, *The Complete Home: An Encyclopedia of Domestic Life and Affairs* (Philadelphia: J. C. McCurdy, 1879), 383.

8. Ibid., 3.

9. Ibid., 4.

10. Ireland, "Compiled Cookbook," 107.

11. Laura Shapiro, *Perfection Salad: Women and Cooking at the Turn of the Century* (New York: Farrar, Straus and Giroux, 1986), 25.

12. Ibid., 15.

13. Evelyn Birkby to Nelljean Rice, Sidney, Ioway, May 27, 1994.

14. Jane Stern and Michael Stern, "Neighboring," *New Yorker*, April 15, 1991, 78–93.

15. Birkby, *Neighboring on the Air*, 42.

16. Robert Birkby, *KMA Radio: The First Sixty Years* (Shenandoah, IA: May Broadcasting, 1985), 23–29.

17. Ibid., 42.

18. Birkby, *Neighboring* 45.

19. Evelyn Birkby, conversation with author, Sidney, Iowa, November 22, 1994.

20. Lori Rohlk, "Iowa's Radio Homemakers," *Iowa Woman* 12, no. 3 (1992): 18–21, 20.

21. Stern and Stern, "Neighboring," 87.

22. Evelyn Birkby, letter to the author, May 27, 1994.

23. Birkby, *Neighboring on the Air*, 229–30.

24. Birkby, *Neighboring on the Air*, 235.

25. Evelyn Birkby, *Up a Country Lane* (Iowa City: University of Iowa Press, 1993), 145.

26. Ibid., 149.

27. Ibid., 150.

28. Ann Romines, *The Home Plot: Women, Writing and Domestic Ritual* (Amherst: University of Massachusetts Press, 1992), 222.

29. Birkby, *Up a Country Lane*, 150.

30. Mary Anne Schofield, Preface to *Cooking by the Book: Food in Literature and Culture* (Bowling Green: Bowling Green State University Popular Press, 1989), 1.

Juana Manuela Gorriti's *Cocina eclectica:* Recipes as Feminine Discourse

This essay is a revised and substantially rewritten version of an earlier article with the same title, which I published in *Hispania* 75 (May 1992): 310–14.

1. Juana Manuela Gorriti, *Cocina ecléctica* (1890; Buenos Aires: Librería Sarmiento, 1977). According to Josefina Iriarte and Claudia Torre, this edition is incomplete, but it was the only one available to me; see Iriarte and Torre, "La mesa está servida," in *El ajuar de la patria*, ed. Cristina Iglesia (Buenos Aires: Feminaria Editora, 1993), 60.

2. Rosario Ferré, "La cocina de la escritura," in *La sartén por el mango. Encuentro de escritoras hispanoamericanas*, ed. Patricia Elena González and Eliana Ortega (Rio Piedras, PR: 1984), 153. Unless otherwise indicated, all translations in this essay are mine.

3. Francine Masiello, "Between Civilization and Barbarism: Women, Family and Literary Culture in Mid-nineteenth Century Argentina, in *Cultural and*

Historical Grounding for Hispanic and Luso-Brazilian Feminist Literary Criticism, ed. Hernán Vidal (Minneapolis: Institute for the Study of Ideologies and Literature, 1989), 527.

4. Aída Martínez Carreño, *Mesa y cocina en el siglo XIX* (Bogotá: Fondo Cultural Cafetero, 1985), 107–27.

5. Margaret Cook, *America's Charitable Cooks: A Bibliography of Fund-raising Cook Books Published in the United States (1861–1915)* (Kent, OH: [privately printed], 1971), 7.

6. Ricardo Rojas, *La literatura argentina. Ensayo filosófico sobre la evolución de la cultura en el Plata,* 2nd ed., 8 vols. (Buenos Aires: Librería "La Facultad," 1925), 7–8: 791. Domingo Faustino Sarmiento, who was to be Argentine President from 1868–74, had earlier traveled to Europe and the United States in order to study educational systems. A former schoolteacher himself, he was intensely interested in normal schools and teacher training and recruited a group of some sixty-five teachers, mostly female, to travel to Argentina in a Peace Corps-like effort to improve especially primary education. With respect to the term "Creole," it is important to point out that in Spanish America this referred to the offspring of the white Spanish settlers, born in the Americas. It did not imply racial miscegenation.

7. Manuals of cooking and housekeeping were very popular in the United States in the late nineteenth century, and Mary Mann (wife of educational reformer Horace Mann), with whom Sarmiento had formed a close friendship, was herself the author of *Christianity in the Kitchen* (1861). See Esther B. Aresty, *The Delectable Past* (New York: Simon and Schuster, 1964), 202–206.

8. Rojas, *La Literatura argentina,* 795.

9. María Luisa Cresta de Leguizamón, "Aportes de Juana Manuela Gorriti a la narrativa argentina," in *Mujeres y cultura en la Argentina del siglo XIX,* ed. Lea Fletcher (Buenos Aires: Feminaria Editora, 1994), 67. Also, see Josefina Iriarte and Claudia Torre, "Juana Manuela Gorriti. *Cocina ecléctica.* 'Un sí es no es de ajo molido,' " in *Mujeres y cultura en la Argentina* ed. Fletcher, 81–82.

10. Susan J. Leonardi, "Recipes for Reading: Summer Pasta, Lobster à la Riseholme, and Key Lime Pie," *PMLA* 104 (May 1989), 343; 342.

11. Gorriti, *Cocina ecléctica,* 15–16.

12. Gorriti, *Cocina ecléctica,* 309; 273–77.

13. Miguel Brascó, in his introduction to the reprint of *Cocina ecléctica* (11), states that one of the reasons why Gorriti's marriage to Belzú foundered was that she was a dreadful cook, without, however, indicating the source of this anecdote. He is quite wrong in this statement, for Gorriti herself told of a culinary rivalry between herself and her dear friend, the Peruvian writer Mercedes Cabello de Carbonera, when the two were on vacation together: "We promised our two gentlemen (Gorriti's son, and Cabello's husband) the de-

lights of an exquisite table, whose menu, selected alternately by the two ladies of the house, would leave nothing to be desired . . . you can just imagine the great care that each of us took to keep up with the other, . . . above all, in culinary masterpieces." See Gorriti's "Chincha," from *El mundo de los recuerdos* (orig. pub. Buenos Aires: Felix Lajouane, 1886), trans. Mary G. Berg in *Rereading the Spanish American Essays: Translations of 19th and 20th Century Women's Essays*, ed. Doris Meyer (Austin: University of Texas Press, 1995), 63–64.

14. Gorriti, *Cocina ecléctica*, 188–89; Clorinda Matto de Turner also waxes poetic about chicha in her famous 1889 novel *Aves sin nido* (Birds without a nest), praising it as a beverage far superior to the more Europeanized beer (63). See also Gorriti, "Chincha."

15. Clorinda Matto de Turner, *Aves sin nido* (1889; Lima: Ediciones Peisa, 1984), 352.

16. Gorriti, *Cocina ecléctica*, 261; 77–80; 231; 234.

17. Iriarte and Torre, "La Mesa," 56.

18. Gorriti, *Cocina ecléctica*, 60; 246; 358–59; 123.

19. Juana Manuela Gorriti, *Veladas literarias de Lima: 1876–77* (Buenos Aires: Imprenta Europea, 1892). As opposed to the laudatory tone of this prologue, Palma apparently minced no words in disapproving of Gorriti's involvement in a cookbook; in his opinion, it amounted to "the beginning of senility" (Cresta de Leguizamón, "Aportes de Juana Manuela Gorriti," 67). See also Iriarte and Torre, "Juana Manuela Gorriti," 81.

20. Gertrude Yeager, "Juana Manuela Gorriti: Writer in Exile," in *The Human Factor in Latin America: The Nineteenth Century*, ed. William H. Beezley and Judith Ewell (Wilmington, DE: Scholarly Resources, 1989), 123–24. Thomas Meehan indicates that there may have been other, somewhat more colorful activities as well: "Curious rumors circulated about wild parties and other strange bohemian activities held during her *soirées*, as, for example, ritual dances by moonlight in the garden of her house, smoking and the practice of spiritualism, much in vogue at the time." See Thomas C. Meehan's "Una olvidada precursora de la literatura fantástica argentina: Juana Manuela Gorriti," *Chasqui* 10 (February–May 1981): 7.

21. Elvira García y García, *La mujer peruana a través de los siglos. Serie historiada de estudios y observaciones*, 2 vols. (Lima: Imprenta Americana, 1924–25), 52; 16.

22. Lily Sosa de Newton, *Diccionario biográfico de mujeres argentinas*, 3rd ed. (Buenos Aires: Plus Ultra, 1986), 17, 251.

23. Leonardi, "Recipes for Reading," 347.

24. It should be noted that in Spanish "huevos" are a euphemism for testicles, so that the name of this dish is unmistakeably racy.

25. I found the same recipe under the heading "To make an Egg as big as Twenty" in a facsimile version of a cookbook printed in Colonial Williams-

burg. It originally came from *Lady's Companion* (1753), owned by "Miss Anna Maria Dandridge, 1756." The title of the facsimile is *The Williamsburg Art of Cookery or Accomplish'd Gentlewoman's Companion: Being a Collection of upwards of Five Hundred of the moft Ancient & approv'd Recipes in Virginia Cookery*, by Mrs. Helen Bullock (Williamsburg: Printed in Colonial Williamsburg, incorporated on the press of August Dietz and his Son, near the Great Prison at Richmond, Virginia, 1938).

26. Iriarte and Torre, "La mesa está servida," 47–84, call attention to the fact that this recipe (as well as several others) is mentioned in other texts Gorriti wrote; Helado de espuma, for example, appears in a short story entitled "The Banquet of Death," in Gorriti *El mundo de los recuerdos* (The world of remembrances), 1886.

27. Gorriti, *Cocina ecléctica*, 349.

Recipes for *Patria:* Cuisine, Gender, and Nation in Nineteenth-Century Mexico

1. Laura Esquivel, *Like Water for Chocolate: A Novel in Monthly Installments, with Recipes, Romances, and Home Remedies*, trans. Carol Christensen and Thomas Christensen (New York: Doubleday, 1992), 57–59, 69.

2. Silvia M. Arrom, *The Women of Mexico City, 1790–1857* (Stanford: Stanford University Press, 1985), 15–26; Jean Franco, *Plotting Women: Gender and Representation in Mexico* (New York: Columbia University Press, 1989), 79–101; William E. French, "Prostitutes and Guardian Angels: Women, Work, and the Family in Porfirian Mexico," *Hispanic American Historical Review* 72, no. 4 (November 1982): 529–53.

3. William H. Beezley, *Holidays . . . Holy Days . . . Mexican Virtue on Parade: The Nimble Mnemonics of Social Tradition, 1821–1911* (Wilmington, DE: Scholarly Resources, forthcoming).

4. *El cocinero mexicano o coleccion de las mejores recetas para guisar al estilo americano, y de las mas selectas segun el método de las cocinas española, italiano, francesa e inglesa*, 3 vols. (Mexico City: Imprenta de Galvan á cargo de Mariano Arevalo, 1831), 1:177 and preface.

5. *Nuevo cocinero mejicano en forma de diccionario* (Paris and Mexico City: Librería de Rosa y Bouret, 1868), x.

6. *Nuevo y sencillo arte de cocina, repostería y refrescos, dispuesto por una mexicana, y experimentado por personas inteligentes antes de darse a la prensa* (Mexico City: Imprenta de Santiago Pérez, 1836), iv.

7. *La cocinera poblana y el libro de las familias. Novisimo manual práctico de cocina española, francesa, inglesa, y mexicana*, 2 vols. (Puebla: Narciso Bassols, 1877), 1:3.

8. Vicenta Torres de Rubio, *Cocina michoacana* (Zamora, Michoacán: Imprenta Moderna, 1896), iii–iv.

9. *Recetas prácticas para la señora de casa sobre cocina, repostería, pasteles, nevería, etc.* (Guadalajara: Imp. del Orfanatorio del Sagrado Corazón de Jesús, 1892), 3.

10. Although later jailed for supporting the French intervention, in the 1830s Galván had employed the founder of Mexican liberalism, José María Luis Mora, to manage his journals. See Miguel Angel Peral, *Diccionario biográfico mexicano* (Mexico City: Editorial PAC, 1944), 292.

11. Torres, *Cocina michoacana*, 347. She was no relation to Vicente García Torres, editor of *El Monitor Republicano.*

12. *Diccionario Porrua de historia, biografía y geografía de México*, 3rd ed., 2 vols. (Mexico City: Editorial Porrua, 1970), 1:833, 2:1434, 1593.

13. Arjun Appadurai, "How to Make a National Cuisine: Cookbooks in Contemporary India," *Comparative Studies in Society and History* 30 (January 1988): 3–24.

14. *Diario del Hogar*, February 9, 1886.

15. See, for example, *Nuevo cocinero mejicano* (1872), 62, 158, 264; *La cocinera poblana* (1877), 1:37; Torres, *Cocina michoacana*, 28, 36.

16. Marianita Vázquez de Celis, "Cuaderno de Cosina," 1874, Centro de Estudios de Historia de México, Condumex Mexico City, Fondo 71–2, 1891; Torres, *Cocina michoacana*, 224, 409, 752. Donato Guerra, a hero of the French Intervention, may have tasted his namesake cod, but Moctezuma never ate the dessert named in his honor, which was made of candied sugar, ground almonds, and bread rolls.

17. Guillermo Prieto, *Memorias de mis tiempos, 1828 á 1840* (Mexico City: Librería de la Vda. de Ch. Bouret, 1906), 287; *Nuevo cocinero mejicano* (1868), 940; *El cocinero mexicano* (1831), 1:177.

18. Prieto, *Memorias*, 15; Fanny Chambers Gooch [Iglehart], *Face to Face with the Mexicans* (New York: Fords, Howard & Hulbert, 1887), 495–96.

19. See, for example, *El cocinero mexicano* (1831), vol. 2; *Manual del cocinero y cocinera* (Puebla: Imprenta de José Maria Macías, 1849), 80–312; *Nuevo y sencillo arte* (1836), 32–134, 162–72, 195–217.

20. Gooch, *Face to Face*, 498.

21. Fanny Calderón de la Barca, *Life in Mexico: The Letters of Fanny Calderón de la Barca*, ed. Howard T. Fisher and Marion Hall Fisher (Garden City, NY: Doubleday, 1966), 55, 156.

22. William Bullock, *Six Months Residence and Travels in Mexico* (Port Washington, NY: Kennikat Press, 1971 [1824]), 253.

23. *Nuevo y sencillo arte* (1836), iv. See also the recipe in the *Manual del cocinero y cocinera tomado del periodicado literario "La Risa"* (Puebla: Imprenta de José María Macias, 1849), 92.

24. Hortensia Rendón de García, *Antiguo manual de cocina yucateca; fórmulas para*

condimentar los platos más usuales en la península, 7th ed., 3 vols. (Mérida: Librería Burrel, 1938 [1st ed. 1898]), 55.

25. Alfred W. Crosby, Jr., *The Columbian Exchange: Biological and Cultural Consequences of 1492* (Westport, CT: Greenwood Press, 1972), 70–71; John C. Super, "Bread and the Provisioning of Mexico City in the Late Eighteenth Century," *Jahrbuch für Geschichte von Staat, Wirtschaft und Gesellschaft Lateinamerikas* 19 (1982): 159–82; Virginia García Acosta, *Las panaderías, sus dueños y trabajadores: Ciudad de México, siglo XVIII* (Mexico City: Centro de Investigaciones y Estudios Superiores en Antropología Social, 1989), 159–82; 29–35.

26. The dozens of different bread soups contrasted sharply with a single recipe for tortilla soup. See *Nuevo cocinero mejicano* (1868), 780–90; *Nuevo y sencillo arte* (1836), 19–30.

27. Bullock, *Six Months Residence,* 106.

28. Valois suspected they picked up the accent from traveling salesmen (Alfred H. Siemens, *Between the Summit and the Sea: Central Veracruz in the Nineteenth Century* [Vancouver: University of British Columbia Press, 1990], 70). See also Calderón de la Barca, *Life in Mexico,* 133.

29. Torres de Rubio, *Cocina michoacana,* 340–50. *Galatinas* continued to appear in cookbooks well into the twentieth century. María Ibarrola de Salceda, *Moderno recetario de cocina mexicana* (Mexico City: Talleres Gráficos "Michoacán," 1929), 62.

30. Archivo Histórico de la Secretaria de Salud (hereafter AHSS), Inspección, box 1, exp. 5, report of sanitary inspector Ildefonso Velasco, August 26, 1872. See also the advertisements in Mexico City newspapers, for example, *Two Republics,* November 28, 1868.

31. Salvador Novo, *Cocina mexicana: Historia gastronómica de la Ciudad de México* (Mexico City: Editorial Porrua, 1979), 125–29; *Recuerdo gastronómico del centenario, 1810–1910* (Mexico: n.p., 1910); Harvey A. Levenstein, *Revolution at the Table: The Transformation of the American Diet* (New York: Oxford University Press, 1988), 96.

32. Quoted in Sonia Corcuera, *Entre gula y templanza: Un aspecto de la historia mexicana* (Mexico City: Universidad Nacional Autónoma de México, 1981), 227.

33. Fernando Cortés, *Five Letters of Cortés to the Emperor,* trans. J. Bayard Morris (New York: Norton, 1991), 97; Bernal Díaz del Castillo, *The Discovery and Conquest of Mexico, 1517–1521,* trans. A. P. Maudslay (London: George Routledge, 1928), 290–91.

34. Teresa Rojas, "La agricultural prehispánica," in *La agricultura en tierras mexicanas desde sus orígenes hasta nuestros días,* ed. Teresa Rojas (Mexico City: Editorial Grijalbo, 1991), 15–138; Woodrow Borah and Sherburne F. Cook, *The Aboriginal Population of Central Mexico on the Eve of the Spanish Conquest* (Berkeley: University of California Press, 1963).

35. Inga Clendinnen, *Aztecs: An Interpretation* (Cambridge: Cambridge University Press, 1991), 162.

36. Juan Pedro Viqueira Albán, *¿Relajados o reprimidos? Diversiones públicas y vida social en la ciudad de México durante el Siglo de las Luces* (Mexico City: Fondo de Cultura Económica, 1987), 132–35.

37. John G. Bourke, "The Folk-Foods of the Rio Grande Valley and of Northern Mexico," *Journal of American Folk-Lore* (1895): 41–71; Gooch, *Face to Face*, 62–64.

38. Ignacio González-Polo, ed., *Reflexiones y apuntes sobre la ciudad de México (fines de la colonia)* (Mexico City: Departamento del Distrito Federal, 1984), 61.

39. Viqueira Albán, *¿Relajados o reprimidos?* 160–62.

40. Calderón de la Barca, *Life in Mexico*, 541–42; Gooch, *Face to Face*, 285, 438.

41. Calderón de la Barca, *Life in Mexico*, 194–99.

42. Prieto, *Memorias*, 106, 115, 121.

43. Ibid., 57, 82–83; Gooch, *Face to Face*, 74, 491.

44. Anne Staples, "Orden y Buen Policia: Nineteenth-Century Efforts to Regulate Public Behavior (Tlacotlalpan, Veracruz, and Mexico City at Mid-Century)," in *Rituals of Rule, Rituals of Resistance: Public Celebrations and Popular Culture in Mexico*, ed. William H. Beezley, Cheryl English Martin, and William E. French (Wilmington, DE: Scholarly Resources, 1994), 115–26.

45. AHSS, Inspección, box 1, exp. 4, proclamation dated June 19, 1854; Archivo Histórico de la Ciudad de México, vol. 3668, exp. 93, Cayetano Teller to Cipriano Robert, September 13, 1870.

46. Prieto, *Memorias*, 104–05, 117.

47. *Nuevo y sencillo* (1836).

48. *Nuevo cocinero mejicano* (1868), 879, quoted in Diana Kennedy, *The Tortilla Book* (New York: Harper & Row, 1975), 98.

49. Quoted by Diana Kennedy, *The Art of Mexican Cooking: Traditional Mexican Cooking for Aficionados* (New York: Bantam Books, 1989), 84.

50. See also *La cocinera poblana* (1877), 2:64.

51. These *tamaladas* were popular among Guillermo Prieto and his companions. See Prieto, *Memorias*, 150.

52. *Nuevo cocinero mejicano* (1868), 940.

53. Prieto, *Memorias*, 286–87.

54. Anne Staples explained these holiday rites in an interview in Mexico City on December 10, 1993. For the recipe, see Kennedy, *Art of Mexican Cooking*, 194–95.

55. Francisco Bulnes, *El porvenir de las naciones Hispano Americanas ante las conquistas recientes de Europa y los Estados Unidos* (Mexico City: Imprenta de Mariano Nava, 1899).

56. Julio Guerrero, *La génesis del crimen en México: Estudio de psiquiatría social* (Mexico City: Libreria de la Vda. de Ch. Bouret, 1901), 148. I thank Rob Buffington for this citation.

57. *La Mujer,* April 15, 1881; *El Imparcial,* July 2, November 30, December 2, 1898.

58. Benedict Anderson, *Imagined Communities: Reflections on the Origin and Spread of Nationalism,* rev. ed. (London: Verson, 1991).

59. Arrom, *Women of Mexico City,* 231–38.

60. *El ama de casa* (Mexico City: Librería de la Vda. de Ch. Bouret, 1899), 1.

61. *El libro del hogar* (Pachuco, Hidalgo: Imprenta "La Europea," 1893), 6.

62. Franco, *Plotting Women,* 23–54.

63. Gooch, *Face to Face,* 494.

64. Simone Beck, *Food and Friends: Recipes and Memories from Simca's Cuisine* (New York: Viking, 1991), 35.

65. José L. Cossio, ed., *Recetario de cocina mexicana escrito por Doña María Luisa Soto Murguindo de Cossio* (Mexico City: Vargas Rea, 1968), 7, 46–47; compare with *Recetas prácticas,* 95–97. Marianita Vázquez, "Cuaderno de cosina," attributed dessert recipes to Maxiana and Jesús Maria; and Carmen Cabrera cooked artichokes using Pachita's recipe. See Eugenio del Hoyo Cabrera, ed., *La cocina jerezana en tiempos de López Velarde* (Mexico City: Fondo de Cultura Económica, 1988), 48. See also Patricia Preciado Martin, *Songs My Mother Sang to Me: An Oral History of Mexican American Women* (Tucson: University of Arizona Press, 1992), 56.

66. *Recetas prácticas* (1892), 3; *Nuestro libro* (1912) in Diana Kennedy's *Recipes from Regional Cooks of Mexico,* (New York: Harper & Row, 1978), 138.

67. Torres, *Cocina michoacana,* 39, 58, 74, 102.

68. Torres, *Cocina michoacana* (1896), 62; *Recetas prácticas* (1892), 103; *Recetas de cocina* (1911), quoted by Kennedy, *Regional Cooks of Mexico,* 138.

69. See the recipes for *chiles fritos, sopa de bolitas, lomo frito,* and *lengua rellena* in Cossio, *Recetario de cocina mexicana,* 24, 25, 49; and *Recetas prácticas* (1892), 144; 13; 32; 55.

70. *Manual del cocinero* (1856), 175.

71. Torres, *Cocina michoacana* (1896), 193, 340–50, 752. On Guadalupine devotion, see Jacques Lafaye, *Quetzalcoatl and Guadalupe: The Formation of Mexican National Consciousness* (Chicago: University of Chicago Press, 1982). For a description of the 1895 crowning ceremony, see Beezley, "Porfirian Smart Set."

72. *La Libertad,* December 23, 1883; Wilhelmine Weber, "The Winter Festivals of Mexico: A Christmas that Combines Aztec and Christian Legends," *Craftsman* 23, no. 3 (December 1912): 266–74; *Excelsior,* December 11, 1926.

73. *Recetas prácticas* (1892), 172; *Nuestro libro* (1912), 40–44.

74. Torres, *Cocina michoacana* (1896), v.

75. *Restaurante,* January 1963.

76. Faustina Lavalle de Hernández M., *La exquisita cocina de Campeche: 400 recetas experimentadas* (Mexico City: Imprenta "Londres," 1939), 19.

77. Jeffrey M. Pilcher, "¡Vivan Tamales! The Creation of a Mexican National Cuisine" (Ph.D. diss., Texas Christian University, 1993), chapter 6.

Cooking, Community, Culture: A Reading of *Like Water for Chocolate*

1. I specifically maintain the Mexican names of the foods mentioned here and I also include both Spanish and English quotations from the novel because I do not wish to appropriate the flavor of the Spanish language for my own (Anglo) theoretical purposes. We must not forget that this is first and foremost a *Mexican* novel / cookbook, although it may have universal implications and uses.

2. Lisa M. Heldke, "Foodmaking as a Thoughtful Practice," in *Cooking, Eating, Thinking: Transformative Philosophies of Food,* ed. Deane W. Curtin and Lisa M. Heldke (Bloomington: Indiana University Press, 1992), 203.

3. Emma Kafalenos, "Reading to Cook / Cooking to Read: Structure in the Kitchen," *Southwest Review* 73 (1988): 2, 6.

4. Anne Goldman, "I Yam What I Yam," in *De / Colonizing the Subject: The Politics of Gender in Women's Autobiography,* ed. Sidonie Smith and Julia Watson (Minneapolis: University of Minnesota Press, 1992), 172.

5. George C. Booth, *The Food and Drink of Mexico* (Los Angeles: Ward Ritchie Press, 1964), 7.

6. Good editions of these texts for study are: Bernardino de Sahagún, *Historia general de las cosas de Nueva España* (Madrid: Historia 16, 1990), and Bernal Díaz de Castillo, *Historia verdadera de la conquista de la Nueva España* (Madrid: Historia 16, 1984).

7. María de Mar de la Cueva, *Así es la comida* (Mexico: Cal y arena, 1991); Leonor Cuesta Soto, *Técnicas culinarias* (Mexico: Escuela Superior de Administración de Instituciones, 1983); and Paco Ignacio Taibo, *Brevario del mole poblano* (Mexico: Terra Nova, 1981). These are just a few of the many titles available.

8. Stephen Mennell, *All Manners of Food* (Oxford: Basil Blackwell, 1985), 65.

9. Susan J. Leonardi, "Recipes for Reading: Summer Pasta, Lobster à la Riseholme, and Key Lime Pie," *PMLA* 104 (1989): 342.

10. Eve Kosofsky Sedgwick, *The Coherence of Gothic Conventions* (London: Methuen, 1986), 9.

11. Laura Esquivel, *Like Water for Chocolate: A Novel in Monthly Installments with Recipes, Romances, and Home Remedies,* trans. Carol Christensen and Thomas Christensen (New York: Doubleday, 1992).

12. Esquivel, *Como agua para chocolate,* 33.

13. For an incisive analysis of popular literature in Mexico and women's reaction to it see Jean Franco, "The Incorporation of Women: A Comparison of North American and Mexican Popular Literature," in *Studies in Entertainment: Critical Approaches to Mass Culture*, ed. Tania Modeleski (Bloomington: Indiana University Press, 1986), 119—39.

14. On a research trip to Mexico City in 1989 I found *Como agua para chocolate* shelved in both the cooking and fiction sections of various bookstores.

15. Just two examples of this emphasis on the visual appear in Plato's analogy of the cave in the *Republic* and in Descartes' use of oracular metaphors in his philosophical texts. Everyday language itself testifies to the degree to which our thinking about thinking has been shaped by visual models.

16. In my use of the word "bricoleur" (tinkerer), I take it for granted that readers, like cooks, engage in this tinkering process that makes reading and cooking such creative and participatory activities—you can bend the rules.

17. Michael Fischer, "Ethnicity and the Post-Modern Arts of Memory," in *Writing Culture: The Poetics and Politics of Ethnography*, ed. James Clifford and George E. Marcus (Berkeley: University of California Press, 1986), 195—96.

18. Goldman, "I Yam What I Yam," 190.

19. Ibid., 190.

20. Debra A. Castillo, *Talking Back: Toward a Latin American Feminist Literary Criticism* (Ithaca, NY: Cornell University Press, 1992), xiv.

21. Esquivel, *Like Water for Chocolate*, 186.

22. Esquivel, *Como agua para chocolate*, 194.

23. Ibid., 53.

24. My translation.

25. José Luis Loredo, foreword to Leonor Cuesta Soto, *Técnicas culinarias* (Mexico: Escuela Superior de Administración de Instituciones, 1983), 9.

26. Guy García, "Seven Lives Later, a Director Starts His Eighth," *New York Times*, August 28, 1994, Arts and Leisure section, 9.

27. My translation.

28. Antonio Marquet, "¿Cómo escribir un best-seller? La receta de Laura Esquivel," *Plural* 237 (1991): 58—67.

29. For more explanation of the concept of the writerly text, see Roland Barthes, *S/Z*, trans. Richard Miller (New York: Hill and Wang, 1974), 4: "What evaluation finds is precisely this value: what can be written [rewritten] today: the writerly. Why is the writerly our value? Because the goal of literary work (of literature as work) is to make the reader no longer a consumer, but a producer of the text."

30. Leonardi, "Recipes for Reading," 342.

31. This is a perennial problem, especially for North American critics of Latin

American literature who do not wish to impose their theoretical, cultural readings on texts. Among the many critics who are conscious of this problem and try to address it are Debra Castillo and Jean Franco, to name only two.

32. My translation.

33. Josefina Ludmer, "Tretas del débil," in *La sartén por el mango: encuentro de escritoras latinoamericanas,* ed. Patricia Elena González and Eliana Ortega (Rio Piedras: Ediciones Huracán, 1984), 53.

34. Sor Juana Inés de la Cruz, *A Sor Juana Anthology* (Cambridge: Harvard University Press, 1988), 225–26.

35. My translation.

36. Sara Castro-Klarén, "La crítica feminista la escritora en América Latina," in *La sartén por el mango: encuentro de escritoras latinoamericanas,* ed. Patricia Elena González and Eliana Ortega (Río Piedras: Ediciones Huracán, 1985).

37. Chandra Talpade Mohanty, "Feminist Encounters," in *Destabilizing Theory: Contemporary Feminist Debates,* ed. Michele Barrett and Anne Phillips (Cambridge: Polity Press, 1992), 76.

38. For the term "deterritorialization" I am indebted to Gilles Deleuze and Felix Guattari, "What Is Minor Literature?" in *Kafka: Towards a Minor Literature,* trans. Dana Polan (Minneapolis: University of Minnesota Press, 1986).

39. Esquivel, *Como agua para chocolate,* 136.

40. Esquivel, *Like Water for Chocolate,* 48.

41. Esquivel, *Como agua para chocolate,* 57.

42. Esquivel, *Like Water for Chocolate,* 48.

43. Esquivel, *Como agua para chocolate,* 57. Also note that in the Spanish text Gertrudis is identified as the "afortunada," the fortunate one, as opposed to the "poor" woman in the English translation.

44. Esquivel, *Like Water for Chocolate,* 224.

45. Esquivel, *Como agua para chocolate,* 232.

46. Esquivel, *Like Water for Chocolate,* 113.

47. Esquivel, *Como agua para chocolate,* 120.

48. See Fredric Jameson "Conclusion: The Dialectic of Utopia and Ideology," in *The Political Unconsciousness: Narrative as a Socially Symbolic Act* (Ithaca, NY: Cornell University Press, 1981).

49. Christian Norburg-Schulz, *Genius Loci: Towards a Phenomenology of Architecture* (London: Academy Editions, 1980), 115.

50. Claude Levi Strauss establishes a useful and provocative dichotomy between raw food and civilization, respectively. In some of the cultures he examines, unmarried women have remained imprisoned in nature and rawness and so are roasted or cooked symbolically by fire: "The conjunction of a member of the social group with nature must be mediated through the intervention of

cooking fire . . . so that a natural creature is at one and the same time cooked and socialized" (*The Raw and the Cooked,* trans. John Doreen [New York: Harper & Row, 1969]), 336. I think that more study of this kind in relation to Esquivel's work could prove very fruitful.

51. Jean Franco, "Beyond Ethnocentrism," in *Marxism and the Interpretation of Culture,* ed. Cary Nelson and Lawrence Grossberg (Urbana: University of Illinois Press, 1988), 514.

52. In actual fact, without a knowledge or background of Mexican cooking, it is very hard to reproduce the recipes as given in the novel. I speak from experience. Tita would, I assume, expect any cook to create his or her own recipe in conjunction with her recipe.

53. Luisa Valenzuela, "The Word, That Milk Cow," in *Contemporary Women Authors of Latin America,* ed. Doris Meyer and Margarite Fernández Olmos (Brooklyn: Brooklyn College Press, 1983), 96.

54. Leonardi, "Recipes for Reading," 347.